There is nothing more difficult to take in hand, more perilous to conduct, or more uncertain in its success, than to take the lead in the introduction of a new order of things.

—Machiavelli, *The Prince*

The Human Side of School Change

The Human Side of School Change

Reform, Resistance, and the Real-Life Problems of Innovation

Robert Evans

 JOSSEY-BASS
A Wiley Company
San Francisco

Jossey-Bass books and products are available through most bookstores. To contact Jossey-Bass directly, call (888) 378-2537, fax to (800) 605-2665, or visit our website at www.josseybass.com.

Substantial discounts on bulk quantities of Jossey-Bass books are available to corporations, professional associations, and other organizations. For details and discount information, contact the special sales department at Jossey-Bass.

Epigraph on p. 3: Reprinted by permission of the publisher from Michael Fullan, *The New Meaning of Educational Change, 2nd edition* (New York: Teachers College Press, © 1991 by Teachers College, Columbia University. All rights reserved.), excerpt from p. 96.

Epigraph on p. 91: E. Schein, *Process Consultation: Lessons for Managers and Consultants VOL II,* © 1987 by Addison-Wesley Publishing Company, Inc. Reprinted by permission of Addison-Wesley Publishing Company, Inc.

Library of Congress Cataloging-in-Publication Data

Evans, Robert
    The human side of school change : reform, resistance, and the real
-life problems of innovation / Robert Evans.
        p.   cm. — (The Jossey-Bass education series)
    Includes bibliographical references and index.
    ISBN 0-7879-0318-3 (cloth)
    ISBN 0-7879-5611-2 (paper)
    1. School management and organization—United States.   2. School
improvement programs—United States.   3. Education change—United
States.   I. Title.   II. Series.
    LB2805.E9   1996
    371.2′00973—dc20   96-25277

FIRST EDITION
HB Printing   10 9 8 7 6
PB Printing   10 9 8 7 6 5 4 3 2 1

The Jossey-Bass Education Series

Contents

*To my wife, Paula, a teacher's teacher, a family's keeper,
who nourishes hope and never gives up;*

*to our sons, Nicholas and Alec, who bring us such
delight;*

*and to my father and late mother, whose lessons and love
live with me every day.*

Introduction

"Oh, great. Another school change book," said the principal, his voice thick with sarcasm. "More of what we're doing wrong? More pie in the sky that we'll never manage? I can't wait." He was teasing—he is a longtime colleague—but he was on target. After all, the futility of school change is legendary. Perhaps no American institution has been reformed more often, with less apparent effect, than the school. Critiques of current performance, calls for radical reform, and ambitious initiatives for change have been chronic, cyclical—and, it seems, ephemeral. Innovative ideas and promising projects have repeatedly failed to move beyond ardent advocacy and local promise to full, broad adoption. The structure of schooling and the practice of teaching have remained remarkably stable. One might say of reform, as Samuel Johnson did of remarriage, that it represents the triumph of hope over experience.

Will the latest wave of school change—"restructuring"—meet a different fate than its predecessors? Since the emergence in the 1980s of a series of reports sharply criticizing our schools and proposing a wide range of reforms in curriculum, instruction, governance, and teacher preparation, restructuring has dominated the discourse about American education. By vividly documenting the deficits of schools and calling for sweeping changes, its proponents have won the support of policymakers, business leaders, legislators, and many parents. But how many of the nation's classrooms are ultimately restructured will depend on how many of the nation's educators make the necessary changes in practice and beliefs—a vast process of adaptation that must be accomplished teacher by teacher, school by school. And educators are the one constituency not captivated by the new improvement agenda. While many have embraced it, a great many more have not. In schools that have supposedly undertaken reform, it is easy to find teachers who have made only minor changes or none at all. And in schools everywhere, it is easy to find those who remain strongly opposed, even when reform aims to empower them. School improvement faces a fierce paradox: its essential agents of change—teachers—are also its targets and, sometimes, its foes.

To accomplish comprehensive change in such a context is an enormous and intricate task—one that falls heavily on school leaders, and one they must undertake with insufficient help from advocates of reform. For beyond their consensus on the necessity for swift, full-scale restructuring, advocates disagree about which are the key problems of schools and how to fix them, about what students need to learn and how they need to learn it. More important, most advocates (and most policymakers) pay too little attention to the central problem that has long plagued school improvement—implementation. With a few notable exceptions, they neglect its practicalities. However accurate their critiques and however appealing their proposals, they show a remarkable naïveté about how people and institutions actually behave, about how to get from here to there. Like their predecessors, they generally prescribe combinations of logic and leverage (explanation, training, mandates) to make teachers relinquish the practices of a professional lifetime. Most see change largely as a rational redesign of the school's goals, roles, and rules. They treat it as a product and, concentrating on its structural frame, overlook its human dimensions.

But change is a generative process (Shahan, 1976, pp. 53–54); it must be accomplished by people. And the people who must accomplish it deserve and require much more consideration than most designers of school improvements give them. If we broaden our perspective on reform to examine its impact on educators, we see that the context of change in schools has never been more challenging. The opportunities are unprecedented, but so are the pressures. Promising proposals abound, but so do demands for rapid results. Expectations for performance in both academic and nonacademic spheres expand relentlessly, as do other complexities of school life—bureaucratic, legal, interpersonal. But resources, both financial and human, fail to keep pace. Never have so many teachers and administrators worked so hard or so long and felt less rewarded or more alone. Never has good leadership been more crucial.

This book tries to help school leaders meet the formidable challenges they face. It is designed for all who take a leading part in school improvement—primarily principals and superintendents, but also teachers, more of whom are assuming active roles as change agents, and school board members and policymakers, whose understanding of the issues explored here is also crucial to achieving real reform. It is not about why schools need to change, or which changes they should adopt, but about how to lead and implement change in ways that truly "take." It presents a way of approaching all school improvement, a conceptual framework for understanding change as a process, educators as people, schools as institutions, and leadership as a craft.

At the same time, this is not a leadership cookbook or how-to manual that glorifies procedure and technique and reduces the implementation of change to pressing the right managerial buttons. On the contrary, it advocates an approach to change that emphasizes people's need to find meaning in their life and work and the role of the school in providing that meaning. It endorses recent calls for a new kind of leadership that emphasizes authenticity, translating the integrity, core beliefs, and natural strengths of school leaders into practical strategies for problem solving. Its aim is to simplify the process of change and the tasks of leadership—not oversimplify them, but reduce them to an essential core. All of this requires a theoretical base. I offer one, but I try to stay close to human nature, to the realities of life in schools, the dilemmas involved in actually implementing change—especially the recurrent problem of resistance—and their implications for leadership.

The Plan of the Book

The book is divided into three parts. Part One reflects on the nature of change itself, revisiting the assumptions that underlie educational innovation. Its three chapters look at the way we conceptualize change and at its relationship to the psychology of individuals and the culture of institutions. Together, these chapters cast resistance in a new light, as the normal, inevitable human and organizational response to reform. Part Two explores the key dimensions of the change process. Chapter Four provides an overview of the transitions that teachers must be helped to accomplish to implement reform. Chapters Five through Eight examine the four main dimensions of organizational change—substance, staff, setting, and leadership. Innovations begin with content, the actual program for change, but their success depends heavily on the readiness of people, the organizational capacity of schools, and, crucially, the kind of leadership that is exerted. Problems in each of these areas are so pervasive in our schools that they create unprecedented dilemmas for leaders of change.

Part Three addresses these dilemmas. It offers a new foundation for administering schools—authentic leadership, which is outlined in Chapter Nine. Authentic leadership is characterized by four key "strategic biases," described in the remaining chapters: clarity and focus, participation without paralysis, recognition, and confrontation. These biases are neither techniques nor rigid rules, but general predispositions that simplify leadership and strengthen leaders' ability to solve problems and foster improvement. The book concludes by recasting our expectations for school improvement. Without abandoning the highest strivings, leaders must honor the practicalities of innovation. They must help their colleagues maintain a twin focus, "reach and realism," and apply this focus to their own leadership as well.

What This Book Is Not

This, then, is not a standard school change book. It is not about student needs and best classroom practice, which are the core and cause of reform, but about educators' needs and best leadership practice, which arc the keys to its implementation. It is not, for the most part, about new theoretical constructs; it is about the most ordinary—and fundamental—facts of human nature and school life, many of which are widely known but widely discounted in educational policy and planning for reform. Though commonplace, they are extremely powerful and must be fully appreciated by anyone who hopes to change our schools.

This book is also not full of easy optimism. Many of the facts I consider confirm the enormous difficulty of achieving innovation in schools. Indeed, the first half of the book concentrates on the obstacles to change. Some readers, especially those strongly committed to school reform, may find this discouraging. Most will, I hope, find it affirming—as a reality check, as a new way of understanding the frustrations they and others have experienced, and as a constructive basis for reducing resistance and fostering change. My aim is not to deny the necessity or promise of reform but to underscore the extraordinary effort it requires, both from those who lead it and from those who must accomplish it, and to build a realistic foundation for achieving and assessing genuine progress. There is, as I hope to show, a crucial, challenging, and ultimately encouraging paradox about leading school change: a genuine respect for the sober realities of experience is crucial to success. Without it, frustration, disappointment, and failure are inevitable. With it, the chances for making a critical difference in America's schools, for achieving a triumph of hope over experience, improve immensely.

Acknowledgments

This book marks a long return to my roots. I started out as a teacher, became a psychologist, and later added school consultation to my psychotherapy practice; en route I became an administrator. Writing this book has permitted me to gather the different perspectives of my career—educational, clinical, organizational, administrative— and apply them to my first love, schools, and my chief interest, leadership. These perspectives have been informed by the generosity and wisdom of many people. First among these are the teachers and administrators with whom I have worked, in both the schools where I have consulted and in the seminars I have led. Though I left the classroom long ago, my contact with schools has been deep and broad. For twenty years I have visited several dozen schools on a regular basis, consulting closely with staff and leaders on issues of all kinds, from troubled students and parent-school communication problems to staff conflicts and major institutional crises. Over the past seven years I have worked with thousands of educators in several hundred seminars across the country on the dilemmas of coping with change. Both kinds of experience have taught me about the range and complexity of the challenges educators face and about their dedication, skill, and courage.

I owe an equal debt to my professional family at The Human Relations Service, where colleagues have taught me to combine psychological and systemic perspectives on organizational issues and how to look for strengths in the midst of even the greatest weaknesses. The agency's trustees have been a steady source of support for all our endeavors and for the writing of this book. And I am profoundly grateful to my great friend and colleague Norman Colb, on whose advice, criticism, and encouragement I have depended throughout and who, had he not become an outstanding school leader, could surely have been an outstanding editor. The flaws, of course, remain mine.

The Author

Robert Evans is a clinical and organizational psychologist and director of The Human Relations Service in Wellesley, Massachusetts. He earned his A.B. degree (1966) from Princeton University and his doctorate (1974) from Harvard University. A former high school and preschool teacher, he has consulted to hundreds of schools and districts throughout America and around the world, has worked extensively with teachers, administrators, school boards, and state education officials. His special interest is in the implementation of change and the resistance it causes.

Part One

The Nature
of Change

Chapter One

Changing Paradigms

> *The revolution we are in is first and foremost a revolution*
> *of the total situation. It is not just new kinds of problems*
> *and opportunities that we are facing, but whole new*
> *contexts within which these problems and opportunities*
> *reside.*
> —PETER VAILL (1989, PP. 2–3)
>
> *The fallacy of rationalism is the assumption that the*
> *social world can be altered by logical argument. The*
> *problem, as George Bernard Shaw observed, is that*
> *"reformers have the idea that change can be achieved by*
> *brute sanity."*
> —MICHAEL FULLAN (1991, P. 96)

At a conference on school reform, the principal of an urban high school, unable to contain himself, burst out, "We've spent all morning discussing which changes are best. In my school, we have too many problems hurting too many kids. We need to change everything—now!"

Many critics of our schools would agree. The rhetoric of school improvement is relentlessly assertive. Advocates may differ sharply about which changes are needed, but most share a common conviction that radical change is both crucial and possible. No matter how complex the problem they diagnose or how dismal the history of previous efforts to treat it, they have a remedy. Indeed, it often seems that the greater the dilemma, the greater their expectations for change. At its best, this combination of impatience and confidence can stimulate and sustain exceptional effort in the face of imposing obstacles. But it also overlooks fundamental truths of human psychology and organizational behavior, and it flies in the face of experience.

Organizational change—not just in schools, but in institutions of all kinds—is riddled with paradox. We study it in ever greater depth, but we practice it with continuing clumsiness. Change itself proves Protean, its implementation Sisyphean. We try to define it, analyze it, plan it—management experts speak of "mastering" it—all in vain. It remains elusive, mutable, never what it seems. When we try to implement it, to actually get an organization to do something new, the result is often painful and futile. Acknowledging these problems, a growing number of observers have shifted the way they think about organizational change. They have turned away from the traditional rational-structural paradigm of change, a paradigm on which decades of organizational and school reform have been based, toward a new strategic-systemic paradigm marked by very different assumptions and emphases. This emerging model has profound implications for efforts to improve schools. It calls on us to revise old assumptions and, ultimately, reaffirm old truths.

Approaches to Change, Gaps in Knowledge

Over the past few decades the knowledge base about school change has grown appreciably. Some scholars feel that we know more about innovation than we ever have (Miles, 1992, pp. 29–30). But although we have surely learned much, there remain two large gaps in our knowledge: training and implementation. The first involves who "we" arc. There may be a group of researchers who have learned more about school change, but such knowledge is not widely disseminated among practitioners. Few school administrators receive the regular training in organizational development and innovation that is common among business executives. One consequence, readily apparent to those of us who consult in both corporations and in schools, is that many educational change efforts fail due to expectable problems that well-trained leaders would anticipate.

The second problem is even larger. Despite what has been learned about implementing change, we—everyone involved in school improvement—still face a major implementation gap, for we are now attempting reforms that are far more extensive and complex than ever before. In 1968 I joined a team of teachers that sought to develop a high school English curriculum that would be both highly relevant for students and "teacherproof," with content so engaging that it would make students want to learn and lesson plans so clear that no teacher, however dull or incompetent, could fail to conduct an interesting class. As comparatively simple as our reform was, it proved futile. Yet, the changes currently under way in schools are far more extensive and sophisticated. One of the central lessons we think we have learned about previous rounds of innovation is that they failed because they didn't get at fundamental, underlying, systemic features of school life: they didn't change the behaviors, norms, and beliefs of practitioners. Consequently, these reforms ended up being grafted on to existing practices, and they were greatly modified, if not fully overcome, by those practices. Dull and incompetent teachers taught the new content dully and incompetently.

The flaw here, as some see it, is that most of these projects aimed at first-order change rather than at second-order change. First-order changes try to improve the efficiency or effectiveness of what we are already doing. Even when these efforts are large in scope (having all the elementary schools in a city adopt a new basal reader, for example), they are usually single, incremental, and isolated. They do not significantly alter the basic features of the school or the way its members perform their roles. Second-order changes are systemic in nature and aim to modify the very way an organization is put together, altering its assumptions, goals, structures, roles, and norms (Watzlawick, Weakland, and Fisch, 1974, pp. 10–11). They require people to not just do old things slightly differently but also to change their beliefs and perceptions. The various school reforms that live under the tent of "restructuring" include an array of efforts at second-order change, altering everything from instructional methods to governance. Some seek overtly to change the culture of the school; the rest require culture change to succeed. These types of reforms are vastly more ambitious than even the large efforts of the past, such as the effective schools movement. Changing a school's culture, for example, is a huge and daunting task, as Chapter Three will show. So, despite what we have learned, our reach for more extensive, complex change means that we still face a disparity between what we know and what we need to know about accomplishing innovation.

In an effort to close this knowledge gap and enhance both the theory and practice of change, a number of keen observers, chief among them Michael Fullan, Matthew Miles, Philip Schlechty, and Thomas Sergiovanni, have offered compelling analyses of the process of school change and its implications for leadership. Their work takes a new paradigm of change that has emerged among experts in organizational development, management, and psychology and applies it to schools. This new paradigm, derived from systems thinking and strategic approaches to organizational development, opposes the rational-structural model that has dominated organizational and school reform for decades and still underlies most restructuring efforts.

The Rational-Structural Paradigm of Change

The traditional—and prevailing—approach to change is rooted in the concept of scientific management. Developed by the famous (and now much-criticized) Frederick Winslow Taylor (1911) in the early twentieth century, scientific management began as an effort to radically improve industrial performance by making work more rational and efficient.[1] Its impact was profound. It sped the development of mechanization, specialization, and bureaucratization, bringing vast increases in productivity and transforming the factory and the office into places where work processes were prescribed and results measured. It also earned Taylor widespread, enduring criticism for degrading skilled crafts into rote tasks and reducing humans to automatons. Even so, decades later its principles abound, not only in the way we organize our workplaces but also in the way we train our athletes and even in the ways we structure our personal and family lives (Morgan, 1986, p. 30). Modern notions of professional management have softened and adapted Taylor's original concepts, but they still share its highly rational, structured, command-and-control mindset. I shall have more to say about these theories when we look at leadership in Chapter Eight. For now, we are concerned with their impact on our thinking about organizational functioning and improvement.

The traditional model of change is rooted in three of Taylor's assumptions: stability, rationality, and structure. Its principal dimensions are summarized in Table 1.1. It assumes that an organization and the environment in which it operates are relatively static entities. The environment, even if it is challenging and not fully under the organization's control, is nonetheless stable and predictable enough that one can measure it and plan accordingly. In this respect the paradigm reflects the basic assumptions of Newtonian physics: the world is an ordered place in which events unfold according to causal, linear laws; everything can be understood, provided enough information is available. Similarly, in this paradigm the organization itself is seen as a fundamentally stable and logical enterprise, to be understood chiefly in terms of its formal properties: its division of labor, structural hierarchy, official roles, and prescribed procedures, all of which should be logical and functional and should foster accountability.

In its planning, the organization depends on rational, objective decision making, quantitative measurement, and the pursuit of long-range goals. Innovation, when it is needed, requires this same objectivity in its development, implementation, and assessment. It is typically seen as an end product or event, a specified outcome (such as a restructured school) that conforms to a step-by-step

Table 1.1. Paradigms of Change.

	Rational-Structural	Strategic-Systemic
Environment	stable	turbulent
	predictable	unpredictable
Organization	stable	fluid
	logical	psychological
Planning	objective, linear	pragmatic, adaptable
	long-range	medium-range
Innovation	product	process
	fixed outcome	emerging outcome
Focus	structure, function	people, culture
	tasks, roles, rules	meaning, motivation
Implementation	almost purely top-down	top-down and bottom-up
	disseminating, pressuring	commitment-building ("purposing")

design developed in advance by experts: "Conventional organizations are analytic and detail-oriented in their problem solving. . . . They enshrine . . . the 'endless planning, flawless execution' model of problem solving, in which a lengthy period of analysis leads to a plan so perfect that any fool could supposedly carry it out" (Hammer and Champy, 1994, p. 112).

Whether the blueprint calls for new outputs or for greater efficiency in current outputs, it focuses on changes in the organization's structure and in its tasks, roles, and rules. The methodology for innovation is almost entirely top-down in nature, a combination of dissemination and pressure. There may be much lip service paid to "participation," but this usually means getting people to "go along," to have a "sense of ownership." The implementation goal is to have staff adopt the expert plan as is. This requires explanation, persuasion, training, and incentives; if these fail to produce the proper results, it requires mandates, requirements, and policies.

Rational-structural assumptions have long dominated thinking in corporate, governmental, and educational spheres in America. They are incarnated in models of management such as PPBS (Program Planning and Budgeting System) and MBO (Management by Objective), among many others. In education, examples of such traditional approaches to innovation range from teacherproof curriculum projects like mine in the 1960s to more recent movements by federal and state governments to impose curriculum standards and competency testing. The mandating of detailed procedures for diagnosing and teaching students with special needs is a classic example of a rational-structural blueprint to be implemented as specified by its developers. At the district level, this approach dominates thinking about professional development. In-service offerings are typically designed by the central office and consist of defect-based "how-to" programs aimed at correcting deficiencies in teachers' performance via technical training in new strategies and materials.

This summary of the rational-structural approach to innovation does not credit the sincerity or diligence of those who have sought change in this way. Although it has become de rigueur for organizational theorists to attack Taylor, scientific management's gravest failings are simply its naïveté and its age: after nearly a century, events have overtaken it. There is nothing wrong with trying to make schools more functional or trying to plan change thoughtfully, and it is surely true that the way an organization is structured significantly affects its performance. There is a natural appeal to the notion that effectiveness ensues when goals and policies are clear, jobs are well defined, control systems are in place, and employees act rationally. Still, there is no denying that change efforts based on the traditional paradigm have compiled a dismal record. The rational-structural perspective may be very good at explaining how organizations ought to work, but it is very poor at explaining why they often don't, why the same kinds of problems recur over and over (Bolman and Deal, 1991, p. 36).

In education, the persistence of the same old problems is famous. Successive waves of school reform, though not nearly as ineffectual as they are often portrayed, have failed to fully realize the improvements they promised, and many staff development programs have developed teachers' cynicism more than their expertise. The typical pattern when reform fails has been to blame teachers rather than designers; it now appears, however, that the designers' assumptions are often at the core of the chronic failure of change efforts. This realization is growing not only among observers of school reform but also more broadly, among experts in organizational development who see that extensive change efforts based on traditional assumptions have failed to improve organizational performance in the corporate sphere. "There has been more of this rationalistic analysis, design, and control of human systems in the last fifty years in America than possibly anywhere else in possibly all of the rest of human history," notes management expert Peter Vaill, yet people everywhere continue to find their organizations "mysterious, recalcitrant, intractable, unpredictable, paradoxical, absurd, and—unless it's your own ox getting gored—funny" (1989, p. 77).

To many critics, the traditional paradigm is riddled with conceptual and practical faults. It ignores the flux and complexity in and around organizations; it overemphasizes linearity, rationality, and formal structure; and it overlooks vital realities of context, human psychology, and the process of change. For truly practical, effective approaches to school improvement to develop, the rational-structural paradigm must give way. In its place we need a conceptual framework that acknowledges the real world of people, institutions, and change.

The Strategic-Systemic Paradigm: Environment and Organization

Though it requires taking some conceptual liberties, such a framework can be fashioned from two current perspectives on organizations: strategic management and systems theory. These two bodies of thought differ in important ways, but because they make similar critiques of the traditional paradigm and because they each have inspired some of the most promising reassessments of school reform, I amalgamate them here into what I call the strategic-systemic paradigm. We may best understand this hybrid by contrasting it with the older model on each of the dimensions in Table 1.1.

The strategic-systemic paradigm begins by challenging traditional assumptions about stability and causality. For both systems and strategic thinkers, conventional notions of organizational functioning are simplistic and unrealistic. Systems theory, rooted in cybernetics, emphasizes the multiplicity and complexity of factors that affect the functioning of any person or group over time. It looks at wholes rather than parts, at "patterns of change rather than static 'snapshots'" (Senge, 1990, p. 68).

Linear notions of cause and effect fail to see that every event is both cause *and* effect, part of an interactive loop of mutual influences; no single element can be altered without affecting the rest. (For example, successful crackdowns on drug dealers may raise a city's crime rate by reducing the availability of heroin, pushing up its price and causing addicts to commit more theft to support their addiction.) It is these loops, these larger systems, though intricate and subtle, that govern behavior, not, as we so often imagine, single events or particular individuals or functional job descriptions. The complexity of these loops is increasing rapidly: we now have the capacity "to create far more information than anyone can absorb, to foster far greater interdependency than anyone can manage, and to accelerate change far faster than anyone's ability to keep pace" (Senge, p. 69). Systems thinkers argue that only by staying focused on the broader, underlying systemic patterns can we solve problems effectively and develop a truly creative, self-renewing "learning organization" that can cope with a changing environment (Senge, pp. 42–54).[2]

Strategic theorists, too, challenge the traditional model's simplistic assumptions about stability and predictability. Their view of organizations concentrates more on "people issues" and on the nonrational aspects of organizational life than does systems theory. It sees more than complexity; it sees chaos without and fluidity within. The rate of both planned and unplanned change—technological, social, economic, and political—is accelerating so sharply that we simply can no longer take for granted the stability assumed by the traditional paradigm, in any aspect of our experience. As it accelerates, change ceases to be incremental; it virtually explodes and becomes discontinuous. "Thirty years ago most people thought that change would mean more of the same, only better. They expected and welcomed this incremental change. Today we know that in many areas of life we cannot guarantee more of the same . . . and cannot even predict with confidence what will be happening in our own lives" (Handy, 1990, p. 6).

Strategic thinkers find in chaos theory a better model for understanding this world of discontinuous change. Chaos theory, a growing body of thought, calls for a sharp revision of Newtonian physics and its assumptions that the world is orderly and predictable and that, given sufficient information and perspective, everything can potentially be understood and explained (a view that many systems thinkers would accept). Chaos theory sees systems as not only complex but also spontaneous and idiosyncratic—and, most importantly, as unpredictable. Systems may in fact be orderly underneath, but that order is often extremely elusive, if not impossible to discern. In books with titles like *Thriving on Chaos* (Peters, 1987), strategic writers trace the dilemmas of leadership when change is so rapid and events so complex that leaders cannot predict long-range trends. They conclude that the very context within which organizations exist has become destabilized, so that we can no longer treat as given the most fundamental things we once took for granted (Vaill, 1989, p. 3).

To describe this destabilized context of discontinuous change and chronic uncertainty, Vaill uses the metaphor of "permanent white water" (p. 2), a river of endless rapids with no stretches of lakelike calm. Examples are legion. The popular business press has chronicled the way in which events have swamped one flagship American corporation after another, from major steel producers and the "big three" automakers to Polaroid, Digital Equipment Corporation, and IBM. In truth, the tendency of organizations to flourish and then falter is not new. Almost all the leading corporations of one hundred years ago—including such giants of the time as the Eastern Buggy Whip Company and the Lobdell Car Wheel Company—are extinct (Malkiel, 1990, p. 89). What is new is the speed and extent of change and the vulnerability of organizations to rapid decline. Many large industrial companies don't live past their fortieth birthday. Fully one-third of the Fortune 500 companies in 1970 no longer existed by 1983 (Senge, 1990, p. 17). The context surrounding organizations is now so full of unplanned, unpredictable change that adapting is extraordinarily difficult.

Like American companies, American schools exist in a destabilized context. The entire educational environment is in flux, as social, economic, and political forces radically reshape the world of schools. As recently as 1980, few educators were anticipating an explosion in the number of non-English-speaking students or accelerating poverty among young children or intensifying divisions between racial, ethnic, and religious groups. Nor are schools themselves immune to the competitive pressures convulsing corporate America. As recently as 1985, few would have taken seriously the idea of companies' running schools for profit, or that Baltimore and Hartford would hire such a company, or that the president of Yale would leave his post to help lead another one for a salary reported to be $800,000 (Stewart, 1994, p. 75).

This external chaos and unpredictability is mirrored in the internal turbulence and variability within today's organizations. Instead of the utilitarian scheme of the organizational chart, with its orderly, predictable logic, the strategic-systemic paradigm sees an intricate human system governed by a complex, nonrational logic that is often paradoxical, if ultimately comprehensible and susceptible to influence (Fullan, 1991, p. 97). Taking a human resource perspective on organizational life, it eyes the gaps between, on the one hand, functional designs and formal procedures and, on the other, the actual behavior of workers, which can vary widely from formally prescribed roles. It sees human nature as complex and malleable, marked by variability in at least two ways. First, the personal lives and needs of staff routinely intrude on their performance—intrusions that can significantly hamper efforts at innovation.[3] Among these personal changes, one of the most important in schools has been the aging of the faculty. The majority of educators are veterans of more than twenty years' experience. These professionals have reached midlife and midcareer, a time when changing attitudes, interests, and energy levels are likely to reduce one's investment in work and one's appetite for innovation—a subject we will explore in Chapter Six.

A second source of variability in staff performance is the sheer social complexity of organizational life itself. The fulfillment of official job descriptions is affected by such things as politics—power struggles between different interest groups and conflicts over resources and status, among other factors. In addition, there is the general refusal of the environment to stand still. When Warren Bennis, an expert on leadership and organizational development, became a college president, he learned that "routine work drives out nonroutine work and smothers to death all creative planning, all fundamental change" and that, "make whatever grand plans you will, you may be sure the unexpected or the trivial will disturb and disrupt them" (1989, pp. 15–16). Anyone who has led a school or any similarly complex organization recognizes instantly what Bennis means.

Planning and Innovation

Strategic theorists oppose the highly objective approach to planning and innovation that has long dominated management and policy making in schools and corporations. They object to the internal rigidities and flaws in what they see as a narrow, limited, overly rational view of organizational development. Relying on long-range forecasting, cause-and-effect thinking, step-by-step problem solving, and statistical measurement; devaluing judgment, intuition, and nonrational aspects of decision making; treating innovation as a fixed outcome—these staples of management constitute what Vaill calls a "technoholic" approach. A technoholic is someone trying to avoid uncertainty, messiness, politics, and the "fundamental back-and-forthness" of human interaction, someone who wants to "front-end a project by imposing a technique or protocol on a stream of organizational events." This rigidity spawns two key problems. One is reification, a tendency for a plan to become an end in itself and to be pursued even when the context changes in such a way as to invalidate the assumptions on which the plan was based. Following the blueprint comes to substitute for addressing the actual problem facing the institution. The second is that traditional planning leads an organization to concentrate on first-order changes, on means rather than ends, on how to do things rather than on why to do things. The "can-do" attitude so prized in America may keep an organization focused on finding better procedures for its current ends rather than reconsidering the very ends it should be pursuing. In a destabilized, rapidly changing context, this can be dangerously shortsighted (Vaill, 1989, pp. 88–89).

At a deeper level, the traditional emphasis on rationality is much less substantive and objective than it seems and much more a matter of ideology and symbolism. We have only to look at an institution in terms of its politics, Gareth Morgan argues, to expose organizational rationality as a myth designed to overcome an inherent contradiction: an organization is not just a system of cooperation but a system of competition, too: "Organizations may pursue goals and stress the importance of rational, efficient, and effective management. But rational, efficient, and effective for whom? Whose goals are being pursued? What interests are being served? Who benefits? . . . These [questions] suggest a reevaluation of the ideological significance of the concept of rationality" (p. 195). To see schools in this way is to be reminded that power issues do indeed influence behavior, that the change process is often not so much a matter of clear, objective improvement as it is a competition for control.[4]

Many organizational experts are discarding what they see as an overreliance on "hyperrationality." This means abandoning traditional long-range master plans—with their specific goals and time lines and their extensive use of statistical measurement—in favor of much more pragmatic, adaptable approaches that acknowledge the nonrational, unplannable aspects of organizational life and the importance of being ready to respond to external change. Strategic planning emphasizes, among other things, adapting to the organization's environment, setting medium-range goals (two to three years), and conducting performance assessments that rely on the judgment of leaders instead of on statistical measurements. Strategic management goes even further. Despite its ring of sophistication and complexity, it de-emphasizes formal planning altogether and relies on experience and intuitive judgment in decision making (Louis and Miles, 1990, pp. 31–32).

These approaches see change as a journey, rather than a blueprint. They recognize that we frequently do not know what we're truly after or appreciate the consequences of pursuing it until we have already begun the effort (Fullan, p. 5) and that "specific organizational achievements are always only approximations of what was intended" (Vaill, 1989, p. 78). This is because they see change as a multidimensional process that involves all aspects of the organization: its structure, its politics, and especially its people. They see it as a process that requires people to learn new technologies, practice new behaviors, and, ultimately, adopt new beliefs. Change is not a predictable enterprise with definite guidelines but a struggle to shape processes that are complex and elusive. Its result is an emerging outcome that will be modified during the process of implementation as internal and external conditions shift, data accumulate, and judgment dictates.

Focus and Implementation

Just as it challenges earlier assumptions of stability and rationality, the strategic-systemic paradigm opposes the traditional model's focus on organizational structure and its heavily top-down implementation methodology. It does not deny the need to change the structure of schools or to redefine the roles of teachers, administrators, and students; instead it argues that structure, though important, is not a sufficient focus for change. Centering innovation on formal tasks and procedures and moving directly to how-to-do-it training ignores much about the process of how people actually change (especially how they alter their beliefs). To strategic theorists, the rational-structural bias of the traditional paradigm stimulates staff resistance but is unprepared to cope with it. After all, a good solution is only useful if people adopt it, if its implementation enables them to really make it their own. Traditional organizational change often fails because its designers, overemphasizing rationality, underestimate the opposition reform generates and the power of staff members to resist. They frequently fail to build a base of support for their innovations, and staff are often unwilling or unable to fulfill the new roles created for them. Instead, they informally redesign their roles "to fit what [they] used to do rather than what they are now supposed to do" (Bolman and Deal, pp. 401–402, 429). In the face of this or other kinds of resistance, structural reformers can only resort to exhortation and pressure, repeated explanations and stricter rules. "When their 'if-then' procedures don't work, they become 'if-only' procedures. . . . [But] wishing for, waiting for, and urging the system to become more rational is in itself irrational—it won't happen" (Fullan, p. 97).

At the core of traditional approaches to change lies an arrogance that invites failure and plays a key role in the inability of those approaches to overcome resistance. Innovation is almost certain to encounter problems when its implementation is defined according to only one reality (its creator's). The reason is straightforward: the subjective reality of the implementer (in schools, the personal experience of the teacher) is crucial to successful innovation; transforming this subjective reality is a key task of change. When change agents assume they have "the right answer" and ignore the processes that foster this transformation, they can be "as authoritarian as the staunchest defenders of the status quo" (Fullan, p. 36).

This hubris has marred many past efforts at school improvement and is embedded in much current restructuring. Having a strong commitment to a particular reform, even having the authority to force people to adopt it, does not guarantee successful innovation. On the contrary, it can prove counterproductive. The conviction of an advocate, even a powerful one, inspires resistance if it simply dismisses the inevitable dilemmas of implementation. Being heavily committed makes one less likely to establish the lengthy procedures vital to implementation, less amenable to modifications, and less tolerant of the unavoidable delays and setbacks that ensue as others struggle to adopt the change. It is not that innovators should not have deep convictions but rather that they must be open to the realities of others, to the necessary modification their ideas will undergo as others encounter them—and to the delays this will surely cause.

Strategic approaches to organizational change begin with these realities and complexities. They emphasize meaning before roles, culture before structure. Implementation depends crucially on the meaning the change has to those who must implement it. As we will see in Chapter Two, our response to change, particularly when it is imposed upon us, is determined by how we understand it, what it does to our attachments and beliefs, and how we can fit it into the sense we make of our world. This is crucial to our motivation; few of us will accept the losses and discontinuities of change unless the undertaking is meaningful to us.

The primacy of meaning leads directly to considerations of culture. The strategic-systemic paradigm emphasizes the importance of organizational culture—the deep, implicit, taken-for-granted assumptions that shape perception and govern behavior. It recognizes that no matter what kind of change is undertaken, these ingrained, second-order features of organizational life influence the outcome. "Culture constrains strategy," as Edgar Schein (1992, p. 382) notes, and trying to restructure an organization without confronting its underlying cultural assumptions is usually futile. Schlechty puts it this way: "Changing the structure of schools—or any other organization—is no simple task. Social structures are embedded in systems of meaning, value, belief, and knowledge; such systems comprise the culture of an organization. To change an organization's structure, therefore, one must attend not only to rules, roles, and relationships but to systems of beliefs, values, and knowledge as well. Structural change requires cultural change" (1990, pp. xvi–xvii). No simple task, indeed. Cultural change, increasingly seen not just as vital to certain programmatic changes in schools but as a goal in its own right, is an extraordinarily complex undertaking. As we shall see, culture is conservative: it works to preserve the status quo. Changing it is vastly more difficult than is popularly imagined.

A focus on meaning and culture calls for implementation that relies on commitment building far more than on carrots and sticks. An enormous amount has been written in recent years about the importance of vision and mission. It is now widely accepted that a clear sense of purpose is vital to productivity and especially to innovation, that leaders invigorate performance and inspire commitment to change by engaging their people in the pursuit of shared goals. "Purposing" is the term coined by Vaill, who defines it as a "continuous stream of actions by an organization's formal leadership that [induces] clarity, consensus, and commitment regarding the organization's basic purposes" (1982, p. 29). Strategic approaches to innovation place great emphasis on building followership—an active, engaged, self-managing commitment to change among those who must implement it. Followership first requires a strong initiative by a leader to articulate a clear sense of purpose—or to lead her staff in the development of one. The strategic-systemic paradigm thus begins with a top-down approach. But it is also a bottom-up model, or, more accurately, a "widen-out" model, for it takes the principle of participation seriously. Its emphasis on flexible, developmental planning and the building of shared meaning demands that leaders listen actively to staff, modify their initial goals to reflect staff experience, and aim toward building innovation that is truly collaborative wherever possible. To change schools, therefore, requires much more than "restructuring" them; it requires reconceptualizing the entire enterprise of reform from the strategic-systemic perspective. In Chapter Two we take a close look at this reframing by examining two fundamental elements of innovation that will concern us throughout the rest of this book: the meaning of change and the role of culture.

Notes

1. Taylor emphasized five principles: make the manager responsible for organizing the work; use scientific methods to discover and specify the most efficient way of working; select the best workers for these specifications; train them well; and monitor their performance closely (Morgan, p. 30).

2. Although systems theory makes a seminal contribution to our grasp of organizational functioning, my approach is primarily strategic. For me, systems theory offers a fascinating and elegant diagnostic lens, but it has fundamental flaws as a prescriptive guide for action. It resembles the traditional paradigm it criticizes in that it is highly focused on structure (albeit a deeper, richer notion of structure) rather than people; and, more important, in that it is overly rational in its orientation. It sees most problems as conceptual, approaching organizations and

change in terms of "mental models" and "feedback loops," and relies on a truly remarkable degree of objectivity, on problem solving through cognitive self-observation. (Senge calls for a "shift of mind," a kind of transcendent objectivity he terms "metanoia," [pp. 13–14]). It assumes not only that individuals can routinely diagnose the longer-term, underlying patterns in which they themselves are enmeshed, but that, through insight, they can change these patterns. As a clinically trained psychologist, I find this inconceivable: it contradicts vast bodies of psychological, sociological, and anthropological data. As a consultant to organizations and a member of an organization myself, I find it more than unrealistic: it ignores the overwhelming evidence of everyday life. Although systems theory does allow for intuition, it virtually disregards the role of emotions, interpersonal dynamics, culture, and other crucial nonrational influences in organizational functioning. Ironically, a body of thought that seeks a higher-order awareness of self and context has a blind spot: it fails to recognize that the prevalence of the shortsightedness it criticizes, the non–systems thinking that predominates everywhere, calls into question its own prescriptions.

3. Tom Bird, reflecting on the turbulence that affects any school change project, observes: "At any time, about half of the persons needed to pursue a solution are getting married or divorced; tending a sick or well relative; going bankrupt or coming into money; just starting, getting ready to leave, or near retirement; taking care of babies or putting children through college; making up or breaking up; getting sick, getting well; getting chronic or dying" (1986, p. 45).

4. Despite its insistence on objectivity, rational management's key components, such as such as goal setting or quantitative measurement and evaluation, often function, Morgan argues, much as magic does in primitive societies. Since our belief systems emphasize rationality, the legitimacy of our organizations depends on their demonstrating that objectivity guides their performance. Thus, we take the setting of goals as essential to organizational life. In truth, it is "a socially constructed necessity, characteristic of a mechanical mentality" (p. 106). Choosing and pursuing goals becomes an end in itself—an organization no sooner achieves one objective than it adopts another—because we have defined it as part of rational management. Think of the scandal if a school district, even one which has enjoyed tremendous success and achieved *all* of its targets over the past five years, were to announce a moratorium on planning or a period of consolidation during which no new goals would be pursued! Measurement and evaluation are even more "magical." The quantitative analysis of modern management

experts, just like the reading of entrails by shamans, is designed to forecast and manipulate the future. Like the shaman, it frequently fails but
is nonetheless allowed to preserve its credibility (in each case, failure
is attributed to unanticipated factors). In many ways, rationality is "the
myth of modern society" (pp. 134–135).

Chapter Two

The Meanings of Change

We live under the spell of ideas, good or bad, true or false.
We may think we are responding directly to events and
changes in the histories of institutions, but we aren't; we
are responding to those events and changes as they are
made real or assimilable to us by ideas already in our
heads.
—ROBERT NISBET (1980, P. 4)

Change leads a doubly double life. There is a fundamental duality to our response to change: we both embrace and resist it. We acknowledge its inevitability, and yet a profound conservative impulse governs our psychology, making us naturally resistant to change and leaving us chronically ambivalent when confronted with innovation. Furthermore, change means different things to different people; in fact, it usually means something different to each and every individual. This chapter argues that the key factor in change is what it means to those who must implement it, and that its primary meanings encourage resistance: it provokes loss, challenges competence, creates confusion, and causes conflict.

Public Ideal: Change as Growth and Renewal

The hearty confidence of school reformers reflects an optimism that has long been a part of our very concept of change. Strictly defined, change simply denotes a difference in the state or quality of something. But its meanings and associations, as used in public discourse, are almost invariably positive, centering on the notion of progress. The language of social change, of which school reform is a notable example, is phrased primarily in terms of growth and renewal. Of all the notions in Western thought about mankind and culture, that of growth is the oldest and most powerful: dating back to the ancient Greeks, a long line of philosophers have compared human society and its institutions to the phases of growth in plants and other organisms (Nisbet, 1969, pp. 7–8). Western theories of social evolution have tended to see change as natural, cumulative, and purposeful, with civilization advancing by stages. This advancement has become axiomatic, needing no proof. From the start of the nineteenth century until relatively recently, "belief in the progress of mankind, with Western civilization in the vanguard, was virtually a universal religion on both sides of the Atlantic" (Nisbet, 1980, p. 7). Though it has resonated throughout the West, this conviction is in many ways classically American. Born through revolution and long marked by a frontier mentality linked to a sense of manifest destiny, the United States has spent much of its history as a young nation extolling growth, development, know-how, and newness. We have felt innovation, growth, and progress to be prototypically ours.

One derivative of this view is the embrace of the faster, more productive life. It is now commonplace to note the ever-increasing speed at which we live. Within a span of two generations, the already rapid pace of American life has accelerated almost exponentially. Virtually every aspect of our existence has been transformed by technology, by the revolutions in computing, mass communication, and travel, by the ever-quicker flow and larger quantity of information we "process." As life grows so much more rapid and complex, requiring greater and greater adaptability, change itself is more often championed as a positive value in its own right. There is a widespread sense not only that we must adapt to current changes right now but also that we must prepare ourselves and our children for even greater rates of change in the future. This is one of the engines that drives systems theory's emphasis on creating organizations that are capable of learning.

Despite all this, the change-as-perpetual-progress view has never been unanimously accepted. There have always been thinkers who have seen growth as cyclical, a metaphor that implies not perpetual development and enhancement of social institutions but instead their flowering, decline, and eventual death. And for all our appreciation of the necessity of change, the late twentieth century has seen a distinct descent in our confidence about growth and progress. From what is now called a "postmodern" perspective, observations of the "failures of modernity" are compelling: "the myth of continuous progress of the human race under the guidance of science and rationality can no longer stand up to the evidence" (Starratt, 1993, p. 99). Many factors play a role here. Chief among them is that so many apparent advances have turned out to produce overall effects—environmental, social, moral, demographic, spiritual—that are at best mixed. Indeed, the solution to yesterday's problem often becomes today's problem. As the paleontologist Stephen Jay Gould has observed, history may overtake past adaptations, so that "what was once a sensible solution becomes an oddity or imperfection in the altered context of a new future" (1991, p. 66). When the automobile came into mass production, for example, newspapers in New York, a city struggling with a massive transportation pollution problem—horse manure—hailed it as an environmental blessing. And today, our early enthusiasm about advances in life-prolonging medical treatments has yielded to growing concern about their cost and their consequences for quality of life.

If we have become ambivalent about some advances in technology, we are in little doubt about the progress—that is, the lack of it—of our social and political institutions. Government is attacked on all sides as increasingly bureaucratized, out of touch, and unable to meet the needs of citizens. Skepticism about our leaders, institutions, and national direction seems universal. Accompanying and feeding our growing doubt about inexorable progress has been the loss of our economic preeminence, the apparent slippage in our competitive strength, and the rise in the costs of maintaining our quality of life (families now need two incomes where once they needed only one). Our schools have been strongly implicated in all of this; they are widely seen as having failed to teach both the basic and the higher-order skills necessary to thrive in a more competitive world. Declining test scores and reading levels, rising dropout rates, and surges in adolescent drug abuse and violence have all been adduced as evidence of their inadequacy.

But if progress can no longer be taken for granted, if our institutions, including our schools, are no longer as competent or trustworthy as they once were—if, in short, advancement is not inherent and inevitable—there is a need for renewal. The current rhetoric of social and economic reform displays a sturdy variant of our traditional optimism about progress. It emphasizes restoration, a revival of our fundamental strengths and a recapturing of our natural competitive advantage. Our worry about regaining the economic initiative has reinforced change as an American icon. It is the key to productivity. It has become a ubiquitous theme in political platforms, corporate missions, and school district visions. It would be difficult to find an organization that does not claim to equip its clients for change. The promotion of and planning for change dominate the popular literature on leadership and the professional literature on management consulting, organizational development, and, increasingly, education. Throughout, change is associated with renewing our productivity and competitiveness. Both require a steady stream of technological innovation, which in turn requires new kinds of organizational behavior and a smarter workforce. Our capacity for changing the way we work—and the way we educate our workers—is regularly described as critical to our ability to thrive in the twenty-first century. Change is also seen as inevitable and its embrace as exhilarating. The cutting edge is not only the place to be but a place we can readily reach. Charles Handy's enthusiasm is typical: "Change, after all, is only another word for growth, another synonym for learning. We can all do it, and enjoy it, if we want to" (1990, p. 5). All we have to do to is "change our attitudes, our habits, and the ways of some of our institutions," to achieve "an age of new discovery, new enlightenment, and new freedoms—an age of true learning" (p. 11).

All of this makes sense. Change does indeed promise growth, mastery, development, and renewal. I would not have written this book and you would probably not be reading it if we didn't see the potential of school improvement. When we think of change as learning we can readily remember the value, the excitement, the pride—and the fun—of new things we have learned in our lives. Every teacher is a change agent, helping students learn and grow over the course of the school year. The concept of change-as-growth is not just a political or theoretical construct; it is genuine.

But though it boasts an ancient lineage and is embedded in the fabric of Western civilization, and though, as renewal, it has recently intensified its hold on our imagination, this aspect of change is countered by another deeply rooted in human nature, a fundamental resistance that has enormous implications for the enterprise of school reform.

Private Reality: The Conservative Impulse

Even though the constancy of change has been among our most persistent intellectual assumptions, we can ask why this should be. After all, daily experience and common sense confirm "the conservative bent of human behavior, the manifest desire to preserve, hold, fix, and keep stable" (Nisbet, 1969, p. 270). In truth, beneath its positive public persona, change lives a very different private life. Though we exalt it in principle, we oppose it in practice. Most of us resist it whenever it comes upon us. We dislike alterations in even our smallest daily routines, such as a highway improvement detour on our route to work, for example, let alone in the larger aspects of our life and career, such as a major restructuring of our workplace. Change is neither natural nor normal, constant nor common. On the contrary, when we look at actual social behavior we find that persistence is far more typical (Nisbet, 1969, pp. 271). This is not to say that people and patterns never change; they do. But most of these changes are slow, incremental, often barely perceptible; they are rarely rapid, formal, or overt—and they are almost never sought. We know that life requires us to adapt, and we sometimes long for a change in our circumstances or in the way others treat us, but for the most part we cling reflexively and tenaciously to things as they are.

This predominance of stability is elaborated in an eloquent work by Peter Marris, *Loss and Change,* on which much of what follows is based. Combining psychological and sociological perspectives, drawing upon a variety of studies ranging from the effects of bereavement among widows in England to the impact of slum clearance projects in America and Africa, Marris makes a compelling case that life depends on continuity and that change usually means loss. In virtually every significant transition of any kind, acceptance and adjustment prove far more difficult than anticipated for all concerned: whether a change is planned or unplanned, personal or professional, welcome or unwelcome; whether we take the perspective of reformers or their targets, of people or organizations, "the response is characteristically ambivalent" (1986, p. 5). Anyone who has ever had responsibility for mobilizing people to implement a major change can attest that "characteristically ambivalent" understates the case, if anything. As psychotherapists have long known in their dealings with individuals, as consultants have long known in their dealings with organizations, and as teachers have long known in their dealings with students, any transition engenders mixed feelings. Understanding these feelings is vital to the successful implementation of change.

Our ambivalence springs from a deep-seated conservative impulse to find patterns in life and preserve the continuity of things. "Conservative" does not refer to political doctrine but to our tendency to assimilate reality according to our existing structure, to create and then cling to patterns. This tendency is recognized by students of human nature in many disciplines. Psychologists emphasize the need for a fundamental psychological security, as in Erik Erikson's famous concept of "basic trust" (1963), the essential confidence about the safety and predictability of the world that an infant develops through a parent's consistent nurturing attention. A need for security continues in different forms throughout the life cycle. At an existential level, adults too need an "ontological security," a core confidence in the orderly nature of things (Starratt, pp. 29–40). We are, as Gould says, "pattern-seeking animals. We must find cause and meaning in all events" (1991, p. 60). This pattern seeking is a fundamental, universal element of human experience.[1] It is vital to our very existence, for our ability to make sense of events and even to adjust to change depends crucially on continuity, on the validity of what we have learned. "The conservative impulse . . . is as necessary for survival as adaptability: and indeed adaptability itself depends upon it. For the ability to learn from experience relies on the stability of the interpretations by which we predict the pattern of events" (Marris, p. 6).

We often see this pattern seeking most sharply in the eccentricities and superstitions of other people (our own, of course, are harder to see). But the repetitive behaviors and circular absurdities of others simply reflect our universal "commitment to stasis . . .

[our] deep loyalty to the familiar" (Mitchell, 1988, p. 273). This need for predictability helps explain why psychologists and medical researchers have persistently found a connection between change and stress. It is now axiomatic that the greater the degree of change one faces—in the original parlance of stress researchers, the more "life change units" one accumulates—the more likely one is to develop physical or psychological symptoms of stress. Change of any kind—not just unwanted, negative change but also apparently positive events such as getting a promotion or a raise in salary, getting married, or having a baby—upsets the pattern we are accustomed to and thrusts us into new roles, new relationships, and new perceptions, challenging the way we cope with life.

Because our capacity to cope and adapt depends crucially on our impulse to seek meaning, to fit new experiences into a familiar pattern, our resistance to change is not only inevitable but also constructive, fundamental to learning, essential to adaptation. Our tendencies to ignore events we don't understand, suppress unexpected behavior, and limit innovation are ways we "defend our ability to make sense of life" (Marris, p. 11). It is natural, even necessary that we should avoid or reshape events we cannot assimilate, for our adaptability depends as much on protecting our assumptions as it does on revising them (p. 16).

Even innovators depend on the conservative impulse, though they rarely think so. They will, after all, ultimately *need* their followers' resistance. Pause for a moment over this scenario: You are a principal seeking radical change in your school. You summon the most resistant teacher on your faculty and tell him that his current practice is all wrong, that you know what is right, and that he must reform straightaway. He says, "OK! I'll change at once. Just tell me what to do. Interdisciplinary curriculum? Let's have a lot of late afternoon planning sessions. Site-based management? Sign me up for a lot of evening meetings with parents. Inclusion? Put more behavior-disordered students in my class." Such a reaction would be bizarre, of course—and it would also be dangerously destabilizing. After all, what would stop such a teacher from changing to something else if his next principal ordered a different set of innovations? Advocates of reform do not want perpetual openness to change if this means shifting like a weather vane. They want movement from the status quo to a new and better state, which they then hope to preserve. Once there, they will depend on people's resistance (though it may then be called "commitment") to maintain it. It is unrealistic and unfair to expect people to be open and flexible now, when we wish them to innovate, and to be firm and resolute only later, when we wish them to persevere.

To say that our response to change depends vitally on its meaning is to speak really of two primary components of meaning: *understanding* ("I see what you mean") and *attachment* to people and ideas ("you mean so much to me"; "this principle matters so deeply to me"). The first is cognitive, the second emotional. There is more to meaning, but these two aspects of it are central. Our lives cannot be meaningful unless we can construct and preserve a coherent, predictable pattern from events and relationships. And we become attached not only to people but also to the concepts and beliefs that structure our life and work. Values "have an emotional charge. [They] mean something to people. They are the family jewels and are not juggled about casually. When [they] are vindicated, the feelings are of elation and triumph. When [they] are ignored or denied, it hurts" (Vaill, 1989, p. 54).

How we experience change depends on how it affects the pattern of understanding and attachments we have already constructed and by which we live. The impact of any particular innovation depends on many factors, including, among others, our individual characteristics (personality, history), the kind of organization we work in, the nature of the change, and the way it is presented to us. But, at best, our reaction is likely to be mixed. For though the public meanings of change are firmly linked to growth and renewal, progress and development, its primary private meanings are quite different: they begin, as Robert Mankoff's cartoon (opposite) suggests, with loss.

Change as Loss

Significant change almost always means loss and causes a kind of bereavement. Since the meaningfulness of life depends on predictability, we are bereaved by an actual or potential loss, whether this is caused by a death or by a "discrediting of familiar assumptions" (Marris, pp. 20–21). We are bereaved if someone we love dies, but we are also bereaved if assumptions we live by and take

"Relax, honey—change is good."

Drawing by Mankoff; © 1993 The New Yorker Magazine, Inc.

for granted are devalued—if, say, staff reductions result in our being transferred to a new school, leaving behind friends and status, or if after years of teaching advanced placement seniors we are suddenly forced to teach freshmen. A major part of our world stops making sense; continuity is disrupted; our connections can no longer be counted on. Virtually nothing is more painful or more threatening to our basic security, our very ability to understand and cope with things. It is natural that we should vigorously avoid and resist such experiences.

Four facts stand out about our construction of meaning, its dependence on continuity, and its vulnerability to change. First, it is cumulative and grows more fixed over time. The longer we live, the more events and experiences we incorporate into our structure. The larger that structure, the more difficult it is to revise; the more profound the changes we are forced to make in it, the greater the loss we experience. This is why most people, as Tolstoy said, cannot "accept even the simplest and most obvious truth if it . . . would oblige them to admit the falsity of conclusions which they have delighted in explaining to colleagues, which they have proudly taught to others, and which they have woven, thread by thread, into the fabric of their lives" (Gleick, 1987, p. 38). It is also a key reason change is less welcome to the old than to the young (Marris, pp. 10–11).

Second, our structure of meaning is rooted in feelings and experiences that have great emotional significance. Hence, our perceptions and purposes can rarely be altered by rational explanation alone; our investment in them is too personal. We cannot simply accept the loss of familiar attachments in the name of "some impersonal utilitarian calculation of the common good" (p. 156). This helps explain why people resist structural, technical, and other innovations that seem perfectly logical to their developers and that are advocated largely on the basis of their effectiveness. People must discover their own meaning in such changes before they can accept them (p. 156).

Third, our structure is formed in a context of specific relationships (with parents, friends, teachers, other significant adults) and circumstances. Goals and purposes are developed in this context, become associated with it, and cannot easily be severed from it and transferred to a new one (pp. 10–11). This is a chief reason innovation often meets resistance, even when it seems to its authors to call for only a minor modification in objectives or methods.

Fourth, the structure can include negative elements—it can, indeed, be predominantly pessimistic. "Meaningful" does not necessarily mean "positive." The pattern we construct builds its meaning by continuity, not happiness. People can incorporate "the defeat of their hopes" (p. 123). Ironically, when they have done so, rather than eagerly abandon their demoralized perspective for a new one, they cling to it even more tenaciously. Hence, it can often be extremely hard to make innovation appealing to those who might seem to be its most promising constituents. When we are trying to understand people's resistance to change, it is never just the logical we are dealing with but the psychological (Vaill, 1989, p. 57). Viewed in this light, assurances like Handy's about the promising pathway to innovation—we just need to change "our attitudes, our habits, and the ways of some of our institutions" (p. 54)—seem wildly optimistic, if not simpleminded.

To bring these four points together, let us say that I am a veteran middle school teacher who chiefly lectures in my classes and that I, like many of my colleagues, find that students these days no longer respond, behave, or achieve as well as in the past. I am increasingly disenchanted. You are my principal, and you are convinced that part of the problem results from students' spending too much time passively listening; you feel that they need to be much more actively engaged as learners. You want me to get into cooperative learning. You see your recommendation as a gift, an addition to my repertoire, an opportunity for growth, and an answer to my own dissatisfaction. But I may feel your suggestion to be a dagger in the heart. Even if you don't criticize me directly, I am likely to feel that you are devaluing what I do and who I am. After all, what it means to me to be a teacher is to be a repository of knowledge, a transmitter of the wisdom of the ages. You are casting doubt on the way I define myself and my role, on the relevance of my practice and the importance of my syllabus, both of which matter to me very personally. You may leave our conversation shaking your head, convinced that I am narrow, rigid, and "resistant to change." Perhaps I am. But it may primarily be that I am bereaved.

Not all change, of course, risks causing such bereavement. Some change is simply substitution. Buying a new, faster computer simply provides a replacement for, or an incremental addition to, something familiar. Recovering from an illness simply brings a return to familiarity. Such change alters neither our purposes nor the way we understand life. And there is also change-as-growth. This includes events that may be quite significant, even intense, but that do not threaten the pattern we have already constructed. Developmental changes of the life cycle (like those of adolescence, for example) may have powerful effects, but they fulfill an innate purpose already pressing for expression and represent a linking of new purposes to familiar circumstances (Marris, p. 148). But although one can technically distinguish these different types of change, in our lived experience the distinctions are rarely absolute: we are likely to perceive many of the changes we encounter as a combination of substitution, growth, and loss (p. 22). And the predominant impact, for changes that are imposed on us, is likely to be loss.

It is not, however, the only impact. There are, as Lee Bolman and Terrence Deal point out, three other closely related ramifications of change that are problematic as well: change challenges competence, creates confusion, and causes conflict.[2]

Change Challenges Competence

In 1967, Eric Hoffer, a social critic and author who had actually lived a working class life as, among other things, a migrant laborer and a longshoreman, wrote of the fear change inspires even when it involves the simplest of skills:

> Back in 1936 I spent a good part of the year picking peas. I started out early in January in the Imperial Valley and drifted northward, picking peas as they ripened, until I picked the last peas of the season, in June, around Tracy. Then I shifted all the way to Lake County, where for the first time I was going to pick string beans. And I still remember how hesitant I was that first morning as I was about to address myself to the string bean vines. Would I be able to pick string beans? Even the change from peas to string beans had in it elements of fear [p. 3].

Change immediately threatens people's sense of competence, frustrating their wish to feel effective and valuable. From a human resource perspective, organizational performance and staff growth and morale depend on responding to the needs and feelings of workers, on finding a good fit between their personal priorities and those of the organization. Alterations in practices, procedures, and routines hamper people's ability to perform their jobs confidently and successfully, making them feel inadequate and insecure, especially if they have exercised their skills in a particular way for a long time (and even more if they have seen their performance as exemplary). It shakes their confidence and makes them doubt their abilities, especially their ability to adapt to the new requirements. As Hoffer discovered, "every radical adjustment is a crisis in self-esteem: we undergo a test, we have to prove ourselves. It needs inordinate self-confidence to face drastic change without inner trembling" (pp. 2–3).

It is important to note that one need not suffer a frontal attack to feel an acute challenge to one's competence and confidence. The threat occurs not only if a principal condemns a teacher's methods as outmoded and inadequate, for example, but simply if he endorses and supports a new and different approach. This alone is enough to redefine proficiency. Each of us constructs an occupational identity based on the accumulated wisdom—drawn from our own experience, that of colleagues, and lessons from predecessors—about how to perform a job. Change often discredits this experience and learning, challenging our purposes and identities and devaluing our skills (Marris, pp. 156–157). This kind of reaction is particularly likely when change affects a core competence, such as, for teachers, instruction.

> In Middlevale, a deteriorating economy and a declining population forced the public schools to consolidate and realign the elementary schools, requiring the transfer of many teachers and the reassigning of two dozen teachers to different grade levels. Although the district offered extensive preparation and training for those reassigned, the change made them feel anxious and inadequate. As one said, "We're struggling like rookies all over again, abandoning things we've developed and depended on. We can't feel confident about ourselves or that we're doing our best for the kids."

I know few teachers who are willing to try to improve by experimenting on students. Like those at Middlevale—indeed, like most people—they cling to their competence.

This natural tendency helps to account for many implementation problems in school reform. To return to our previous example about cooperative learning, let us say that despite my misgivings, I decide to take your suggestions and try it. I sign up for workshops and read the books and manuals and even visit a few colleagues' classes. Some months later, pausing at my classroom, you see the students now clustered in small workgroups. Each workgroup has been assigned a different role, as the method calls for, but they are still listening to a teacher-centered lecture from me. The students are now practicing what might be called cooperative *listening*. I have adopted the form without the substance. You may again dismiss me as resistant or rigid or stupid ("He just doesn't get it!"), but it might well be that I am trying hard to combine two things: your wish for me to change and my need to preserve my competence. Most educators cannot feel good unless they feel they are giving students their very best. Hence, they are quite likely to re-graft old branches onto new trunks.

Of course, many go further. To change metaphors, they do make Hoffer's switch from peas to string beans, and they emerge the better for it. I know a number of teachers who, looking back, acknowledge that a particular change they were forced to face, even such a difficult one as an involuntary reassignment to a new school or grade level, turned out far better than they feared and helped them grow professionally. They mastered new skills and developed greater confidence. Yet this appreciation is only in retrospect; they still recall vividly their own version of Hoffer's "inner trembling" at the time of the change, when their competence was at risk.

Change Creates Confusion

Whatever improvements change may promise, it almost always increases confusion and unpredictability. From a structural perspective, organizational performance depends heavily on the coherence of the organization's design, the clarity and appropriateness of its formal roles, rules, and policies. These structural components provide the security of predictability, which, as noted, is vital to our sense of meaningfulness and, as we will see in Chapter Three, is a key benefit of organizational membership. During change, "people no longer know what their duties are, how to relate to others, or who has the authority to make decisions. The structural benefits of clarity, predictability, and rationality are replaced with confusion, loss of control, and the belief that politics rather than policies are now governing everyday behavior" (Bolman and Deal, p. 382). Structural stability is undermined, even when structure is not the direct target of innovation (which it often is in school reform efforts). With roles and rules uncertain, it is often unclear who is responsible for what. Staff become confused and often distressed.

When rising enrollment forced the Overton Public Schools to move its sixth-grade classes from the elementary schools to its junior high school, principal Ted Collins decided the time was ripe to adopt a true middle school model. Some of his best teachers had been eager for such a change, though many others were not. After six months of planning, including visits to schools in nearby communities that had made this kind of transition, Collins and a planning group decided to begin by implementing a team model for the new sixth grade. Incoming students would be grouped into "houses," each taught by its own team of teachers. This meant not only reorganizing the schedule but also finding common planning time for the teachers involved. This in turn required relieving them of certain duties and distributing these among other teachers who were not involved in the project.

As this redistribution unfolded, some felt that Collins was protecting his favorites rather than assigning these burdens evenly. Then, as the year began and the sixth-grade teams started to meet each week, it became apparent that they were quite unclear about the scope of their authority. Some teachers felt that all important decisions about students and about house functioning should be deferred to the administration; others felt this disempowered the teams and insisted they were entitled to take greater initiative. Teaming began to become a source of frustration, and many of the teachers involved, most of whom had supported the innovation, started to become disheartened.

As this example illustrates, when an organization is being restructured, all staff—not only those who preferred the status quo but also those who pressed for change—experience the stress of uncertainty. Even when the elements to be changed are heartily disliked by a majority of staff and are the object of chronic complaints, the change itself commonly provokes more upset and distress than anyone anticipated.

Change Causes Conflict

Innovation is almost always sold as being better for everyone—school reform will benefit students, teachers, administrators, parents, and employers. The reality is almost certain to be quite different. Change almost always generates friction, both between individuals and between groups, because it invariably produces winners and losers, especially at first. Viewed in terms of their political dimensions, organizations are arenas in which groups with opposing interests routinely and appropriately oppose and compete with one another; these groups are affected differentially by innovation. From this perspective, conflict does not automatically signify that something is wrong. On the contrary, it is both natural and inevitable whenever resources are limited and there are competing priorities at stake (Bolman and Deal, p. 199).

When conflict is natural and inevitable, power is the crucial resource. Competition and jockeying for power mean that coercion, negotiation, and compromise are vital ingredients in organizational life. This is particularly true when resources are especially scarce relative to performance demands—a chronic condition in most schools, as we shall see in Chapter Seven. This natural friction occurs between the faculty and administration and also among staff. Any significant innovation increases this friction, because it affects not only roles and skills but also power relationships and status. Often, staff see change as something imposed by administrators for their own purposes and that complicates classroom life. This is particularly true in schools where there is a history of distrust between the faculty and the administration. In many large urban school districts it is often the "downtown" bureaucracy that is the object of this distrust. But in all schools, even in those that enjoy generally good labor relations, innovation increases friction. Even if in the early excitement of reform many staff seem ready to commit themselves to change, sustaining this commitment often proves difficult. When it comes to actually implementing an innovation, all sorts of conflicts, many quite unexpected, may emerge. As change becomes real rather than merely theoretical, some staff inevitably begin to benefit more than others. Some see their goals and philosophy validated; others see theirs discredited. Some gain influence and authority; others lose. These losses include those that are obvious and official (termination of a program, removal from a position) and those, such as a loss of face, that are implicit and informal.

In addition to creating new sources of friction, innovation rekindles old wounds and resentments. Every staff "family" that has been together for some time has a history of disputes and disagreements, personal hurts, jealousies, and betrayals; most of these we learn to endure, and they may recede in importance—but we don't forget them. We may still like or love those who have wounded us, but we remember the hurt they caused or the unfairness they got away with. Change reawakens these wounds. So, it is common to find that change results in increased tension and diminished cooperation.

At Doubleday High School, new principal Harry Smythe found the school to be suffering from years of a "do your own thing" mindset and rampant "feel-goodism." Impressed by E. D. Hirsch's *Cultural Literacy* (1987), Smythe undertook to restructure the curriculum and course offerings to, as he put it, "reemphasize fundamental subject matter and the major disciplines." His proposals split the staff, with some, who came to call themselves traditionalists, supporting him and others, who were sometimes called liberals, in strong opposition. As Smythe began to implement his ideas, power began to shift and conflict to grow. He angered the liberals by abolishing the principal's council, a volunteer advisory group that they had dominated. He began to ignore and bypass an assistant principal—well liked on all sides and a successful mediator of staff differences—who had voiced mild concerns about his new direction. As it became clear that she had lost the principal's ear, she became marginalized: teachers, too, began to bypass her, no longer seeking her opinion and help. Eventually, old disagreements that had previously divided the faculty began to reemerge. These included widespread resentment at English teachers' workloads (they taught four classes instead of five) and the math department's bitterness about a reorganization nine years earlier in which it lost choice classrooms to the science department. The tone of faculty meetings grew more sullen; grumbling and sarcasm increased, and cooperation and collegiality diminished, not only between traditionalists and liberals but within each camp.

Leaders and staff alike may try to ignore or paper over such frictions. The issues they involve are often unseemly (particularly in schools, where there is a strong tradition of conflict avoidance). But trying to quash or simply smooth away the very real differences innovation provokes is counterproductive: it neither resolves the conflicts nor enhances innovation. It simply drives issues underground, where they are likely to enhance divisiveness and hamper change.

Double Duality

Loss, incompetence, confusion, conflict—these meanings of change reveal a double duality in innovation. This duality expresses itself first and most obviously as a public gap between what change means to its authors and what it means to its targets. Designers of reform may have some awareness of this disparity—they typically offer at least a token acknowledgment that change is difficult—but on the whole, they are prone to energetic optimism. Swept up in the urgency of a problem and the promise of a solution, they can overlook and underestimate the effort and agony of the people who must adapt, "the advantages lost and the penalties inflicted by opponents . . . the humiliation of becoming a raw novice at a new trade after having been a master craftsman at an old one, and . . . the deep crisis caused by the need to suppress ancient prejudices, to put aside the comfort of the familiar, to relinquish the security of what one knows well" (Kaufman, 1971, p. 13). Too often, we approach innovation with a powerful double standard: we see the value of change *by other people*. Change that we seek from others we understand in the positive terms associated with growth; change that others seek from us we experience in the negative terms associated with loss. We readily make the case for innovation—on the part of someone else. For ourselves we are likely to resist it stoutly.[3]

But the duality of change begins as an interior, personal issue. The different meanings change has for its advocates and its targets mirrors a fundamental division within each of us, between our overt embrace of change and our conservative inner impulse to resist it. Though the significance of a particular innovation will depend in part on the unique characteristics of person, institution, and situation, we can see that the prototypical response to change is strongly ambivalent. We can also observe that this is true whether change is desired or opposed, planned or unplanned, individual or institutional, and we can see that it afflicts the advocates of change as well as its targets. But as we have also seen, this ambivalence is natural, necessary, and even vital to adaptation. Rooted in the most profound depths of the human psyche, our ambivalence—especially our resistance—needs to be seen as part of the solution, not just part of the problem; it demands the attention and respect of all who seek innovation.

Notes

1. The neurologist Oliver Sacks notes that even at the level of our physical senses, this patterning is basic: "When we open our eyes each morning, it is upon a world we have spent a lifetime *learning* to see. We are not given the world: we make our world through incessant experience, categorization, memory, reconnection" (1993, p. 61, emphasis in original).
2. This summary of the three consequences of change—incompetence, confusion, and conflict—is drawn chiefly from Bolman and Deal, pp. 375–401.
3. Fullan asserts bluntly that this "neglect of the phenomenology of change"—how people actually experience it as opposed to how it is intended—is at the heart of the "spectacular failure" of most social reforms (p. 4). Although designers of change reap more rewards than costs, for implementers the reverse is true, and this is a major source of resistance (p. 127).

Chapter Three

The Culture of Resistance

*Like almost all other complex traditional social
organizations, the schools will accommodate in ways that
require little or no change. . . . The strength of the status
quo—its underlying axioms, its pattern of power
relationships, its sense of tradition and therefore what
seems right, natural, and proper—almost automatically
rules out options for change.*
—SEYMOUR SARASON (1990, P. 35)

It is not only as individuals that we seek patterns, stability, and
meaning but also as groups. In fact, the conservative impulse is perhaps seen nowhere more clearly than in the phenomenon we call
culture. In the late twentieth century, analyzing organizations
through the lens of culture has achieved a prominent place in
American management. The concept of organizational culture is
now used liberally throughout both the private and public sectors,
not only by academics who study organizations but also by practitioners themselves, businesspeople and educators alike. Its ubiq-
uity reflects its utility, but it has also led to problems of clarity.
There are literally hundreds of definitions of culture (Morgan, p.
359) but no single, universally accepted definition. What it actually is and its role in organizations can be controversial topics and
the focus of exaggerated expectations. The growing recognition
of the importance of culture to innovation has brought with it not
only much sophisticated analysis but also much glib prescription
and facile advice about how an organization's culture can be
rapidly transformed through creative, heroic leadership. But a

careful look at the true nature and functions of organizational culture reveals that it operates at a profound level, exerting a potent influence over beliefs and behavior to preserve continuity and oppose change.

Defining Organizational Culture

Definitions of organizational culture range from the simple to the complex. Many people use it to describe an organization's traditional practices and modes of operating or its climate and general ambience. An elementary school principal who resigned after his first year at a new school exemplified this usage when he explained, "I didn't fit their culture. My style is very assertive and theirs is laissez-faire." A superintendent, seeking help for a high school whose faculty was sharply divided over a major restructuring effort, said, "The culture there is terrible. They've hated one another for years, and they all just look out for themselves." These uses of *culture* are not inappropriate, but neither are they correct. Though in everyday parlance we need not be exact about the meaning of the term, when we attempt to make fundamental change in the way a school operates, precision becomes much more important. We need to know what we're trying to change.

The most authoritative student of organizational culture, Edgar Schein, defines it as "the deeper level of *basic assumptions* and *beliefs* that are shared by members of an organization, that operate unconsciously, and that define in a basic 'taken-for-granted' fashion an organization's view of itself and its environment. These assumptions and beliefs are learned responses to a group's problems of *survival* in the external environment and its problems of *internal integration*. They come to be taken for granted because they solve those problems repeatedly and reliably" (1985, p. 6, emphasis in original). As these assumptions and beliefs permeate an entire organization, they become invisible; they become so accepted, so automatic and ingrained in the organization's routine practices that they are automatically taught to its new members, by both precept and example, as "the correct way to perceive, think, and feel" about problems (Schein, 1992, p. 12).

The two essential characteristics of organizational culture are depth and structure. An organization's culture should be distinguished from closely related phenomena such as its climate, norms, formal philosophy, customs, and symbols (Schein, 1992, pp. 8–10). All of these emanate in part from culture and reflect it, but none of them are the same thing as culture. For one thing, they reflect the impact of other influences, such as the external environment or the ethos of a particular profession rather than a particular organization. For example, much of the way doctors deal with their patients and with one another results from their training and initiation into the role of physician and the world of a given hospital. But the main reason for not treating these features as culture is that they do not operate at the same level. Culture is the construct that gathers these other phenomena into a unique, profound structure. To call something "cultural" is to say not only that it is shared but also that it runs very deep, that it is stable, and that it is integrated into a larger gestalt. Culture "implies that rituals, climate, values, and behaviors [form] a coherent whole. This patterning . . . is the *essence* of what we mean by 'culture'" (Schein, 1992, pp. 10–11, emphasis in original).[1]

There are three levels of culture: artifacts and creations, values, and basic assumptions. It is the first two that are often referred to indiscriminately as culture itself. The former is the most tangible level of culture, the physical and social environment. Included here are a school's physical space, its language, its style of dress, its climate, its norms of behavior and mores concerning the display of emotion, its myths and stories, its customs, rituals, and ceremonies. One has only to walk into a school to begin noticing these characteristics. How is the building decorated? How are the classrooms arranged? How do people acknowledge one another in the hall? How are meetings run? These kinds of artifacts and behaviors are the most visible features of an institution's culture. A visitor immediately begins to compare them with those of other schools and starts to form certain impressions about what they "say" about this school. But though these features are easy to notice and offer intriguing clues about a school's culture, they can be difficult to interpret because they may not mean what we think they mean. Until we know the school much better, we cannot fully comprehend them.

The second level, values, is more complex. Values develop as problems are solved. When a solution to a problem works reliably, it becomes invested with special significance. It comes to be seen as "the way to do it." It begins as a hypothesis, but ultimately it becomes accepted as a reality; it is transformed into a shared value or belief that is taken for granted (Schein, 1992, p. 21). Values that become ingrained in this way can be of several types and can operate at a higher or lower level of awareness. In many schools, faculty can describe the values that guide their work and their collegial behavior. In all schools, as in all organizations, there are some values that members of the organization are not usually aware of that affect decisions and behavior. In addition, some of the values that members are aware of are what Chris Argyris (1976) calls "espoused," that is, values people profess but do not typically practice. In most organizations, there are principles to which people merely pay lip service. In many schools, for example, the concept of equity has received considerable attention in recent years. "Every child can learn" and "respect for individual differences" are themes commonly proclaimed in school mission statements or cited if a visitor asks about a school's guiding values. In some schools these are truly enacted and vigorously pursued; more frequently, however, they are simply ignored, even when they are stated with real force.

Finally, at the deepest level of culture, are an organization's basic assumptions. These are fundamental, underlying shared convictions that guide behavior and shape the way group members perceive, think, and feel. They operate at what we might call the *truly* cultural level—that is, the most unconscious, implicit depths. They are invisible and nearly invincible. Cultural assumptions and beliefs are much harder to grasp and understand than the surface artifacts that emerge from them and hint at them. Vaill underscores this point by defining culture as "a *system* of attitudes, actions, and artifacts that *endures over time* and [produces] among its members a relatively *unique common psychology*" (1989, p. 147, emphasis in original). Though we may draw inferences about the unique common psychology of a school by studying its artifacts and values, we can understand it only by participating in the life of the school for a long time. But it is this unique common psychology— fundamental similarities in thinking and feeling, perceiving and valuing—that gives meaning to the attitudes, actions, and artifacts of a school's culture.

Functions of Culture

Organizational culture is both product and process, effect and cause. It represents the collective knowledge of our predecessors, and it is perpetually renewed as we initiate new members, who eventually initiate others, and so on (Bolman and Deal, p. 250). Once established, it not only shapes people's behavior, perception, and understanding of events, it provides the template for organizational learning. Culture exerts a profound impact on the induction and orientation of organizational members and on the way an organization responds to changes in its environment. Most institutions make sure that new recruits "learn the ropes," which includes the elementals of task performance and a variety of formal and informal roles and procedures. But they also teach and model a fundamental way of seeing, understanding, and responding. In giving meaning to people's experience, culture dictates how they interpret and react to events (Deal and Peterson, 1991, p. 8). In providing this framework, it helps them not only to define and respond to problems but also, more broadly, to master new events by assimilating them into the structures of meaning they have acquired. In so doing, it provides an important source of security for both individuals and the organization as a whole.[2]

Culture thus serves as an enormous conservative force, the collective expression of the conservative impulse within individuals. It reflects "our human need for stability, consistency, and meaning" (Schein, 1992, p. 11). Hence, the culture of an institution strongly supports continuity. Indeed, it is as if this were its chief purpose. As Herbert Kaufman points out, "The logic of collective life . . . has a conservative thrust," and organizations by their very nature have "an aversion to unpredictability" (p. 80). In this regard they generally serve their members well. Though the rhetoric of social reform typically castigates institutions for their resistance to change—and much of the rhetoric of restructuring in education follows suit—one of the chief benefits people seek in their organizational affiliations is protection from change. The routines of any school provide a basic security, a framework within which people can come to count on one another and trust the world to be the way it is supposed to be. Indeed, this "comforting assurance that the immediate environment will not change significantly all at once" (Kaufman, p. 80) is a primary reason why people put up with the many irritations of organizational life. Whatever we may think in the abstract about the need for change in other people's organizations, we usually look to our own for predictability.

From this vantage point, what is surprising is not that institutions resist innovation but that anyone should expect them to welcome it. In fact, there do exist organizations that are inventive and creative, that "break the mold" in the way they operate, but these tend to be new or young. As they succeed and grow, they typically become more conservative, hierarchical, and structured. Among mature organizations there are those that develop innovative solutions to internal or external problems—even some that achieve a real renaissance—but it is extremely rare for them to reinvent themselves repeatedly over a long period of time. For institutions of all kinds, just as for individuals, stability, far more than change, is the rule. Organizations are "social systems in which people have norms, values, shared beliefs, and paradigms of what is right and what is wrong, what is legitimate and what is not, and how things are done" (Bennis, 1989, p. 30). These "forces for conservatism" support the status quo and discourage both dissent and innovation. One achieves status and power only by accepting them. Organizations must also contain a means for development so as not to become paralyzed, but there is persuasive evidence that the conservative thrust of organizational culture, including the cultures of strong, effective organizations, rarely encourages such development.

Strong Cultures, Old Cultures, Weak Cultures

Influenced in part by research on school climate—efforts to identify the characteristics that make a school both a good workplace and a good learning environment—some of the writing on school culture tends to try to identify the qualities of a good (or "strong") culture so that we might export these to other schools with what are sometimes called "weak" (that is, negative) cultures. This approach overlooks two problems: healthy, positive cultures are almost never flexible and are typically quite resistant to change— and so too are supposedly weak, negative cultures!

The benefits of a positive school culture are evident. It offers an effective means of coordination and control and a center of shared purposes and values that provides "inspiration, meaning, and significance" for members of the school community (Sergiovanni, 1991, p. 222). However, there is considerable evidence that excellent organizations, those that achieve and sustain high levels of performance, do so in part because of their members' unswerving commitment to their goals. Having become sure of the rightness of their goals, believing that they have created an approach that works and is effective, they are prepared to stay the course (Vaill, 1989, p. 66). More generally, any strong culture tends to be quite conservative simply because "a coherent statement of who we are makes it harder for us to become something else" (Weick, 1985, p. 385). And such a culture resists not only new ways of approaching problems but also new blood as well. No strongly cohesive group admits newcomers freely, especially those who challenge its values and practices. The stronger the culture, the more firmly it resists new influences.

In addition to the stability that is bred by success, there is the further fact that, like a person, a culture tends to grow more conservative with age. During an organization's birth and early growth, its culture begins as a distinctive competence, a source of identity, the "glue" that holds things together. When an organization reaches maturity—the stage that characterizes most schools—its culture generally becomes a constraint on innovation and a defense against new influences (Schein, 1992, pp. 314). Traditional patterns of doing things have become so ingrained that they seem to have a momentum of their own. If the institution has enjoyed a history of success with its assumptions about itself and its environment, people will not want to question or reexamine them, "because they justify the past and are the source of their pride and self-esteem" (Schein, 1985, p. 292). Thus, for all their advantages, strong cultures can be "backward, conservative instruments of adaptation" (Weick, p. 385). They can suffer from rigidity; they can be slow to detect changes and opportunities and slow to respond once opportunities are sensed.

It may be understandable that the members of an old, successful organization would resist change. It seems much less sensible that the members of a weak, ineffective organization should do so. Indeed, many school reform proposals seem to assume that it is precisely because schools are such dispirited, ineffective institutions that fundamental change is not only necessary but welcome to teachers. For example, proposals for school-based management and collegial, shared decision making expect teachers to respond eagerly to the chance to throw off old practices and habits. However, as teachers (like workers in many occupations) have proved, this rarely happens. In fact, many teachers, even if they dislike their current school, are not hungry for change; they cling to their culture. Like most people, they depend on their organization for stability, and even disadvantaged members of a group routinely acquiesce in the systems that treat them badly. As the Founding Fathers noted in the Declaration of Independence: "All experience hath shown, that mankind are more disposed to suffer, while evils are sufferable, than to right themselves by abolishing the forms to which they are accustomed."

To an objective observer, such behavior may seem foolish and self-defeating. But culture serves a vital anxiety-reducing function, and so people grasp it tightly even after it becomes dysfunctional (Schein, 1985, p. 320). When strongly held, a basic assumption provides security and makes action based on any other premise virtually inconceivable. Learning something new in this context requires us to resurrect, reexamine, and revise fundamental aspects of our worldview. This "destabilizes our cognitive and interpersonal world" (Schein, 1992, p. 22), causing intense anxiety. Rather than tolerate such anxiety, we interpret events around us to be congruent with our assumptions, even if this means "distorting, denying, projecting, or in other ways falsifying to ourselves what may be going on around us" (p. 22). So-called weak cultures may seem irrational and may fail to support efficacy or self-esteem, but they fulfill a function we cannot live without and so turn out to be remarkably tough.

Culture as Prison

This persistence means that culture can be a kind of prison (Morgan, pp. 199–202). It can sharply confine both our perspective and our approach to problem solving. From the time we join the faculty of a school and begin to become acculturated, as we learn the school's traditions and customs and adopt its perspectives, as we master our tasks and fulfill a role, we make a trade-off that helps entrench the power of the school's culture. As Freud showed long ago, to live in groups requires us to repress powerful individual impulses, both conscious and unconscious. Though we do so, these impulses nonetheless influence the workplace cultures we establish. Moreover, we find ways to gratify these impulses in sublimated form. Wishes to be powerful (or even immortal), for example, can be satisfied by membership in organizations, which are "larger than life and [last] for generations" (Morgan, p. 213). In becoming identified with the organization we work for, we come to find meaning and permanence; and "as we invest ourselves in our work, our roles become our realities" (p. 213). We define ourselves by what we do. To have an identifiable occupational role is to be a "who" and a "what" (Levinson, 1991). Consequently, we are loath to tolerate any interference in these roles. We may become dependent on culture in a way that causes us to oppose any innovation that threatens our dependency (Morgan, p. 230). A school may be a chronically troubled and demoralized workplace and yet still provide for many of its teachers and administrators gratifications they will not willingly abandon.

The trouble with this dependency is that culture becomes a self-fulfilling prophecy: "False assumptions, taken-for-granted beliefs, unquestioned operating rules . . . can combine to create self-contained views of the world that provide both a resource for and a constraint on organized action. While they create a way of seeing and suggest a way of acting, they also tend to create ways of not seeing and eliminate the possibility of [other] actions" (Morgan, pp. 199–202). One need not embrace the metaphor of a prison to see that culture is much more complicated than is acknowledged by popular notions about managing or changing it. Though leaders may influence its evolution, they can never shape it in the way that many management books suggest. It is so pervasive that it is "not amenable to direct control" (pp. 137–138), and an organization's beliefs and ideas about itself, its mission, and its environment are much more likely to perpetuate themselves and resist change than is commonly imagined.

Culture Change

For those who are persuaded of the necessity of changing the culture of schools, all this may be quite dispiriting. Is there no hope, they may wonder, for deep, systemic change in schools? The answer is that culture change can occur, but it is a vastly more difficult, lengthy undertaking than most people imagine. To a related question—Is there any hope for rapid culture change in schools?—the answer is no. Many educational leaders have been victimized, just as managers in the private sector have been, by the promise of a quick culture fix. Unfortunately, as Vaill (1989) suggests, the idea of culture has been misused. As it becomes ever clearer that cultural patterns determine much of what happens in organizations, there is a tendency to shift from talking about culture to thinking about what can be done to culture to move it toward particular goals. Even some of the sharpest observers of schools who have correctly identified the importance of cultural change have underestimated the difficulty of accomplishing it. However, for many of the reasons advanced above, Vaill argues that it is likely that organizational culture cannot be changed and that trying to do so simply strengthens the culture and stimulates resistance. There is, to begin with, an obvious difficulty: any organization that sets out to change its own culture remains powerfully influenced by that culture even as it attempts the change. Even those who seek to create new settings are armed with—and disarmed by—the ways of thinking that led to the very conditions they hope to remedy (Sarason, 1972, pp. xii–xiii). We don't, after all, "just put on and take off these gestalts, these big pictures, these paradigms, casually. . . . It is a major achievement to get outside one's gestalt and experience the world as those with other gestalts are experiencing it" (Vaill, 1989, p. 104).

In part because of this difficulty, much of what is called a change of culture simply is not. Real culture change is "systemic change at a deep psychological level involving attitudes, actions, and artifacts that have developed over substantial periods of time" (Vaill, 1989, pp. 149–150). The changes that most schools are currently undertaking are generally far more superficial, even when they are novel. Many involve simply setting new criteria for measuring performance, as when a school district announces a new portfolio-based assessment program but makes no changes in the instructional goals that will be measured by the new scheme. This kind of shift may prove to be important and to be one element of an eventual culture change, but it does not by itself constitute such a change. Similarly, creating participatory, collaborative structures (site-based management and peer coaching programs, for example) may produce what some call "contrived collegiality," but they do not by themselves change underlying norms, assumptions, and values about professional collaboration and collegiality. Calling such shifts "cultural" misrepresents. It creates the expectation that the basic assumptions, core beliefs, and behavior of teachers and administrators—their unique common psychology—will change. In reality, their unique common psychology is likely to ignore most of the new criteria and changes, bend slightly to those that are not too challenging, and resist those that amount to a direct confrontation (Vaill, 1989, p. 150).[3]

In light of the perspective this chapter provides, the eager optimism of apostles of culture change is misguided and misleading. Unfortunately, however, the facile assurance of popular management tracts seems to have found its way onto the agendas of major educational conferences and into the goals for reform adopted by states, school boards, and administrators. Though the weight of the evidence confirms the difficulty of accomplishing true culture change, there are many who hugely underestimate the task. If anything, such change is even harder in schools than in corporations, since schools are by their very nature less entrepreneurial and more bureaucratic and since most are mature rather than new institutions. The gravitational pull of culture is stronger in them. We should anticipate that the enthusiastic embrace of change and the rapid transformation of norms and values will be rare, an exception to be wondered at. Not only should we see school culture as a force acting against change, we should also remember that this opposition is sensible, even when the necessity for change may seem compelling from an external perspective. No institution can readily abandon the deep structures on which its very coherence and significance depends. Thus, we find repeated at the collective level the same conservative impulse we saw among individuals—an impulse as vital as it is profound and which reform, if it is to succeed, must respect.

To acknowledge the forces that support the status quo is neither to endorse the status quo nor to absolve us of the duty to address serious problems embedded within it. No matter how insistent the conservative impulse, we can still make critical judgments about the adequacy of our institutions and our own performance. We can see that our system of schooling needs improvement in many areas. Indeed, I have reviewed the psychological and cultural obstacles to change not to argue that reform is impossible but to counter naive assumptions about innovation and to assert that reform, if it is to succeed, must accept the realities of human nature. The next step on our path is to look at the implementation of innovation in light of these realities.

Notes

1. As Morgan observes, an organization's culture always runs much deeper than its mission statement and its members' behavior. The characteristics that "decorate the surface of organizational life" merely give clues to "a much deeper and all-pervasive system of meaning" (p. 133).

2. "All human systems," says Schein, "attempt to maintain equilibrium and to maximize their autonomy vis-a-vis their environment. Coping, growth, and survival all involve maintaining the integrity of the system in the face of a changing environment. The set of shared assumptions that develop over time in groups and organizations serves this stabilizing and meaning-providing function. The evolution of culture is therefore one of the ways in which a group or organization preserves its integrity and autonomy, differentiates itself from the environment and other groups, and provides itself an identity" (1992, p. 298).

3. This does not mean that culture cannot change or that leaders cannot shape it, only that the changing and shaping take a very long time. There are many steps that can make a real difference in a school's climate and performance and that can *eventually* become part of the culture. The leadership biases I outline in the latter part of this book facilitate such changes. See also Deal and Peterson (1991) and Saphier and King (1985).

Part Two

Dimensions
of Change

Chapter Four

Implementation: Tasks of Transition

Any change comes down to people: first how you help them face it and then how you help them move with it.
—PRINCIPAL

This chapter begins our focus on the actual ingredients of the change process. It outlines the tasks of implementation, the transitions that leaders must help teachers accomplish individually and collectively. It offers a framework for conceptualizing any school improvement and assessing its goals—the fundamentals a change agent needs to keep in mind. The beginning task is to make the case for innovation, to emphasize the seriousness of a problem and the rightness of a solution. This frequently involves challenging teachers' acceptance of and comfort with the status quo. It involves, in essence, provoking the four problematic aspects of change discussed in Chapter Two: loss, incompetence, confusion, and conflict. This can be difficult and unpleasant. It is, however, just the beginning. One must then help staff address the four dilemmas, help them move from loss to commitment, from old competence to new competence, from confusion to coherence, and from conflict to consensus. Table 4.1 summarizes these tasks.

Unfreezing

One cannot hope to implement change without persuading people that it is necessary. This is a task of daunting proportions that

Table 4.1. Tasks of Change.

Task	Goal	Key Factors
Unfreezing	• Increase the fear of not trying • Reduce the fear of trying	• Disconfirmation • Appropriate anxiety and guilt • Psychological safety
Moving from loss to commitment	Make change meaningful	• Continuity • Time • Personal contact
Moving from old competence to new competence	Develop new behaviors (skills), beliefs, and ways of thinking	Training that is coherent, continuous, and personal
Moving from confusion to coherence	Realign structures, functions, and roles	Clarity regarding responsibility, authority, and decision making
Moving from conflict to consensus	Generate broad support for change	• A critical mass • Pressure • Positive use of power

must often start by challenging people's view of themselves, their performance, and their clients. The most thoughtful, realistic approach that I have encountered is Schein's concept of change as "unfreezing."[1] This approach recognizes the tendency of people and systems to maintain a homeostasis. Innovation requires the learning of something new, usually in place of something old, which unavoidably makes people anxious. As we have already seen, people naturally cling to their current skills and are afraid to try new ones, especially when the changes involved are large and complex or when the time frame is short or the tolerance for error is low—all conditions that apply in schools today. In such a context, it becomes easy to rationalize the value of the tried and true and the impossibility of the new. Unfreezing is a matter of lessening one kind of anxiety, the fear of trying, but first of mobilizing another kind of anxiety, the fear of *not* trying.

Unless something increases the cost of preserving the status quo, the conservative impulse and the cumulative impact of culture and past learning are too strong to permit innovation. People must be sufficiently dissatisfied with the present state of affairs—and their role in maintaining it—or they have no reason to endure the losses and challenges of change. Someone must make the case for change by "disconfirming" people's reading of their situation and their satisfaction with their current practices. This does not mean castigating and blaming them, but it often means challenging people to face realities they have preferred to avoid. Often, teachers experience this approach as negative and critical because it confronts a school with its shortcomings, with the gaps between its professed goals and its actual achievements, and asserts the need for change. One must usually raise people's guilt by noting how their performance violates a shared ideal ("We say we believe that every child can learn, but more and more students are dropping out and we're doing nothing to help them") or raise their anxiety by noting how their performance violates a shared goal or threatens their well-being ("We asked for new staffing and materials to improve literacy, but our results are no better; if they don't improve, we will lose the staff and funding and return to our old class sizes").

This kind of confrontation can be crucial, especially at the outset of an innovation; but as abundant evidence shows, it is incomplete. Disconfirmation alone does not motivate change. If one only threatens people, they resist in all sorts of ways, overt and covert, conscious and unconscious. Disconfirmation can engender much fear and loathing—so much that people often dismiss the information as irrelevant, which lets them repress any anxiety or guilt. This is why in many schools and organizations disconfirming data about performance exist for a long time but are denied or devalued: "If the change . . . threatens my whole self, I will deny the data and the need for change. Only if I can feel that I will retain my identity or my integrity as I learn something new or make a change, will I be able to even contemplate it" (Schein, 1992, p. 300). What is also needed is to reduce the anxiety surrounding change, the fear of trying.

This can only be accomplished by preserving psychological safety. That is, the confrontation about the need for change must avoid humiliation, ad hominem attacks, blanket condemnations, and demands that people admit they were wrong. The change agent must make clear his caring and support, his commitment to working with people to take the difficult steps toward new learning. He must reaffirm connection and help make the change meaningful to people by finding the familiar in the new and strength amidst weakness. He must convey two essential, contrasting messages. The first is, "This is very serious, the risks of inaction are very real, and we must change." The second is, "I value you as people, and I will help you get where we need to go." He must straddle a fault line between pressure and support, change and continuity—confirming his commitment to the people who must accomplish the change even as he expresses his commitment to change and urges them to act. No wonder Schein calls unfreezing "one of the most complex and artful of human endeavors" (1987, p. 98).

From Loss to Commitment

Unfreezing is the start—and only the start. Most innovations flourish only if staff adopt them actively, becoming vigorous, engaged participants. Hence, the second task of change is to help those who must implement it move from loss to commitment, from a letting go of the old to a true embrace of the new. This principle has for far too long been overlooked in school reform. It is especially vital now. Many improvement proposals call not just for new curricula taught in a traditional fashion or for a few new wrinkles in pedagogy but for markedly different ways of conceptualizing learning and teaching. For example, Theodore Sizer (1984) and his colleagues in the Coalition of Essential Schools have sparked a growing interest in a far less teacher-centered classroom, one that emphasizes the twin concepts of student-as-worker and teacher-as-coach. They have also pioneered efforts to rethink assessment, emphasizing the need to have students demonstrate their grasp of what they learn through real-life exhibitions rather than traditional tests. None of these changes can be accomplished to any significant degree by teachers who simply try to tolerate them or who "go along" passively; all require active commitment and participation on the part of teachers.

Given all we know about the natural resistance to change, helping people move from loss to commitment may appear a truly daunting task. It is, but it is not an impossible one. For if the obstacles to change are formidable, it is equally true that there are tendencies within the individual that support adaptation. Moreover, we have recently gained some knowledge about steps in the change process that not only provide psychological safety but also facilitate transition and the development of commitment.

This knowledge begins with Chapter Two's observation that resistance is not only inevitable but also an integral part of adaptation. Although change usually represents loss, from such loss comes not only despair but also innovation. Indeed, despair is often the root of innovation. The strength of our tendency to seek patterns, the tenacity with which we cling to purposes and relationships, leads us at first to resist change, often fiercely; but it also inclines us, ultimately, to accept it. When a loss is permanent, we must reinterpret our purposes and attachments. To do this, we must first accept the loss not merely as an event that has happened but as part of "a series of events that we must now expect to happen. . . . The conservative impulse will make us seek to deny the loss. But when this fails, it will also lead us to repair the thread [of continuity], tying past, present and future together again with rewoven strands of meaning" (Marris, p. 21). Given the chance to revise and broaden the framework by which we understand things, our need to preserve continuity moves us to incorporate a change into our pattern of meaning and adapt to it.

For this adaptation to occur, we must be able to make sense of the loss caused by change. Meaning is the core issue that determines how people cope. Coping hinges crucially upon such questions as, Is the loss intelligible? and, Can some rewarding purpose be drawn from it? (Marris, pp. xiii–xiv). That is, assuming one could adapt to the new requirements successfully, does one want to? Workplace restructurings commonly lead some staff to decide that they do not wish to adjust, even if they could, because their changed roles would not be meaningful enough. Thus, three veteran teachers in an elementary school decided to take early retirement after their state and then their school district each adopted extensive new curriculum requirements. One said, "It's just not worth it anymore.

They're dictating most of what I teach. I could do what they're asking—it's not complex—but I wouldn't be a *teacher* anymore. I'd be a robot or a puppet." More often, people decide that they want to stay. For both groups, there is loss. But for the second, those who must adapt and must implement the change, coping requires working out new meanings, making enough sense of the loss so that they can come to accept new functions and assume new roles. This is a kind of grief work. The conditions that are required for adaptation are those necessary for resolving grief, chief among them continuity, time, and personal contact.

Change agents tend to conceive of their improvements as substitutions—replacing something old and worse and irrational with something new and better and logical. But people cannot resolve their grief simply by substitution; they must work their way through it. They must learn to reformulate the purposes and attachments that are threatened by change (Marris, p. 158). This process is complex, both cognitively and emotionally. It needs continuity. People must be helped to link the new with the old, to see the future not as disconnected from the past but as related to it. Ideally, they need to see the future as fulfilling traditional values in new ways: "Confidence in the original commitment is restored by extracting its essential meaning and grafting it upon the present" (p. 92). This requires an affirmation of the enduring importance of the original commitment and a search for ways in which investing in its new definition will be worthwhile.

This search involves a period—often lengthy—of distress and ambivalence as people try to grasp the full extent of what is being lost and modify their pattern of meaning to incorporate the new. But until this search is complete, it is "the only deeply meaningful activity in which the bereaved can be engaged" (Marris, p. 92). It cannot be hurried, and each person must do it for himself. Efforts to jump-start change, to preempt opposition or conflict by thorough planning and rational explanation, are likely to be futile. No matter how reasonable a proposed innovation may appear to its authors, no matter how readily they might think staff can or should adapt to it, the process of implementation "must still allow the impulse of rejection to play itself out" (p. 155). For it is only by expressing this impulse, by reworking (often, again and again) our experience of loss and the necessity to adapt that we come to accept change and commit ourselves to something new.

Respecting people's need to process loss and to fashion their own meaning of change includes allowing them the time they need to achieve these milestones. Responses to change are so highly personal that all the individuals who will be affected by it must have the chance to work it through, become familiar with it, see how it fits, and discover what they can gain from it as well as what it will cost them (Fullan, p. 127). This takes time. When we seek genuine commitment and changes in belief, the people doing the changing, not us, are in control of the transformation. This is particularly true when the ultimate goal of innovation is to affect not just teachers' behavior but the very ways they think about schooling. If the change agent tries to bypass or suppress what teachers value— to hurry things along with a hard sell or by simply imposing a set of changes or techniques or a new ideology—the result is likely to be paradoxical: resistance will stiffen, and the old values will resurface at a later point (Morgan, p. 222).

Though no one can do grief work for another, considerable experience confirms that progress from loss to commitment benefits enormously from personal contact between the leaders and targets of change. Those who are being asked to adapt respond better when they have regular attention from, and access to, those who are responsible for it. This contact serves two key functions: the obvious one is to help in the learning of new skills (see the following section). The less obvious—but equally important—aspect is to assuage the very personal losses innovation provokes. Not least among these is the severing of personal attachments as people leave and relationships are altered. This is in itself a source of bereavement. Because attachment is so vital to our security in childhood, it becomes permanently ingrained in our sense of safety and reward henceforth. Thus, changes that upset our attachments "disrupt [our] ability to experience life as meaningful, and plunge [us] into grief, however rational these changes may seem [to] someone with other attachments" (Marris, p. ix). When the three elementary school teachers discussed above resigned, their departure intensified the loss felt by the teachers who stayed on, even those who approved of the new curriculum guidelines. One of them said, "I actually think the new requirements are OK, but I miss those three terribly. They left huge holes in this building." A key way that teachers' needs for continuity can be sustained is by regular contact with a sympathetic principal who will acknowledge the distress they are experiencing even as she reconfirms the promise of change and reinforces the necessity and promise of the new skills required. Personal contact that is oriented toward both task performance and emotional adjustment rather than just one or the other facilitates staff progress from loss to commitment.

Taking this notion one step farther, one can argue for the importance of overt public acknowledgment and specific rites of mourning when the people in an institution suffer significant loss.

> In 1989, the Fulton County school system in Atlanta, Georgia, closed twenty-three schools. They accomplished this highly difficult task with little of the turmoil that typically overwhelms efforts to terminate programs, divisions, or units. They succeeded, in part, because they encouraged each school to provide opportunities for teachers, students, administrators, parents, and others to share their grief, let go, and move on. One elementary school, for example, invited the entire community, as well as graduates and retirees, to attend the closing ceremony. The principal gave a speech, students read poems, and teachers, alumni, and others shared memories from the school's rich history. As the ceremony drew to a close, the custodial staff wrapped the entire school with a large red ribbon. The next day a crew demolished the brick building. Later, each person who attended the closing event received a brick tied with a red ribbon, and a videotape, taken from a helicopter, that showed the custodians wrapping the school for its last picture [Bolman and Deal, 1991, p. 393].

Unfortunately, neither continuity, time for grief, nor personal contact come naturally to many change agents. As we saw in Chapter Two, innovators tend to concentrate on the potential benefits of their recommendations and overlook the effort and pain of adapting. They can easily assume a very moralistic tone: change is right, the status quo is wrong. Because they rarely acknowledge the loss provoked by innovation, they rarely attend to the grief of those it affects. They tend to be impatient to get on with progress and to see implementation as a matter of persuasion and power: leaders should explain the rational necessity for the change and then use appropriate combinations of carrot and stick to induce or, if necessary, compel compliance. But to rely on these alone is to overestimate the influence of the leader and to underestimate the realities of adaptation.

It is also an example of self-defeating hubris. After all, reformers who press staff to innovate have already assimilated the reform and found their own meaning in it. They have already worked out a reformulation of purposes and practices that makes sense to them, which may have taken them months or years to accomplish and may have caused them real distress. Denying others the opportunity to make a similar journey, criticizing them for not responding to explanations about change, dismissing their resistance or hesitation as ignorance or prejudice expresses arrogance and contempt for the meaning of other people's lives (Marris, p. 155). This contempt, which denies people the respect and the time necessary to move through loss toward commitment, does little but intensify opposition and impede implementation. In Chapter Ten, we will examine positive ways to address the need for continuity and contact.

From Old Competence to New Competence

Closely related to the building of new commitment is the building of new competence. Change redefines proficiency. It devalues current skills, even if they have been applied artfully—and even if those who have been applying them still see them as valid and successful. Implementation requires staff to move from what has become at least old competence (if not incompetence) to what is now defined as new competence. When, as with restructuring, the scope and sophistication of such change go far beyond minor modifications, this transition is especially challenging.

Of all the aspects of change, this need to help staff acquire new skills is perhaps the most obvious and the most widely acknowledged, and I shall not dwell on it. The extensive history of school reform has offered researchers ample opportunity to study the training that supports innovation. The findings are straightforward: to help teachers develop new competence, training must be coherent, personal, and continuous. *Coherent* refers to the design and sequencing of the training content. Sessions must be relevant to the innovation and unfold in a logical way that provides teachers with both an overview of the larger goals and a walk-through of the specific objectives and the methods for achieving them. *Personal* refers to the importance of tailoring training to the current knowledge, practice, and felt needs of teachers. Credible, easily accessible technical assistance has proven vital to the successful implementation of all sorts of school reforms. New practices depend crucially on the amount of personal assistance teachers receive and how user-friendly this assistance is (Elmore and McLaughlin, 1988, p. 46). As we have previously seen, change threatens people's self-esteem and their need to feel effective, valued, and in control. Technical training must meet them where they are and nurture their confidence. Explaining, training, modeling, and practicing must be more individual and intimate in proportion to the size and complexity of the change. It is an axiom of organizational development that the greater the change, the more interaction it requires.

To be effective, training must also be continuous. That is, it must not only precede innovation but also accompany it through the early and into the middle stages of implementation. Mastery of new concepts, materials, and methods, though typically the unique focus of staff development efforts, is actually the last stage of a complex cognitive and affective process. The first stage is survival, as teachers try to cope with new curriculum or pedagogy. The second is consolidation, as they try to integrate the various aspects of their new training into their traditional roles and routines. Negotiating these two stages requires, among other things, persuading teachers that new practices will make them better educators, opportunities for safe rehearsal of new approaches, systematic feedback about their progress—and time, both to reflect and interact with colleagues and simply to manage the business of new learning while maintaining current daily routines (Elmore and McLaughlin, pp. 45–46).

All training should be coherent, personal, and continuous, but this is especially vital to improvements that ask educators not just to change their materials and teaching techniques but to change their basic beliefs and the way they conceptualize their work. Getting teachers to embrace new curricula and methods is complex enough; getting them to accept new beliefs is even more so. It challenges their core values about the very purposes of education. Restructuring initiatives press teachers to expand and modify some of their most basic assumptions—those lodged deep at the implicit, cultural level—about who can be educated and how and about the range and nature of their own professional responsibility. For example, the mainstreaming of special needs students involves new materials, a greater range of curriculum goals, and a wider variety of teaching approaches—but what it demands most is a new conceptualization of learning and teaching, one that radically broadens a teacher's definition of her responsibility. She must accept special needs students as properly hers and capable of meaningful learning, not as "special ed kids" who really belong in a separate class and are an obstacle to covering the "regular" syllabus with her "real" students. Basic assumptions are deeper and less tangible than skills and cannot be changed by didactic instruction anymore than by mandate (although, as noted below, they can by influenced by requiring people to try new behavior). But training must include continuing opportunities for teachers to consider, discuss, argue about, and work through changes in their assumptions. Without this, the technical changes they are exposed to during training are unlikely to make a deep, lasting impact on their practice.

All of this may seem quite obvious. But although the importance of training is axiomatic, the actuality frequently falls far short of the ideal. In the first place, a great many districts seem to assume that the primary key to innovation lies in technical training and, where they can be afforded, technical resources (materials, time to meet and plan, and chances to practice). These are absolutely vital but not sufficient; they are secondary, not primary. Strong technical support encourages experimentation and is crucial to its ultimate implementation, but it rarely inspires initial commitment. Committed staff respond well to how-to-do-it training (they even seek it out) and make effective use of resources. Uncommitted staff do neither.

Of course, too often training is weak rather than strong. There isn't enough of it, what there is it isn't good enough, and it usually ignores the matter of beliefs and assumptions.[2] Much of it aims at marginal improvements, not fundamental change, at "making conventional teachers a little better at what they conventionally do by making them more conscious of what they have been doing all along" (Schlechty, 1990, p. 107). Trainers may preach the necessity of rethinking students' needs and redefining best practice, but teachers rarely get the opportunity to explore these issues in any extensive, meaningful, interactive way. Without the opportunity to build a new conceptual platform there is little to support new classroom practice.

From Confusion to Coherence

Reform may promise many improvements, but it always causes uncertainty and confusion, especially during the early stages of implementation. As we have seen, a school's formal roles, policies, and procedures provide guidelines for task completion, for the coordination of work, and for role definition. Even when they are widely disliked they structure daily experience, providing a pattern that is vital to the meaningfulness of educators' work and relationships. However, as we have also seen, innovation undermines these structural properties, particularly when, as with "restructuring," the very design of the school itself is a direct target of change.

There are no "surgical strikes" in reform, no improvements that only affect an isolated problem without producing any side effects elsewhere. The consequence for staff, as in Overton's conversion to a middle school model (Chapter Two), is confusion, uncertainty, even suspicion. Often during innovation there will develop misunderstandings about responsibility and authority ("I thought you were handling that"; "This decision is ours, not yours"). A chronic complaint by faculty is that their input is solicited but then ignored ("The administration doesn't listen to us and respect us"), while administrators feel faculty are shortsighted ("We did listen, we just didn't agree"). Confusion and mistrust in these areas are among the largest sources of distress and cynicism in schools. Change agents must help faculty to resolve such uncertainty, to move from confusion to coherence, to a new clarity in structure and function and in roles and relationships.

Whatever the nature of the improvement effort in a particular school, all those whose roles will be affected need to become clear about the new structural alignment and its implications for responsibility, authority, and decision making. They need to know what will be expected of them and what they can expect from others. They need to know how the school will be organized, where power will reside, and how choices will be made. Designers of change need not only to think these things through in advance but also to do so from the point of view of implementers. Of course, simply being clear, being able to lay out the new structure and roles at meetings and on paper, is insufficient—people need time and repetition to really "get it"—but it is essential. Says a teacher of her school's conversion to an accelerated school (Levin, 1988), "One thing that made change easier for us is that our principal is great at topic paragraphs and topic sentences. She could give us, up front, the big picture of what was involved. When someone asked her whether this meant more work for us and would change our team functioning, she could say, 'Yes. Here's what it means and here's what the payoff will be.'" Not being able to answer such essential questions increases the inevitable early confusion and, with it, resistance.

Decision making is improved by clarifying roles and responsibilities as well as procedures. One method for addressing the former comes from a procedure known as responsibility charting, or RASI. Leaders identify key participants according to one of four roles. *R* designates the person with responsibility for seeing that a decision is carried out. For each decision, there can be only one such person. *A* designates anyone who must approve (and who can also veto) the actions of *R*. *S* designates anyone who must provide support and resources to help *R*'s action (even if *S* doesn't agree with it). *I* designates anyone who must be informed about the decision and *R*'s actions (Beckhard and Harris, 1987, p. 104–105). Whether or not one is actually this specific in labeling the participants, innovation will be smoother and the troubleshooting of problems more effective when implementers are clear about who is responsible, who must approve, who must support, and who must be informed. It is equally important for people to be clear about decision-making processes, to know which decisions are the leader's and which are matters for collective input, for true consensus, and so on. Reforms that affect governance or require significant changes in relationships between subgroups of the school community will especially benefit from clarity of this kind.

There is much more to say about establishing coherence in change and about the who and how of decision making in restructured schools; we shall turn to this topic again in Chapter Eleven. Here I will just point out that many school reformers call for decision-making processes and roles that are markedly more democratic than they ever have been, with power struggles and political maneuvers replaced by shared governance and professional isolation by collaboration and collegiality. These advocates tend to view power in negative terms, to see traditional uses of power as part of the problem, not as a natural part of organizational life (and certainly not as part of the solution to problems). Their goal is for power to become decentralized and, at the school level, shared, with teachers (and sometimes parents) taking leading roles in governing and decision making and, in turn, sharing power with students in classrooms, encouraging them to become bold questioners and active learners. Implicit in this view is the expectation that large numbers of teachers are eager to be empowered and are able to handle the authority empowerment promises, that they are eager for collegial interaction and able to manage its complexities. These expectations are unrealistic; in my experience, they have complicated and wounded many school improvement efforts, often leaving many people unclear about the criteria and ground rules for particular decisions. The art, as we shall see, is to balance the liberating potential of participation with the legitimate need for leadership.

From Conflict to Consensus

Change causes conflict among individuals and groups largely because it creates winners and losers and upsets existing power arrangements. In Chapter Two I noted that a certain level of conflict is normal in any organization: people and groups naturally compete for position and influence. In many schools these tensions are already elevated by a chronic imbalance between rising demands and diminishing resources—a problem we will explore in Chapter Seven. Because it brings added responsibilities and always benefits some people more than others, change usually makes these tensions more salient, increasing friction and diminishing cooperation, opening new wounds and reopening old ones.

Moreover, the whole premise of unfreezing is that few of us are open to change if we are satisfied with our current performance ("Our students get into good colleges") or feel that the problems we encounter are the fault of others ("Today's students don't have good work habits"). Whenever they must engage in unfreezing, change agents are in the position of challenging people's self-satisfaction ("We're not really teaching even our brightest students to think. We're not reaching a whole set of non-college-bound students in a meaningful way"), of delivering messages that are often heartily unwelcome and can provoke real anger. Innovation must confront these types of issues. It must anticipate friction, address it constructively, and resolve it sufficiently to build an optimal level of harmony among stakeholders. To accomplish this requires, among other measures, building a critical mass of supporters, exerting pressure, and, throughout, making appropriate use of power.

The ultimate goal may be a true schoolwide consensus for change, but the first and most crucial target is a critical mass of committed supporters. What is a critical mass? It depends on many factors and is impossible to quantify. It is the right number of the right people. In some situations this means a majority of the stakeholders, in others, a smaller number of respected, influential people. In either case, when innovation reaches this critical mass and has recruited a range of advocates, change acquires a momentum of its own and moves into the mainstream of discussion, perception, and practice. Much of the resistance that emerges in the early stages of implementation begins to recede. Largely for this reason, the building of commitment among a critical mass of staff ranks among the most important goals change agents can set for themselves.

This means that planners need to decide who must be committed to the change and how to reach these key people. Realistically, not all staff will become committed, nor will those who do become committed reach the same level of commitment in the same way at the same time. To convert a majority of any institution's members to significant reform is a lengthy, difficult, uneven process. Although many restructuring goals require the highest levels of active involvement by teachers, it is naive to expect fervent participation from large numbers of faculty, especially at the outset. Nor is this necessary. What is necessary is to know who must become part of the critical mass and to what extent they must become invested. One way to conceptualize this task is suggested by Peter Senge's portrait of seven different degrees of support people can have for an organization's vision (1990, pp. 219–220):

Commitment: Wants it. Will make it happen. Creates whatever "laws" (structures) are needed.

Enrollment: Wants it. Will do whatever can be done within the "spirit of the law."

Genuine Compliance: Sees the benefits of the vision. Does everything expected and more. "Good soldier."

Formal Compliance: On the whole, sees the benefits of the vision. Does what's expected and no more. "Pretty good soldier."

Grudging Compliance: Does not see the benefits of the vision. But, also does not want to lose job. Does enough of what's expected because he has to, but also lets it be known that he is not really on board.

Noncompliance: Does not see the benefits of vision and will not do what's expected. "I won't do it; you can't make me."

Apathy: Neither for nor against vision. No interest. No energy. "Is it five o'clock yet?"

A simpler distinction can be made between three basic levels of commitment to change: make it happen, help it happen, and let it happen. What is needed from each person is the minimum level of engagement that will result in a critical mass of support (Beckhard and Harris, p. 94). However one frames the stages or levels of commitment, it would be ideal to have most staff in the upper reaches; but, as Senge notes, the genuinely compliant behave much like the enrolled and the committed. Indeed, "an organization made up of genuinely compliant people would be light-years ahead of most" in its performance (p. 221).

It is one thing to identify ideal members of a critical mass and another thing to engage them. Change agents need ways to help key participants reach a consensus for reform and then, with their help, expand this consensus throughout the school community. One way to think about any such agreement, whether of a critical mass or of a larger community, is in terms of individual commitments multiplied. All real change is personal, which means that it has to be accomplished person by person. Thus, the measures summarized above that aid unfreezing and the development of commitment, competence, and coherence are all relevant to the building of consensus. But though essential, they are insufficient. To rely on them alone to motivate change incrementally among a critical mass, let alone throughout an entire school, would take so long as to be self-defeating. Consensus needs not just support but also pressure.

Though we think of pressure as bad and support as good, pressure is vital to almost all innovation. The unfreezing outlined above is an example of early pressure used to arouse dissatisfaction. It usually needs to be sustained. When the ultimate goal is a change in beliefs and assumptions, something that cannot be imposed, it is often necessary to insist on a change in behavior, which can be. Changes in behavior lead to, as well as flow from, changes in belief (Fullan, p. 91). It is true, as argued above, that simply imposing change stiffens resistance (for example, forcing a group of teachers to team together doesn't make them good—or even willing—collaborators). But it is also true that experimenting with a new behavior is often a prerequisite to acquiring new learning (they will never grasp what teaming can offer or how to collaborate if they don't try it). Finally, pressure also helps make change inevitable and thus spurs the process by which we finally accept loss and reformulate our pattern of meaning.

Pressure, of course, implies the use of power. Despite the strong bias against power and politics that informs much of the school reform agenda, in studies of school innovation the presence of a powerful, adroit leader is repeatedly found to be vital to success (Elmore and McLaughlin, p. 22). However, power need not mean only coercion and exploitation; it can also mean exerting influence to pursue visions and goals, to move an organization toward a larger good and its members toward growth. In fact, David McClelland (1975) offered a famous distinction between these two aspects of power, sometimes known as power *over* versus power *to*. Though pressure includes coercion, coercion need not be an end in itself; it can be a means to fulfill a larger vision that takes into account the needs of all. Viewed in this way, it is quite compatible with support. In fact, the two are complementary: "Pressure without support leads to resistance and alienation; support without pressure leads to drift or waste of resources" (Fullan, p. 91). Successful innovation combines the right amount of both. We will return to this theme in Chapters Twelve and Thirteen.

These five tasks of change are not exhaustive. Nor are they the only way to conceptualize the requirements of innovation. Nor are the lists of factors I have linked to each task complete. But no matter how one might expand the catalogue of transitions facing people who must adapt to change, those I have traced here are crucial. New learning cannot occur without unfreezing, and loss, incompetence, confusion, and conflict are central obstacles to the success of innovation. No reform can germinate without raising the risks of not trying and reducing the risks of trying; none can flourish without helping people rebuild commitment, renew competence, restore coherence, and resolve conflict. Similarly, though there may be other factors that support school improvement, those sketched here—disconfirmation that preserves safety; respect, time, continuity, and personal contact; training that is coherent, continuous, and personal; clarity about responsibility, authority, and decision making; nurturing a critical mass of support, working through conflict, and making positive use of pressure and power—are all essential. Above all, to think about school change in this way is to keep our focus firmly where it belongs: on the realities of the people who must make change happen. Schlechty reminds us that to improve the performance of any "knowledge-work enterprise," such as a school, "one must invest in people, support people, and develop people. Indeed, human resource development becomes the linchpin upon which all improvement efforts are based" (1990, p. 139). As we explore the key factors in implementation and then leadership, this focus on people and the realities of their responses to change will continue to be our guide.

Notes

1. Developed from Kurt Lewin's theory of social change (1952), unfreezing is discussed by Schein in several places (1987, pp. 92–114; 1985, pp. 252–256, 294–295; 1992, pp. 298–303; 1993, pp. 88–90).
2. Training tends to be characterized by "well-intentioned 'ad hoc-ism'" (Fullan, p. 84): a few one-shot workshops by outside experts prior to

the start of curricular or instructional change. There is often little continuity from session to session, and it is rare to find follow-through as teachers move into implementation. Also, it is generally provided in large group settings with little opportunity for participants to personalize their learning through interaction and with little emphasis on actually practicing new behaviors.

Chapter Five

Substance: New Agendas, Old Problems

Planned change to these teachers is not the cumulative development of a comprehensive strategy. Rather, it is "one damned thing after another."
—PAUL BAKER, DEBORAH CURTIS, AND WAYNE BERENSON, 1991, P. 13

The dimensions of the change process begin with the substance of the change, the specific content of an actual innovation. Every attempt at significant reform will raise issues of loss, incompetence, confusion, and conflict, but the character of these issues will be shaped in part by the particular nature of the change itself (for example, beginning the full inclusion of special needs students will stir a different mix of concerns than initiating site-based management). The substance of a change program has four chief characteristics: its focus and clarity, its scope and complexity, its desirability, and its feasibility. The first two are properties of the initiative itself. Innovation is easiest to accomplish when its ends and means are sharply delineated and neither too extensive nor too intricate. The second two refer to the relevance of the innovation to those who must implement it. Teachers and administrators are most likely to find change desirable and feasible when it responds to a perceived need in a way they find promising and practical. Included in their assessment of need, promise, and practicality is credibility—especially whether the change is espoused by someone they trust.

Unfortunately, in all four of these areas, the reforms we call restructuring, far from appealing to most teachers, disappoint them. Historically, when reform has failed the blame has fallen on the school: the treatment would have worked but the patient was uncooperative. Now, a number of critics are challenging the assumptions of reformers, pointing to flaws in the design, origin, and emphasis of their proposals that make teacher support and widespread implementation unlikely. This perspective helps make teachers' resistance to reform more understandable. I pursue it in this chapter not to denigrate efforts at reform but to counter false optimism, to introduce more realism into what too often begins as a heady mix of hope and hype promoted by those outside schools and ends with the blaming of practitioners. Restructuring's substance, as it reaches educators, cuts sharply against the grain of their experience, concerns, and priorities and therefore lacks the credibility that would invite their consideration, greatly complicating the tasks of implementation.

Focus and Clarity

An innovation, particularly one that requires radical change on the part of those who must implement it, is unlikely to succeed without its being focused and clear, that is, without all key participants' knowing its "why, what, and how"—why the reform is being pursued, what it actually consists of, and how it is to be implemented—and its "how important"—how it ranks relative to other projects in which they may be involved. Public sector institutions rarely experience such focus and clarity, in part because they are caught between the demands of multiple constituencies. As Kaufman puts it, "Given the ceiling on their resources and the sleaziness of the filter that is supposed to screen demands" (p. 28), they routinely find themselves undertaking more programs than they can manage or fund and are unable to eliminate some so as to concentrate on others. In the context of school reform, this problem is greatly compounded because restructuring, both as a general movement and as particular projects in particular schools, lacks focus and clarity.

Though we speak of it as a single entity, restructuring is actually a potpourri of proposals with widely varied foci. It is seen "as a

synonym for the market mechanism of choice, or teacher professionalization and empowerment, or decentralization and school
site management, or involving parents more in their children's
education, or national standards in curriculum with tests to match,
or deregulation, or new forms of accountability, or basic changes
in curriculum and instruction, or some or all of these in combination" (Tyack, 1990, pp. 170–171). Within each of these categories,
proposals diverge and recombine in various ways. For example,
some school governance reforms call for holding all schools to
national performance goals; others prefer goals set by the states;
still others want them determined by local communities. Most
advocates of school choice want to give parents and students wide
freedom to choose their school, but some want to allow them virtually no choice of elective subjects in these schools (p. 171). The
many proposals cut across each other so many ways that it is hard
even to group them conceptually.[1] But however one frames it,
restructuring requires "a sophisticated array of activities, structures,
diagnoses, teaching strategies, and philosophical understanding"
(Fullan, pp. 70–71). In their profusion, complexity, and conflicts,
restructuring's many different foci can be understood—and misunderstood—in many different ways.

The problems here are far from just semantic. Though critics
of schools appear to agree on the need for swift, radical redesign,
they disagree fundamentally about which problems need redress
and what kind of redress they need. Their divergent views have
produced a rash of rival proposals. Few are comprehensive, and
each addresses a different part of the educational system. Some
focus on the ends of schooling, some on the means, some on both.
Many are in conflict. Consequently, restructuring has become a
muddle of multiple reforms competing for scarce dollars and educators' allegiance. Schools, as Fullan says, "are faced with overloaded
improvement agendas" (p. 69). Hence, the question is not just
whether a specific problem or a specific improvement is important
but also how important it is in comparison to others. However, pri-
oritizing is difficult, for people are reluctant to neglect any goals,
no matter how unrealistic it is to address them all. In fact, most
schools seem unable to concentrate their energies, or else they are
not allowed to. Many are pursuing four, five, or even six initiatives
at the same time. In my experience, this tendency used to be more

common in wealthier schools that make strong claims to excellence, as if advancing on all fronts at once were a way to confirm superior quality, but it is now ubiquitous. The result is a press for what one principal calls "simultaneous multiple improvement. We're tackling major curriculum revision, cooperative learning, technology, authentic assessment, full-tilt inclusion, and site-based management. Each gets less than a day of in-service a year, and their various meetings conflict with one another. We don't know what to focus on or how to do it all." Another principal says simply, "We're suffering from too many good ideas."

Simultaneous multiple improvement reaches its greatest futility when a district pursues projects that are sharply opposed to one another philosophically or procedurally—especially when it imposes these on top of previous reforms that failed to flourish but linger in some vestigial form (layering an accelerated school project on the remains of an effective schools structure, for example). Wherever it occurs and whatever its mix, the result of simultaneous multiple improvement is almost invariably dispiriting: no single project receives adequate attention, resources, planning, or dissemination; staff time and effort are fragmented; frustration abounds.

Closely related to the problem of focus and priority is a problem of clarity. For reform to work, everyone involved must be clear about its purposes, policies, and procedures. Communication about these subjects needs to be lucid, vigorous, and repeated. For change agents, this burden can be relentless: explaining, clarifying, training, seeking feedback, troubleshooting, modifying, reexplaining, reclarifying. (One of most draining aspects of change for a leader is the seemingly endless need to correct misimpressions, to answer the same questions yet again, long after she had thought everyone understood.) When reform is multiple and complex, its ends and means are even more difficult to convey clearly. Hence, in school after school restructuring goals remain too broad and diffuse and implementation plans too vague. I have been in scores of schools where sizable proportions of teachers, even in the second or third year of an improvement project, could not articulate its what, why, and how.

One widespread problem that ensues is "false clarity," which occurs when people interpret change in an oversimplified way, adopting it without truly understanding it (Fullan, p. 70). There are many teachers who sign on to reform enthusiastically without being fully clear about what it involves. They make a surface-level change, endorsing new goals (sometimes articulately), using new materials, and imitating new behavior, but *without specifically understanding the principles and rationale of the change [and] their implications for practice*" (p. 40, emphasis in original). They teach the new text and try the new method, but without incorporating key elements of the reform and clinging, often without being aware of it, to familiar techniques and understandings.[2] Because this is such a common phenomenon, we will return to it at several points in future chapters.

Restructuring's own lack of focus and clarity complicates each of the four tasks of change facing educators. The lack of focus makes it hard for practitioners to move beyond loss to develop commitment, because they often can't understand exactly what they are losing or what is replacing it and thus can't fit the change into their own patterns of meaning. It hampers the development of new competence, not only because it requires new beliefs as well as new behavior (as we saw in Chapter Four) but also because it seeks multiple (and sometimes conflicting) new beliefs and behaviors. And when reforms that are in themselves confusing and divergent are implemented simultaneously, the burden of building coherence and cohesion among implementers is exacerbated.

Scope and Complexity

The larger and more complex an innovation is, and the greater the quantity and quality of change it requires of individuals, the greater its potential—but the more difficult it is to implement. Much of the rhetoric of reform emphasizes the need for boldness, for change that is both radical and comprehensive, no matter how challenging this might be. There are those who argue that ambitious reforms, precisely because they press teachers and schools more than smaller, simpler initiatives, result in greater change even if they don't reach their stated goals. The more a reform attempts, the more change it achieves, even if it doesn't fulfill all its goals. On the other hand, schools routinely overtax themselves, falling far short of improvements that are far beyond their capacity.

Restructuring may ultimately prove to stimulate widespread significant change and reap the rewards of its ambition, but it surely runs the risk of overreaching.

Beneath its fervent calls for renewal, the new agenda envisions changes that in their nature and extent are unprecedented. For example, many initiatives seek major reforms in curriculum and instruction. Yet, these have historically been the aspects of schooling that are most intractable. Indeed, a core dilemma throughout decades of educational reform has been that changes that deal with the essentials of schooling—teaching and learning—seem to prove weak and temporary, but changes that enlarge and enhance the administrative bureaucracy seem to prove strong and enduring (Elmore and McLaughlin, p. 4). In fact, if one looks at long-term trends in actual school practice and not at "waves of policy talk (usually called periods of reform)," as Tyack says, "the development of American schools looks much more linear and consistent than changes in rhetoric might suggest—and [it] goes counter to major tenets of restructuring" (pp. 183–184) in such areas as curriculum, grouping, and governance, among others.[3] The strength of historical trends does not mean we must simply accept them as perpetual givens. It does mean that when we seek to overcome them we must appreciate the scope of the task.

Apart from opposing the historical tide, the changes sought by the new agenda are in and of themselves extraordinarily difficult. They redefine the very notion of what knowledge is: "Teachers must not simply absorb a new 'body' of knowledge [but also] a new way of thinking about knowledge and a new practice of acquiring it. They must cultivate strategies of problem solving that seem to be quite unusual among adult Americans. They must learn to treat knowledge as something they construct, test, and explore, rather than as something they absorb and accumulate. [To accomplish all this] they must un-learn much of what they know" (Cohen, 1991, p. 46). When such change is accompanied by changes in decision making, the overall package is truly immense. Teachers as coaches of students who become active, questioning learners, and teachers as vital participants in school governance are both concepts with powerful potential. Schools where either takes root can be exciting places. But as inspiring and promising as they are, to persuade, prepare, and support the faculty of a whole school for either (let alone both) could hardly be a more difficult undertaking. As we will see in Chapter Eleven, altering teachers' assumptions about decision making is far from easy. And as many reformers have discovered, teachers can find it equally hard to see the value or effectiveness of empowering students in the learning process. Both changes challenge deeply embedded behavioral regularities of classrooms and schools and require teachers to abandon the beliefs, assumptions, habits, and roles of a lifetime. For both, the tasks of building new competence and creating coherence out of confusion are enormous.

Desirability

A change may be focused and clear and of ideal scope and complexity (substantial enough to challenge, simple enough to manage), and yet people will not embrace it if it does not appeal to them. Desirability depends crucially upon dissatisfaction and relevance. To even begin to be open to a change, people must first be unhappy with the status quo in some way and must then find the change relevant to their concerns. Innovation, in other words, must meet a perceived need in a promising way. In the previous chapter I proposed that a primary task of change is often to make the case for it, specifically to disconfirm people's satisfaction with their present performance. But even when this is accomplished there remains the need to devise an appealing solution to the now-perceived problem. When change comes from outside the organization there must be a match between the agenda of its authors and that of its implementers. Unhappily, in the case of most current school reforms this match is poor. Though there is abundant evidence, as we shall see in Chapter Six, that many teachers are deeply dissatisfied with their schools, there is little evidence that most of them see restructuring as addressing their concerns. On the contrary, many find it unwelcome, irrelevant, even hostile.

Teachers' openness to changes in practice turns heavily on service to students or the transmission of knowledge within a discipline (Elmore and McLaughlin, p. 43). Teachers' questions about change tend to be quite pragmatic: Does the change address a need? Will it interest students? Will their learning improve? Is there evidence that the change does what it claims? Is it clear what the teacher will have to do? What will it require in terms of time, energy, and skill? How much will it interfere with current programs and priorities? (Fullan, pp. 127–128). In recent years, as conditions in many schools, especially those in urban areas, have worsened appreciably, teachers' concerns have turned toward changes that will improve their own work situations and increase outside support for their efforts. In my seminars I often ask teachers to list their priorities for improving their school. Their answers almost invariably focus on working conditions, on resources and supports, and on the larger social context of students and families. Their most frequent recommendations include smaller pupil-to-teacher ratios, more "teachable" classes (more homogeneous grouping, fewer difficult or special needs students), more time to plan and prepare and cope with change, larger budgets for books and supplies, fewer nonacademic requirements, more support from parents and the public, and greater attention to, and control over, students by their parents. This last is of growing importance to educators everywhere. Indeed, in 1993, greater parental involvement in their children's education topped the list of policy priorities in the annual Metropolitan Life Survey of the American Teacher (Chira, 1993, p. 1). Most teachers, in short, seek "external" changes (that is, changes external to themselves) that will help them do better what they have traditionally been trying to do.

By contrast, restructuring, regardless of its specific meaning, usually includes a heavy emphasis on defects within teachers and schools and seeks in a variety of ways to get teachers to perform and think very differently, to unlearn what they know. Virtually every recent improvement initiative contains a significant criticism of the current performance of teachers and schools. In some cases this criticism contains a strong tone of censure and blame, and the reform consists of pressuring teachers to change by modifying requirements or incentives. Examples include plans that promote teacher professionalization by requiring recertification (and, in some cases, abolishing tenure), plans that seek free market competition through school choice vouchers, and plans that heighten accountability through state or national curriculum mandates and competency testing. Advocates of some of these proposals, like former U.S. Secretary of Education William Bennett, are strident critics of teachers' performance. Others, like Theodore Sizer, are genuinely sympathetic to the stresses and dilemmas faced by teachers and call for significant improvement in their working conditions; but they still diagnose problems in teachers' practice and recommend changes that relatively few teachers seek on their own, such as making curriculum more outcome-driven, pedagogy more student-centered, grouping more heterogeneous, and assessment more accountable.

The extent of the mismatch between the reform agenda and the agenda of those who must make reform work is best illustrated by elaborating briefly on two key areas of difference, heterogeneous grouping and accountability. With regard to heterogeneity, despite academic research that tends to support its advantages for most students, moral arguments made for it on grounds of equity and social responsibility, and periodic reports from schools of remarkable successes, teachers continue to oppose it overwhelmingly. For one thing, heterogeneous classes are harder to teach than homogeneous classes of equal size. Since few districts cut class size when they change grouping patterns, heterogeneity makes teachers' lives more difficult. Moreover, the range of heterogeneity is expanding as the student population becomes more diverse and as inclusion introduces into classrooms greater numbers of special needs students with major learning and behavior problems. I vividly recall a biology teacher in an urban high school describing what restructuring meant to him: "Over the summer, our high school was detracked. Just like that. In each of my five classes, I still have thirty-three kids, but they now speak eight different languages, their reading levels go from the 97th percentile down to the third, and there are at least four or five—in every class, mind you—with serious behavior or emotional problems. I'm almost totally reduced to multiple-choice worksheets. Some days I'm furious; others I'm depressed."

Even in situations that are nowhere near this extreme, teachers feel inadequately trained to manage and instruct large, diverse groups—and, often, they don't want such training. Philosophically, many educators, particularly at the secondary level, where there tends to be a strong investment in one's subject area, are reluctant to accept changes that they see as compromising quality and debasing standards without really helping lower-achieving students.

Efforts to improve schools' accountability via statewide competency testing and curriculum mandates also dismay teachers, because they diminish their autonomy and deprofessionalize their work. Some critics of schools are convinced that such trimming of teachers' freedom is precisely what is needed, that external pressure is required to improve and direct their performance. But to the extent that these efforts make teachers more like assembly line workers, they are likely to generate resistance—active or passive—not enthusiasm. There are positive and negative mandates. The former "provide direction, define meaning, and promote significance in one's work" (Sergiovanni, 1991, p. 239); they are motivating and inspire commitment. The latter reduce professional prerogatives, decision making, and control; they are demoralizing and lead to detachment and alienation. Some states, such as Vermont, have sought a constructive approach to accountability by trying to incorporate authentic assessment into their competency testing (including portfolios and exhibitions of students' work, not just standardized test scores), but the majority of requirements emerging from statehouses, like most calls for national standards, are of the more narrow, prescriptive type that demotivate teachers.

The dilemma of desirability is complicated by problems of credibility. The antipathy between teachers and their critics is not new. A breach has been growing for several decades between practitioners on the one hand and policymakers and academic experts on the other. This schism has bequeathed to school improvement a serious credibility gap. People assess the desirability of any change not just by its "what" but also by its "who." A change proposed by someone we trust and respect is more credible than it would be if proposed by someone we distrust. Credibility is especially important if the idea itself challenges deeply held assumptions and long-standing practices. Unfortunately, the authors of restructuring—almost exclusively policymakers and academics—do not enjoy great respect among educators. While reform might theoretically begin at any level of the educational hierarchy, in practice it almost always begins with policy. This stems in part from academics' and policymakers' growing distrust of practitioners' judgment and from a concomitant desire to exert political control over schools (Elmore and McLaughlin, pp. 9–10). Teachers return this distrust in spades. Anyone who has worked in schools is familiar with the cynicism and suspicion teachers feel toward those who, over recent decades, have so frequently told them what to do, so rarely acknowledged the difficulties of doing it, and so regularly blamed them when it failed.

In their reform proposals, the experts, it must be said, have done little to ease teachers' antipathy and enhance their own credibility. Despite their claims, the substance of what they propose contains little that is really new. On the contrary, most measures now called restructuring have been tried before with different names—and are generally seen to have failed, with experts' attributing the failure to poor implementation by practitioners. The "new" measures thus join a long tradition, the "carousel of reform," in which earlier initiatives reappear in new guises—merit pay plans as career ladders, decentralization as school-based management. This recurring cycle of past mistakes "rewarmed, relabeled, and reapplied without considering other alternatives" (Deal, 1990, p. 6) has bred skepticism and outright cynicism among practitioners and has demoralized schools as institutions. "Every few years," says a teacher, "these 'experts' propose something 'revolutionary' that we've seen before and that didn't work then. And when it doesn't work again, they'll blame it on us again."

Just as the content of most proposals is not new, neither are their approaches to implementation. Most plans still exemplify the traditional paradigm of change that has foundered so frequently before: imposing highly rationalized, structural improvements according to a top-down, externally devised plan. Most current reforms, rather than seeking to make teachers into co-developers, simply call for them to carry out experts' prescriptions (Elmore and McLaughlin, p. 24). This flies in the face of what we know about motivating people to change and helping them develop "ownership" of an innovation. History shows that the content of successful school reform is almost always generated—or heavily adapted—by local practitioners. One reason is that "most adults act on solutions crafted from their own experience and practical judgment, informed by what they can learn from others whose judgments they trust. If they have no investment in the change, then their willingness to make it work is limited. People develop an investment in change by applying their own skills"

(p. 36). Instead of trying to help practitioners develop ownership of reform, however, many restructuring plans, as noted, rely on external pressure to produce change in local schools. Even when well intended, this rarely produces more than "brittle compliance" from teachers, at best (Cuban, 1984, p. 265), and it is often counterproductive, actually diminishing their motivation and commitment.

Feasibility

Desirability's close companion is feasibility. Teachers must not only want to implement a change, they must feel that they can achieve it. They need to see change not only as appropriate for students and as promising better learning but also as something practical that they and their school can manage. To be practical, changes must not only address important perceived needs, be focused and clear, and seem to be of manageable scope and complexity; they must also come with useful how-to-do-it measures (Fullan, p. 72). Of course, any professional faced with change has practical concerns and is likely to resist changes that interfere with existing, apparently successful teaching methods and do not lead to ready results. The pace and press of school life intensify this tendency among teachers. But the context in which teachers work adds a special intensity. "Immediacy," Schlechty says, "pervades school life" (1990, p. 91). The pressure of having to manage so many clients and cover so much material naturally inclines educators toward the pragmatic rather than the theoretical and toward the short-term rather than the long-term. And there is another key pressure: teachers must innovate en route. Implementation happens during the school year and after the school day—there is no closing the factory to retrain the workers. Schools must change themselves on the fly. Practicality is essential.

So, too, is security. Letting go of an old competence and learning a new one involves a substantial risk, one teachers must be encouraged to take. To succeed at change, people must be free to fail at it, to explore, experiment, err, and try again without penalty. They must be permitted downs as well as ups. Because of the great immediacy of school life, teachers may need extra encouragement and permission to tolerate fluctuation in the results of their own new learning. Consequently, change agents must provide them with a strong basis of security (Schlechty, 1990, p. 91). That is, change must be accompanied by a high degree of both psychological safety and professional safety. Without this, change is unlikely, no matter how intensely people are pressured to alter their practice.

From our discussion of desirability it will be clear that restructuring promises neither the practicality nor the security teachers need. With regard to the latter, since much of the rhetoric of reform contains strong criticism of schools and urgent calls for radical—and rapid—change, and since some of the plans call for intensifying the pressure on practitioners, restructuring hardly provides much sense of safety for them. Moreover, the fact that many of the proposals simply repeat previous efforts does not make them seem more practicable. But it is with respect to the former that restructuring seems most unfeasible. Perhaps the feature that makes it most impractical (and unwelcome) to teachers is an aspect of its emphasis on accountability—its enlargement of the school's responsibility. Restructuring exaggerates the causal role and curative reach of the school.

One of the few common threads among most proposals—and the chief way they differ from past reform movements—is their emphasis on "the school as the unit of improvement" (Goodlad, p. 31). Where earlier reformers focused both on schools and on larger societal problems, current advocates blame the infamous "rising tide of mediocrity" solely on the school (Elmore and McLaughlin, p. 53). They argue that improving education depends directly on improving classroom instruction and the functioning of schools. The idea has natural appeal, promising direct action where it really counts and clarifying accountability. But the accountability, though clear, is excessive, and to teachers it appears punitive. Far from solving the problem of reform, the focus on the school as the unit of improvement simply narrows the target: "[Now] every policymaker's preference for curriculum content, teacher competency, and student performance standards [must] be accommodated within the confines of every school. . . . Instead of reforming and renewing schools from the inside out, school people will be given the task of translating competing and often unreasonable demands into practical solutions that may or may not be consistent with effective practice" (pp. 59–60).

But even before they attempt this translation, many educators fault their critics for acting as if key problems affecting student performance were mainly of the school's making and were fully under its control. Poor scores and high dropout rates reflect not just the shortcomings of schools and teachers but also the decline of family, the dissolution of community, the spread of poverty, and the growth of diversity. I shall elaborate on some of these factors in Chapter Seven. For now, I merely note two. First, as families and communities have steadily abandoned the child-rearing functions they once fulfilled, more and more children have been denied the basic nurture and structure on which psychological health, effective learning, and, ultimately, social behavior depend. Children now spend so much less time with parents and other adults that "we are eroding the intergenerational exchanges on which maturity is successfully built" (Howe, 1994a, p. 10). This depletion of our "social capital" is alarming (Coleman, 1987, pp. 36–37).[4] Second, with respect to diversity alone, the problems facing U.S. schools are extraordinary. America's heterogeneity is unique in the world. Though it can bring great benefits when a school finds a way to truly instill cross-cultural learning and respect, its implications for instruction and staffing are well beyond what most communities can afford.[5]

It is one thing to expect our educational system to improve its capacity to educate children despite the issues posed by accelerating social, economic, and political problems or even to be an instrument of social change. It is quite another to expect individual schools to master these challenges rapidly: "The assumption that to raise our academic achievement we must simply change the schools is wrong for all kids, not just for those from disadvantaged families. . . . The schools, no matter how much we reform them, cannot make up for the support children are losing because of changes in families and communities" (Howe, 1994a, p. 10). For their part, teachers react bitterly to the view that, as one puts it, "We cause it all and should cure it all." Exaggerated expectations about changes that do not seem feasible do little to foster commitment and less to encourage the development of new competence.

This chapter has not focused on all the achievements of the restructuring movement. There is much in it that is compelling, from some of its diagnoses of the ills that plague our schools to some of its imaginative and thoughtful solutions. Advocates of most of the reforms developed since the mid-1980s can cite successes or at least start-up efforts that have encouraged them. The networks of accelerated schools and essential schools, for example, have grown rapidly and have shown some very impressive results. They also allow for substantial autonomy and control of implementation by practitioners. But the issue here "is not whether *some* American schools can teach students effectively or . . . nurture innovative practices; there have always been promising experiments and small oases of excellence and creativity in individual schools across the country. The challenge is to implement and then sustain those ideas *broadly* in schools with different kinds of students, resources, and community preferences" (McDonnell, 1989, p. 1, emphasis added). We must assess restructuring in terms of its potential for success on a broad scale; when we do this, its very substance emerges as, at best, problematic. It contains substantive flaws that repeat past errors, make teacher support unlikely, and make the four tasks of change especially hard to accomplish. No one would expect practitioners in other professions to welcome innovations that are vast and complex, lack focus and clarity, and seem neither desirable nor feasible. Why, then, should we expect this of teachers? Why should they embrace reforms that reach them as competing sets of unrealistic and unfair demands, that are proposed by authors they mistrust, that they had no role in developing, that ignore or oppose their own concerns, and that they see as having previously failed?

In this regard, it is apposite to return to the distinction between change as substitution and growth versus change as loss. Even small, incremental change can be more disruptive than we anticipate (and few restructuring proposals are so modest). Even change as growth, which many proposals claim to offer, requires both some intrinsic appeal of its own and an openness among participants. Even then, it can still be turbulent and difficult. But change as loss, which this chapter suggests is the primary meaning of restructuring to practitioners, must surely provoke resistance. Thus teachers' skepticism and reluctance should not surprise us, and leaders of reform underestimate it at their peril.

Notes

1. Schlechty (1990, pp. 7, 17–28) identifies three competing conceptions of the purpose of schools that have influenced restructuring: as a tribal center (to transmit cultural enlightenment and traditions and norms of citizenship), as a factory (to select and sort students for future occupations according to standardized measures of performance), and as a hospital (to redress the pain and suffering imposed on children by society and to equalize opportunity). Each proponent of a particular reform, he argues, assumes that schools would improve if one of these traditional purposes were at the top of the education agenda. Richard Elmore (1990, p. 11) divides restructuring into changes in teaching and learning, changes in the occupational situation of educators (including conditions of entry and licensure, school structure, and decision making), and changes in governance and in the power relationships of schools and their clients. For her part, Lorraine McDonnell (1989, p. ii) divides it into four: decentralizing via school-based management, more professional teaching conditions, and greater parental choice; accountability via public reports and testing; major curriculum reform; and strengthening links between the school and the larger community via formal alliances with parents, social service networks, and business and industry.

2. David Cohen (1991) offers a brilliant, detailed example of false clarity in his portrait of Mrs. Oublier, an elementary school teacher who believes she has implemented a revolutionary approach to mathematics but who handles novel activities and materials in the most traditional fashion.

3. Among the tenets that are swimming against the tide of history are (1) focusing on fewer subjects in greater depth and detracking so that all students are exposed to this richer instruction—this "goes against the grain of almost a century of differentiation of curriculum to fit the supposed abilities and later destinies of students," (2) site-based management—schools and districts have grown consistently larger and more centralized, and supposed decentralization "often turns out to be little more than another layer of bureaucracy," (3) paring down middle management, regulation, and paperwork—these have actually been "growth industries"; non-teaching personnel have increased sharply and regulations have mushroomed (Tyack, pp. 183–184).

4. Coleman defines social capital as "the raising of children in the norms, the social networks, and the relationships between adults and children that are of value for the child's growing up" and argues persuasively that "the social capital in family and neighborhood available for raising children has declined precipitously" (pp. 36–37).
5. In view of this, argues Seymour Sarason, the real question is not "why schools are as bad as they are but rather why they are as good as they are" (1990, p. 8).

Chapter Six

Staff: Understanding Reluctant Faculty

*I have found over and over again that the acceptance of a
new point of view . . . has much less to do with the
validity of that point of view than with [one's] readiness
to consider any alternatives whatsoever.*
—EDGAR SCHEIN (1987, P. 107)

Resistance may be the normal, necessary human reaction to most
change, and the substance of a particular reform may itself be
likely to invite resistance, but there is more to the picture. People
and organizations vary in their responsiveness to innovation. On
their own, educators as individuals and schools as institutions may
be more or less ready to consider and adopt a change program. As
obvious as this seems, few developers of reform—and few of their
critics—acknowledge it. Many improvement schemes, rooted in
the rational-structural paradigm of change, concentrate on the
diagnosis of current illnesses and the prescription of ideal cures,
cures that emphasize positions, policies, and procedures rather
than people. They pay little attention to the lived realities of the
educators who must accomplish change or to the practical problems of institutional innovation. This blind spot is more than just
unfortunate; it is often fatal. Overlooking and underestimating the
human and organizational components of change has routinely
sabotaged programs to improve our schools (and, for that matter,
programs to improve our corporations and government agencies,
as well). If we have learned nothing else from these efforts, it

should be this: no innovation can succeed unless it attends to the realities of people and place. In this chapter we consider the first; in the next we will turn to the second.

In schools, the need to acknowledge people realities has always been acute, because innovation depends hugely on the attitudes of teachers. But restructuring faces an extraordinarily complex human resource problem: to make new schools with mostly older teachers. Most of America's educators are veteran practitioners who are not eager to embrace a new round of innovation. Their natural human aversion to change is intensified by three factors: their stage of life, their stage of career, and what demographers would call their "cohort factor"—their unique composition as a group and the unique historical context in which they have worked. Their resistance is thoroughly normal, but it presents an unprecedented challenge to innovation, one that cannot be met by standard recommendations for staff revitalization or the implementation of change.

Readiness and Resistance

One's openness to innovation depends on a combination of factors, chief among them one's personality, life experience, and career experience. Too often, when educators prove reluctant or unwilling to change, their behavior is interpreted psychologically, as a kind of character flaw ("She's a resistant person"; "He's rigid"). At the individual level, when a change agent faces opposition from someone, this can seem reasonable: the resistance often feels quite personal. And in most schools of any size we can expect to find a few teachers who might fairly be called obsessive or oppositional. But when we encounter resistance to change among a large group of teachers in a school or among large numbers of teachers more generally, it is misleading to generalize about their personalities and unhelpful to dismiss them as "stubborn" or "resistant" (Sarason, 1990, p. 108).

To begin with, as I have been arguing, all of us are resistant to change, especially when it is conceived and imposed on us by others. Psychologizing resistance also repeats the hubris of the reformer we previously noted (the assumption that an innovation is, by definition, rational, right, and healthy and that therefore any opposition must be irrational, wrong, and neurotic). In addition, it offers no guidance for implementation (people are not about to change their personalities). We need to move beyond such criticisms and consider the larger patterns of people's life and career development.[1]

The Greyer—and Grimmer—Faculty

I often ask audiences of educators to imagine that they are responsible for a brand new, significant change in their school and to describe the characteristics of the ideal staff they would want to implement it. Their answers usually include lofty qualities such as investment in the school, a commitment to excellence, devotion to students, and creativity. They always include practical traits like energy, flexibility, and openness. And as we list these characteristics, someone usually adds, "young," a response that often begets some rueful laughter, as there are rarely many young people in the room.

Looming behind every aspect of the debate about schools is a profound demographic shift among educators: almost en masse, they have become a veteran, middle-aged, immobile group. During the late 1960s and early 1970s, when most of America's current teachers began their careers, a school's faculty typically included a range of age and experience levels, from young beginners in their twenties to ten- and fifteen-year veterans in their thirties and early forties and older, senior-level practitioners. No more. This balanced mix has vanished. The teaching force is now composed mainly of people in middle age and in mid-to-late career who have been teaching in their current school for twenty years or more. In schools everywhere one sees mostly veteran teachers in their mid-forties and older. Teachers' average age is nearly forty-five (in 1973, it was thirty-four); only 5 percent of teachers are under twenty-five (versus 17 percent in 1970).[2] A snapshot of a typical school's faculty would show, as one high school teacher told me, "a large group of us who look 'very veteran,' a small group who look young enough to be our children, and very few in between."

Although teachers' average age is not exceptional relative to other professionals, their modal career pattern is. Teachers are much less mobile, changing occupations and employers much less frequently than other college-educated workers. Fully three-quarters of all teachers have been teaching for at least ten years; two-thirds have been teaching for at least fifteen years, and one-quarter for at least twenty years. (Administrators are older than teachers and have worked in education longer. Superintendents average forty-nine years of age and twenty-five years of experience; principals, forty-six years of age and twenty-three years of experience). And teachers' career stability is remarkable: half have taught in only one or two schools, two-thirds still live and work within 150 miles of their birthplace, and the largest single reason they cite for changing jobs is involuntary reassignment.

Despite this stability, too few veteran educators seem to be enjoying or displaying the benefits of age and experience. As anyone who talks with them regularly can attest, disenchantment is rampant among them. It is increasingly rare to meet teachers who radiate enthusiasm or principals who praise their competence. Although their well-being and outlook are obviously essential to reform, their stress and alienation have never been higher. They complain about low levels of salary, support, and recognition; about deteriorating conditions in the schools and diminishing readiness among pupils; and about growing demands made on them, both instructional and noninstructional. Many surveys have shown sharp declines in teachers' morale and job satisfaction. Up to 50 percent report that they would not choose teaching if they had it to do over again, more than 25 percent are actively considering leaving the field, and attrition among teachers during their first five years averages nearly 50 percent.[3] For their part, administrators complain that staff are coasting (or worse) in the classroom and participating less in the life of the school. A principal I have known for twenty years summarized it this way: "There's not much tread left on the tire around here. Many people are still OK in the classroom but are just doing the minimum. And as soon as school's over, everyone disappears. We need a shot in the arm." The need for staff revitalization is inescapable. Whether this need will prove to be compatible with restructuring is far less clear.

In the view of many observers, teachers' dissatisfaction is broad and deep but is closer to passive resignation than to active indignation, closer to dejection that deflates energy than to anger that inspires action. And, as noted in Chapter Five, it is focused on external impediments rather than on teachers' own shortcomings. Roland Barth describes it this way:

> Teachers are dejected. Many would not enter the profession if again given a choice. They commonly report a sense of discontent and malaise; they feel unappreciated, overworked, and demeaned as professionals. They feel little trust for or from either school and district administrators or the public. They are even alienated from one another. They feel trapped in their jobs, powerless to effect change, and frustrated at the never-ending nonteaching demands. . . . Many would agree with what one fourth-grade teacher told me recently: "Excellence is no longer a goal toward which to aspire. Now I'm satisfied if I can do it all, let alone well." . . . A bumper sticker appearing in parking lots of many public schools sums it up: I Feel Better Now That I've Given Up Hope [1989, p. 227].

Barth's teachers may not yet qualify as burnt-out, but they are well on the way.

Burnout, of course, has become a buzzword. There cannot be an educator unfamiliar with the term. Burnout is the culmination of a progressive disillusionment and lack of efficacy in which early enthusiasm and dedication ultimately yield to depletion and a loss of caring (Farber, 1991, p. 25).[4] Key to burnout is the sense of "inconsequentiality," the growing conviction that one's efforts to help others are unsuccessful, that the task is both endless and unrewarded in terms of either achievement, appreciation, or advancement. There is much research to confirm the importance of a sense of efficacy—the sense of making a meaningful difference, of true accomplishment—in teachers' motivation and performance. Among other benefits, a strong sense of efficacy inclines people to persist in the face of challenge, which is vital to the implementation of change. Conversely, when one's sense of efficacy is low, whether as a result of internal psychological issues or of external pressures and constraints, one's effort, engagement, and persistence weaken.

Burnt-out teachers can be divided into three main types: the worn-out, the frenetic, and the underchallenged (Farber, pp. 86–87). The first have been beaten down by repeatedly dealing with problems beyond their control. They have essentially acknowledged defeat and act as if no matter how hard they try they will be unable to reach their goals. The second are crusaders who redouble their efforts in the face of adversity, marshaling "frantic energy . . . on behalf of their students," exhorting colleagues to try harder. They are "true believers," either "in social justice or the ameliorative effects of education on poverty or the therapeutic effects of simple caring" (pp. 90–91). Refusing to concede defeat or to settle for modest success despite the frustration of their efforts, they work themselves into exhaustion—and, ultimately, into despair.

The underchallenged are far less dramatic, but in my experience far more common. They are neither excessively fatigued like the worn-out nor excessively driven like the frenetic; they are bored. Their dissatisfaction stems more from the sameness and lack of stimulation in their work than from impossible obstacles. "Disinterested rather than fed up" (Farber, pp. 94–95), they find their work unfulfilling: it doesn't tap their talents. They may complain about a lack of challenge, but they are too disengaged to press for real improvement. In essence, they preserve their self-esteem by severing it from their work, reducing their investment in school to a perfunctory level. I have met hundreds of teachers who fit this definition, and I hear repeatedly from principals, superintendents, and teachers seeking significant reform about their fruitless struggles even to pique the interest of these passive, uninvolved individuals, let alone to challenge or revitalize them.

Most of the veteran teachers I meet acknowledge in themselves many of the characteristics of burnout that Farber summarizes. How do we account for this negative cast to teachers' attitudes? We must begin with the enormous odds against which they struggle, particularly in urban schools. Burnout is a normal response when conditions guarantee inconsequentiality. We have already touched on some of these conditions (rising demands, diminishing resources) in the last chapter and will return to them in the next. Here our interest is in the factors within teachers themselves that contribute to their alienation. Teachers' complaints are substantive and reflect real issues about schooling, and they may also reflect a new awareness of stress (now that burnout is officially labeled and widely discussed, individuals are more likely to decide they have it). But they also reflect changes in perception, experience, and behavior that are common to veteran professionals in midlife and midcareer

(Evans, 1989, pp. 10–15). A grasp of these characteristics is essential to understanding teachers' morale and performance problems and their readiness—or lack of it—for change.

Midlife

Midlife is clouded in myth. It has come to be fixed in the public imagination as an era of inevitable distress. In fact, the infamous midlife crisis, in which people, especially men, abandon career, spouse, family, and friends to seek renewal, is far from the norm. It is an example of an exploratory social science concept trivialized by popular culture.[5] The reality of midlife is both less dramatic and less negative. Much of what middle age means is being calmer and wiser, exercising better judgment, applying a broader outlook to life, enjoying a deeper understanding of others. Years of practice enhance one's problem-solving ability. Relationships reach a richness bred of shared history. Many people report a tranquillity they previously lacked, as they begin to acquire the peace, perspective, and freedom that can come with advancing age. As George Sand wrote to Flaubert: "When you feel your own 'self' getting less intense, you love people and things for what they are in themselves, what they represent in the eyes of your soul, and not at all for what they will contribute to your destiny" (Gray, 1993, p. 87). Contentment may not be the norm in midlife, but it is almost certainly more common than crisis.

The many blessings of middle age are quite real but easily overlooked, and I will overlook them in what follows, for two reasons. First, whatever their advantages, they do not stimulate innovation or increase one's appetite or readiness for change. Second, there are definite stresses in midlife, and they do exert a profound—and negative—influence on teachers' motivation, performance, and response to planned change.

Crisis is not inevitable in our middle years, but ambivalence is. Life after forty combines "a curious blend of resurgence and decline" (McAdams, 1993, p. 197): many of us are at the peak of our power in work, family, or community settings and perform with confidence and competence, but we are also encountering the unavoidable signs of aging. These, coupled with the scars of experience and the sense of time passing, affect our basic outlook:

"Optimistic adults are not transformed into brooding pessimists [but the] experience of being at the halfway point in life, of living through important losses and compromises and anticipating many more to come, gradually changes identity's color. From the bold primaries and light pastels of the first half of adulthood, we move to darker mixtures that suggest ambiguity, ambivalence, complexity, and a new uncertainty about the world" (p. 200). Though in our twenties we may be "often wrong but never in doubt," as the saying goes, in our forties and fifties we find life less simple: "Neither the passion of youth nor the power of reason is quite enough for mid-life, for they cannot handle the paradox, irony, and contradiction facing the man or woman who is now moving through the middle and anticipating the end" (p. 201).

As the years pass, life grows more complex. We must continue to make all sorts of important choices, but we must also learn to live with the consequences of our earlier choices—no small task. Periods of serenity and satisfaction are punctuated by intervals of upset and distress, often connected with the passage of psychologically significant milestones, such as the "big" birthdays (forty, forty-five, fifty, and fifty-five), and with important personal and family transitions, such as the departure of children and the illness or death of parents. As we begin to slow down, time seems to speed up. We often feel surrounded by change, much of it problematic, quite apart from whether or not our workplace is restructured. Our concerns, interests, priorities, and perceptions begin to shift, some subtly, others sharply. We adjust to most of these, but they can preoccupy us mightily, disrupting our ability to work effectively (at times, our ability even to be at work), and they greatly reduce our tolerance for change at work.

The major preoccupations of midlife begin with mortality. Midlife may be defined chronologically as beginning at about age thirty-five or forty and extending to fifty-five or sixty, but it really begins when something makes it clear to us that someday we'll be dead—not theoretically clear, as it is to children, but emotionally clear (Schein, 1978, p. 180). Young people are immortal. Adolescents could be locked in a classroom for a week and instructed around the clock about the danger of AIDS and how to prevent it, and many could still walk out saying, "Yes, but not me." We all live with this ability to deny mortality until we suffer an important loss, whether this is the actual death of a parent or someone else close to us or a disappointment that is like a death, such as the loss of a marriage or a job or a dream we have pursued. Once it does become clear to us that our time is limited, many things change. We aren't transformed into totally different people, but our perspective on life and work shifts. The world is not the same again. An English teacher put it this way: "I'd taught John Donne's 'never send to know for whom the bell tolls' for years. When my father died, the shock of finding that the bell *really* tolls for me, too, was intense. Things I had worried about—how old my car was—suddenly seemed trivial. And things I had tolerated—useless faculty meetings—suddenly became unbearable."

Having the reality of our mortality thrust upon us catalyzes our awareness of self and time, helping to precipitate a range of changes in perception and priority. We grow more absorbed in ourselves, beginning with our awareness of bodily change: in midlife, everyone, without exception, sags. Vision and hearing weaken, hairlines and gums recede. Waistlines expand and veins protrude. Short-term memory deteriorates. Sleep grows more fragile and fragmented: we rest less soundly at night and nap more often during the day, particularly in the afternoon. (This universal tendency has enormous educational implications, since training for innovation is routinely conducted after the school day—at nap time!) We acknowledge these infirmities indirectly through jokes and teasing, but we rarely discuss them directly, even though their impact on our sense of self is broad and deep.

Another important set of midlife preoccupations arises out of changes in family composition and roles as one's children leave home and one's parents age. The picture here is, again, different from its stereotype. The "empty nest" syndrome, in which parents, particularly mothers, supposedly fall into depression as children leave home, is even more of an exaggeration than the midlife crisis.[6] But family stresses can still be considerable: raising children, losing them as they leave home, and attending to the elderly. The extension of the life span brings with it many good things, but it also makes those currently in middle age a "sandwich generation," caught between raising children and caring for parents. Like Americans in all walks of life, more and more educators are tending to, supporting financially, or otherwise concerned about their aging parents.

The passages and preoccupations of midlife exert three pressures against innovation. First, they mean that most people are coping with considerable change, some of it quite unwelcome and much of it quite absorbing, before they even come to school. When we prescribe reform, we too often act as if it were the only change people were encountering and hence as if everyone should be readily open to it. In reality, most people usually look to their work as one constant that *won't* change. Second, they make people less likely to throw themselves wholeheartedly into *any* new movement. If veteran staff seem doubtful about promises of rapid, radical change, we must think not first of rigidity or resistance but of a perspective on life that no longer sees the world in terms of black and white, that has become more sophisticated and more skeptical. Third, they leave people much less likely to pursue activities that do not fit their personal priorities. Few people can invest themselves in an idea, plan, or project that does not truly appeal, least of all those to whom time and energy are increasingly precious.

Stability

If midlife requires us to adapt to many changes, is it also a time when we ourselves change as people? This question has important implications for school reform, which requires so much change on the part of educators. There is a popular, appealing answer and a harder, less attractive one. The best known life-span writers, drawing mainly on case studies of small groups of people, agree that development occurs throughout adulthood. Although they differ sharply about its exact course and key features—whether it occurs in phases or stages, how it differs for men and women, and so on— they generally portray development as increasing the breadth of one's perspective and the richness of one's experience, as tending toward what Erikson calls "generativity," the ability to remain a source of growth and giving in our later years. George Sand described it to Flaubert this way: "On the day I decided to put youth behind me I immediately felt twenty years younger. You'll say the bark of the tree still has to bear the ravages of time. I don't mind that—the core is sound and the sap goes on doing its work, as in the old apple trees in my garden; the more gnarled they grow the more fruit they bear" (Gray, p. 87).

This idea of adulthood as a time of continued growth supports our view of ourselves: we like to see ourselves as developing personally even if we are declining physically, and most of us do have the sense not only of gaining wisdom but of making changes in the course of our adult years, whether in what we think or what we believe, the way we do our work or the way we see the world. The notion that we keep growing seems not only flattering, but factual.

Other researchers, who study large populations over long intervals, disagree. Tracking and testing individuals over decades on core personality traits—independence, shyness, assertiveness—they find very little change; consistency is the clear norm. From this perspective it is not we so much as the roles we take on that change (Costa and McCrae, 1989, pp. 48–49). An adult typically moves through a series of roles dictated by social conventions and biology: marriage, career entry, child rearing, career advancement, the departure of children, the death of parents, retirement, grandparenting, and so on. This sequence involves changes but not necessarily "development." That occurs only when the changes "affect the psychology of the individual—when the person adapts and grows with experience" (p. 50)—in short, when personality develops. But, with rare exceptions, personality changes barely at all. Our characteristic ways of thinking, feeling, and acting, "our basic emotional, interpersonal, experiential, attitudinal, and motivational styles" (p. 53) are firmly established by early adulthood. As we saw in Chapter Two, the way we understand the world, our construction of meaning, is cumulative and solidifies over time; by middle age, it is firmly entrenched. This portrait of adulthood as fixed and stable confirms our experience of other people: they don't change. My mother was not a researcher, but she knew this well. "As you get older," she used to say, "you get more like yourself."

Though they present a less optimistic view, these findings about stability help to account not just for the general fixity of human behavior but also for a tendency that grows more prominent in midlife: we become attached to our burdens. Over the years, though we vary according to our personalities and our experience, each of us comes to accept a measure of helplessness in some areas of life and work, acquiescing in recurrent frustrations and disappointments we suffer at the hands of others. These range from the petty, such as habitual annoyances that spouses or colleagues fight about, to the significant, such as chronic injustices that keep people from fulfilling their dreams. But most often we don't reconcile ourselves to the unfairness. We complain, and we dream of being understood, of rationality and rightness prevailing, of our position's being confirmed: it is not we who should change, it is others. But though we dream, we don't assert ourselves sufficiently to break the pattern. Instead, we engage in repetitive rituals of accusation and surrender, sometimes even provoking the very responses we dislike.

These rituals are, of course, easier to perceive in others than in ourselves (we could readily make a list of the self-limiting, self-defeating behaviors of our family, friends, and colleagues, just as they could of ours). Though they may not make rational sense, they tend to be deeply embedded in the patterns of our lives. In fact, the tendency to cling to our burdens can become generalized and entrenched. When it does so, it makes a person what psychologists call a "help-rejecting complainer"—someone who is chronically dissatisfied but resists all assistance and advice. As we shall see in Chapter Seven, this syndrome is too evident in too many schools.

How, then, do we reconcile these divergent views about the potential for growth in midlife? Few of us would want to abandon the promise of adult development, yet we see daily evidence that people not only don't change but also that they help perpetuate the very situations in which they are chronically disappointed. One answer, I think, is to distinguish content from structure. We may, with difficulty, change *what* we think and the goals we pursue, but we are much less likely to change *how* we think or the *way* we pursue our goals. A devout Baptist may convert to Catholicism, and her conversion may constitute a profound personal change, but she is likely to end up as devout a Catholic as she was a Baptist and to worship in her new church as fervently as she worshipped in her old one. It is no small thing to change the content of a belief, but to change the way one actually approaches the world or characteristically behaves is something even more difficult and far more rare.

Midcareer

Most people in midlife are also in midcareer. They contend not only with personal stresses and the effects of growing older but also with professional pressures and the effects of staying in the same job for a long time. In my experience, these have tremendous implications for efforts at school reform but are almost entirely ignored by those proposing to restructure our nation's schools. They deserve special attention.

Researchers generally divide a person's career into three phases. The first is *entry*—an initial period of up to five years in which one explores an occupation, struggles with its demands, and learns to master them. This is followed by *midcareer*, a period when one has learned the ropes, is established in one's position, and exercises regularly the competence one learned during entry. It eventually yields to *exit*—a period of several years of progressive disengagement in which one prepares to leave or retire. Midcareer, then, can be quite lengthy. It usually parallels midlife, but not always. (For example, women who return to teaching after years at home raising children are in midlife but not in midcareer.)

All professionals in midcareer are prone to two kinds of tendencies that limit their readiness to innovate: demotivation (boredom, a loss of enthusiasm, diminished job interest) and a leveling off of growth and performance, especially when they have remained five years or more in the same role (Schein, 1978, p. 36). As unflattering as they sound, these terms describe a nearly inevitable consequence of staying in the same job in the same place for a long time. The growth curve flattens out (particularly for those who do not move into new positions), and energy, interest, and job investment diminish, affecting performance. Much research shows that career satisfaction typically begins at a high level during entry, drops during midcareer, and, though it may recover somewhat, rarely reaches its previous high. Career success, meanwhile, begins at a low level and increases steadily into midcareer, whereupon it also starts to decline (Cytrynbaum and Crites, 1989, pp. 67–68).

Demotivation and leveling off are reflected in four characteristics.[7] The first is a shift from the primacy of the work role in people's lives toward a primacy of their personal roles. As contrasted to the start of one's career, a time when mastering a job assumes great importance, in midcareer one's focus shifts to include a growing preoccupation with personal and family concerns. The midlife issues summarized above exert a stronger pull on one's energy and attention and affect one's investment in one's job: priorities move away from work issues and toward personal issues. As a new teacher at twenty-two, I was free to be totally involved in my work. I didn't have children to raise, a mortgage and a college tuition to pay, or illness among parents or in-laws to concern me. In midlife, though I remain strongly engaged in my work, I have other concerns and responsibilities that divide my attention and allegiance. This shift is especially common for men and for those women who have been teaching full-time for a long time. Having devoted themselves primarily to their career for several decades, they are often ready to reduce their work commitment and devote greater energy to personal or family interests.

A second prominent midcareer tendency is a growing focus on material (as opposed to intrinsic) job rewards. One becomes less exclusively centered on the innate satisfaction of one's work and more concerned about salary, benefits, and related matters. As a new teacher in 1967, unencumbered by midlife's complexities, I didn't worry about how little I was earning ($5,000). I took for granted such things as health insurance premiums, and I was totally disinterested in pension benefits, sick-day allowances, and tenure. The thrill of having a lesson work, of seeing a student grasp a concept I had taught, was reward enough. Recently past fifty, I have grown more concerned about salary, benefits, and the like. Indeed, there would be something wrong with me if I hadn't; I would be failing my obligations to my family. An increased emphasis on material rewards does not mean one no longer cares about one's work. It does mean that, in contrast to the entry phase of one's career, when the thrill of mastering the craft is paramount, one's focus has become more self-attuned in midcareer, so that one is less totally centered on performance outcomes.[8]

The third, and in many ways most crucial, characteristic of midcareer is the double price people pay for mastering their craft: challenge dwindles and recognition plummets. Inevitably, mastery reduces the challenge—and with it the excitement and intensity—in any activity. No matter how dedicated or gifted he might be, no professional in any field sustains his early rate of growth throughout his career. All who teach can remember the tension, anxiety, and fear of starting out and the pleasure and pride of becoming proficient. But while many teachers continue to find their work both challenging and rewarding through the years, it is a rare few who continue to find it *as fully* challenging and rewarding. Professional growth necessarily comes to mean fine-tuning, not great leaps of new competence, and for most practitioners maintaining competence and extending it at the margins is less stimulating than initially achieving it.

The development of new competence is not only rewarding in itself, it is also rewarded. As one demonstrates new skills, recognition from others flows readily. But if with mastery challenge diminishes, recognition withers. One's competence comes to be assumed, and feedback of all sorts is reduced. This stems from a basic fact of human nature: over time, we come to take one another for granted. Any long-standing relationship, no matter how close, is subject to this tendency. A relationship may grow deeper and richer and more profoundly important to us, but we come to expect of the other person a certain response, and as we do, we stop rewarding it. Indeed, we tend to notice it only when it disappears. This ingratitude is inevitable: one cannot keep thanking others day after day, year after year for all the things they routinely do—nor can one can avoid surprise and disappointment if they stop doing these things. I recall an elementary school in which, for years, a third-grade teacher baked special coffee cakes and pastries for the faculty room each week. When she first began, and for some time thereafter, her colleagues were vocal about her gifts and their pleasure. Eventually they came to expect her offerings, and their thanks dwindled to occasional, perfunctory acknowledgments. When, one spring, she just stopped baking, they were incensed.

In incidental areas an absence of recognition may not be critical (although even here people are quite sensitive; little things have a big impact on morale), but in core performance areas it is crucial. To sustain performance everyone needs feedback. Without it, there is little to confirm one's professional adequacy. This is not the primary recognition problem in education—for many reasons schools as institutions are extraordinarily poor providers of recognition, as we will note in Chapter Seven and explore in Chapter Twelve—but in concert with this deficit, the loss of recognition stemming from midcareer changes exerts a powerful negative impact on educators' ability to sustain performance, growth, and morale.

A final characteristic of midcareer is a separateness, a growing isolation among colleagues. The changing priorities and habits of people's lives reduce their contact, professional and social, with one another. Given the rise in personal and family demands and the drop in work motivation and interest, veteran staff are more likely to limit their time at work to the essential, if not the minimum. They are less likely to come early or to stay late to meet with one another, and they are less likely to "talk shop" during their breaks. And since middle-aged people tend to go out socially less often than younger adults, there is less personal connection among colleagues over the years. (This is another way to calculate the onset of middle age: everyone can go out on Saturday night, but only the young go out on Friday night, too. The rest of us stay home and are glad to be there—and lucky to be awake after 9:00 P.M.).

This does not mean midcareer faculty don't like or care about one another. They may experience their relationships as quite deep. It does mean that they spend less time together, are less familiar with one another's work, and draw less support from one another. (It also means that efforts to promote collegiality and shared governance, which we will explore in Chapter Eleven, swim against the developmental tide for many veteran teachers.) Their isolation has a related consequence: all these developmental issues I have just summarized, though very real, are rarely talked about. Beyond rueful jokes and teasing about waistlines, hairlines, and the like, the preoccupations and concerns of midlife and midcareer are rarely shared. This leaves many people with the sense that they are undergoing a unique dilemma. In presenting programs on this topic in several hundred schools, I have been struck by the number of teachers who have sought me out afterward to tell me, in essence, "I thought it was just me."

The Midcareer Continuum

As they cope with these career issues, veteran professionals in all fields may be divided into recognizable types along a continuum of competence, involvement, and growth. Figure 6.1 shows four points along this range. On the high (left) end are *key members,* people who seem immune to most of the issues enumerated above. They are the stars of the organization, people who are both engaged and engaging, energetic and creative, endlessly self-renewing. In education, they are on the cutting edge of their dis-

Figure 6.1. Midcareer Continuum of Growth and Performance.

High Growth			No Growth
←			→
Key Member	Contributor	Stable and Stagnant	Deadwood

cipline, eagerly attending professional conferences, reading widely in their field, and exploring new forms of practice in their class-rooms. They sustain their enthusiasm and their performance at exceptional levels. Colleagues, students, parents—everyone knows who these teachers are. They stir admiration among many col-leagues, envy among some. If we could clone them, our schools wouldn't need restructuring.

Somewhat farther down the scale we find a much larger group: *contributors*. These are solid professional performers who provide a genuine service to their students and their schools. They are not on the cutting edge, not as deep in their commitment nor as broad in their skills as the key members, but they are competent profes-sionals. They care about their work, they can be relied upon for extra help in a pinch, and they often make good mentors for new-comers. Every strong, successful school depends on a solid core of contributors.

As we cross the midpoint of the scale, dropping into the zone where growth has slowed markedly, we come to teachers whom some call *stable and stagnant* (Krupp, 1988). These are staff who are not developing, who are at best passable, who mostly go through the motions. Several principals have described them to me in the same way: "They haven't taught twenty years, they've taught one year twenty times over." If they were on page 248 of the text last May 7, they are likely to be on page 248 this May 7. "I can live with them because there aren't too many of them and because I have no choice," one principal told me, "but not because I'm happy with them. I'll be glad when they retire."

Finally, at the lowest end of the continuum we find the *dead-wood*. They are usually a small group, but they can exert a dispro-portionate influence on the tone and morale of a school. Rarely do they have any history of good performance; they are almost never key members whose performance has deteriorated. On the contrary, in most cases they were never more than marginally competent, but instead of being denied tenure they were spared by the kindness—or cowardice—of supervisors. They have apparently decided that their retirement *off* the job will be greatly enhanced if it is first preceded by some years of retirement *on* the job. Just as everyone knows the key members, so too do they know the deadwood. In schools, they are the teachers who make tenure a travesty, the ones whom students and parents try to avoid and about whom guidance counselors and principals must lie when students are assigned, pretending they are not as bad as everyone knows they are.

It would be ideal to find vast numbers of teachers on the higher side of this continuum, at the level of contributor and above. The available evidence suggests that the reality is otherwise. In addition to the data about teachers' attitudes cited above and the anecdotal evidence readily available to anyone who visits widely in schools, the few studies that have focused on the career cycle of teachers confirm the portrait I have offered here. The most notable of these, by Michael Huberman, found a clear pattern: with age and experience teachers became progressively more conservative and fatalistic, progressively less willing to invest themselves heavily in their careers and in change initiatives.[9] This "focusing down" was most pronounced among twenty-year veterans. They narrowed their interest and activity in a range of ways, such as concentrating "on a preferred grade level, subject matter, or pupil type; disinvesting in schoolwork and increasing outside interests; reducing contacts with peers other than those of one's most convivial group; avoiding additional administrative tasks or off-hours commitments; . . . not getting involved in future schoolwide innovations . . . reducing commitments, using seniority to carve out a comfortable schedule" (1989, pp. 49, 51).

Focusing down can take one of three forms (or, more accurately, tones), ranging from serene to embittered. None of them welcomes innovation. In the most optimistic—positive focusing—a teacher's tone remains firmly constructive, "but there is a clear sense of pulling back, something even of a narcissistic entitlement: 'I've done my share; now leave me alone to do what I want'" (Huberman, 1989, p. 49). In the second—defensive focusing—teachers are withdrawn and critical, more disgruntled with the changes that have occurred during their career, and their tone is notably more negative about their work. In the third—disenchantment—teachers are withdrawn and bitter, their attitudes toward administrators, students, and parents even more negative and cynical. Whatever their emphasis, with age and experience, teachers, even the most creative and dedicated, become less motivated to change their practices and beliefs. Understating the case, Huberman concludes that "ambitious projects of school improvement may be 'out of phase' later in one's career" (p. 50).

The Sixties Cohort

The concepts of life stage and career stage both seek to describe something universal and integral to human experience, something rooted in psychology and, ultimately, biology. But there is a third influence on teachers' motivation, performance, and responsiveness to change—the cohort factor, or the composition of a particular group and the influences of the historical period in which it exists. This is particularly relevant for those of us who began our teaching careers in the late 1960s and early 1970s. Many of us may not have considered how truly unusual our situation was, but our group of teachers was unique in its composition, and so was the social climate in which we started out. Both factors have increased our vulnerability to stress and burnout and diminished our current readiness for innovation.

Three facts stand out about this cohort. First, it is the first large group ever to make a full career out of teaching. For most of this country's history, teachers typically stayed in the field for only a few years (education was overwhelmingly the work of women and only before they married and started families). However draining the demands of teaching, few practitioners stayed at it long enough to develop the symptoms of stress. Because they are now staying longer, teachers are experiencing more stress (Farber, 1991, p. 50). Second, this cohort includes a higher-than-usual proportion of male teachers, who show greater evidence of burnout than their female counterparts and are more vocal and defiant about their dissatisfaction (pp. 146–147). Third, for many, the profession may have not been a good fit. Education was not the first career choice for up to one-third of the current teaching force, including many men who entered the field to avoid the Vietnam military draft

(p. 148). It is an axiom of career theory that occupational satisfaction and achievement require congruence between the characteristics of the individual and those of the work environment. When the match is poor, personal fulfillment and professional performance are both likely to suffer.

Distinctive in its composition, the current group of midcareer teachers is also the product of a most unusual period in American history, the 1960s. Each generation is affected by the zeitgeist that surrounds it as it comes of age; people cannot avoid the influence of the times in which they live, even when they oppose the predominant trends of the period. But in retrospect, the 1960s emerge as a most atypical interval. The professional lives and values of many educators were shaped by the "magical and mythical qualities of that era, its promises of 'radical' social transformation, its optimism, its good intentions, its surrealistic character" (Farber, p. 127)—all of which laid a solid foundation for eventual disillusionment. These characteristics of the times fostered, for example, a marked increase in the idealism of beginning teachers—the fervor of youth was magnified by an urgent belief in the possibility of enormous social change. This stimulated stirring ideals of service, but it also encouraged wildly optimistic hopes. The sixties also bred unrealistic expectations about student achievement, administrative support, and the need for personal rewards—most of us were naive about the functioning of institutions and the realities of overcoming entrenched patterns of economic and social injustice. And there were the dramatic, sordid misuses of power during the Vietnam War and Watergate, which contributed mightily to cynicism and a general distrust of institutions. As hopes for change failed to materialize and social institutions came under intense criticism, teachers became targets of anger, "the most resented and frequently criticized of all professionals" (p. 134).

Many of the teachers caught between such high early hopes and such sober later realities are what Thomas Bowman calls "the last of the suffering heroes"—people who "tried to make *any* system work, even at the sacrifice of their own personal lives. They expected few rewards and little recognition. They tolerated poor management and inadequate facilities. They tended to be bright, creative individuals who viewed education as a noble calling [and] accepted the role of suffering hero willingly" (1991, p. 251, empha-

sis in original). Many of these heroes, it appears, feel they have suffered too much for too little and have abandoned hope of their
sacrifices' bearing fruit. When I shared Bowman's metaphor with
a group of dedicated, talented veteran teachers who meet regularly
in a voluntary study group and could never be thought of as burnt-
out, one said: "I used to make dumb jokes about teaching being a
dramatic adventure: 'Nerdy Clark Kent, the English teacher, is
really Superman, saving our civilization.' But at some level, I
believed it. Now, all of that looks young and foolish. I'm much
wiser, but I've lost something. I do what I can, but I'm just not up
for a whole new educational revolution." Around the room, heads
nodded in melancholy agreement.

Coping: Individual Tasks

As the foregoing makes clear, the changes of midlife and midcareer diminish teachers' appetite for change at work. But they go
further, contributing to a sense of depletion, a lack of efficacy, a
feeling that rewards and supports are inadequate, that one gives
more than one gets. In short, they make teachers not just less ready
for change but more vulnerable to the stress and burnout Farber
describes. The greater the number and extent of the changes people face and the larger the gap between the demands made upon
them and the resources available to them, the more prone they are
to the physical and psychological symptoms of stress. The transitions of midlife and midcareer are a prototypical instance of this
formula for stress. The success of school improvement efforts will
depend heavily on helping educators master them.

The masterly solving of this problem, however, must begin at the
personal level: the issues outlined above are not the fault of the
schools; they stem from staying alive, staying employed, and living in
a particular era. In truth, we are lucky to have them—the alternative
is to be dead—and each of us must take responsibility for solving
them. Schein (1978, pp. 174–180) identifies a set of developmental
tasks each person in midcareer must master. Five are relevant here.

1.   *Specializing versus generalizing.* Over the course of a career,
there is a logical progression from being a learner to being a contributor in a particular area. In midcareer, we must decide whether

we will continue to concentrate on these skills or seek a broader, more general role, such as in leadership. Education, with its flat occupational structure, offers relatively few choices for teachers to broaden out and assume more responsibility. Still, each teacher must decide whether to keep improving skills in a given subject or grade level or to expand into wider realms of activity.

2.   *Establishing an organizational identity and area of contribution.* Everybody needs a niche. All of us need to achieve a place, establish an identifiable role, make a recognized contribution in our workplace. This means both that we must provide something significant or distinctive and that others must acknowledge it. The veteran staff member who has not earned such a place and does not make an identifiable contribution (whether as part of her official job duty or more informally)—or who goes chronically unrecognized for what she does offer—is likely to be disgruntled and unhappy.

3.   *Modifying career dreams.* Midlife is a time of self-assessment in which we ask ourselves "whether our career progress has been consistent with our goals, ambitions, and dreams, and if not, how to resolve the discrepancy"—a question that "exposes the trade-offs" we have made over the years (pp. 177–178). Some people confront the reality that their early dreams will never be fulfilled. They must decide whether to persevere or to revise their initial goals. Others face the vacuum that follows when goals have already been achieved. They must find new sources of meaning for their work.

4.   *Achieving a balance between work, family, and self-development.* The personal and professional changes of midlife and midcareer require us to reassess our investments in the different areas of our life. Looking to the future, how much do we want to be involved in our work, with our family, or in the pursuit of our personal interests? Many people, especially men, who have sacrificed family participation and avocational interests to invest heavily in their careers alter this pattern in midlife. Thus in schools everywhere it is harder to find teachers who want to contribute afternoon and evening time to student activities and to coaching, because so many want the time for themselves. Though this kind of withdrawal from work presents a problem for a school as an institution, it often makes excellent sense within the context of an individual's life.[10]

5.   *Maintaining a positive growth orientation.* Having less time left and fewer opportunities open, having to accept the repercussions of past errors and the prospect of future losses—these make it easy to exaggerate our lot, to become attached to our burdens, to assume that we are trapped and unable to improve things, to give in to depression and passivity. To sustain a positive, constructive outlook on life and work, people must find a way to keep developing their strengths, to treasure and celebrate their successes, to appreciate what they can achieve, to pass on to others what they have learned. To become generative, to avoid premature resignation when options for growth remain, is a core issue of midcareer and of sustaining happiness as one ages.

Revitalization and Reform

Though the responsibility for mastering these tasks is primarily individual, the success of school improvement efforts will nonetheless depend heavily on helping educators cope. This means that school leaders face a double dilemma: not just to reform schools but to revitalize staff. Are the two compatible? There is an obvious connection in that both involve renewal. Some proponents of reform see the need to pursue this linkage. Though the first wave of restructuring proposals, which emphasized broad philosophical questions about schooling's structure, mission, and methods, paid little attention to the realities of the teaching force, proponents of second wave restructuring have focused much more heavily on teachers themselves, stressing the need to enhance their morale, motivation, and participation. Their approaches tend to emphasize increased funding for schools and improved working conditions for staff; teacher empowerment; and site-based management.

Despite these efforts, innovation is at best a two-edged sword, as Fullan says: "It can worsen the conditions of teaching, however unintentionally, or it can provide the support, stimulation, and pressure to improve" (p. 126). As an example, he suggests that systems of teacher appraisal and clinical supervision can lead teachers to become more narrow and superficial in their work, or they can stimulate real improvement: "Good change processes that foster sustained professional development over one's career and lead to student benefits may be one of the few sources of revitalization and satisfaction left for teachers" (p. 131). The proposition is hopeful, and as a statement of potential, true. In practice, such good change processes are not easy to find.

Too frequently, schools' responses to veteran staff who present performance problems and resist innovation are limited to measures that seem intuitively correct or "businesslike" but ultimately prove ineffective. Sticks and carrots (often in that order) appeal to some school leaders (especially those who have become frustrated by staff resistance to change efforts) and to some school board members (especially those who are businesspeople). Of these methods, we have already considered one, retraining, in Chapter Four, noting that school in-service programs typically suffer from a lack of continuity and coherence and often fail to address teachers' felt needs. A second common step is the assertion of greater central-office control over planning and policy. To compensate for a lack of initiative and response among teachers, districts move away from more collaborative models of redesigning curriculum, instruction, and governance and turn instead to top-down structural solutions to compel improvement. These measures diminish teachers' autonomy and damage their morale, particularly among veterans, who find them especially demeaning. (States, of course, often act in a parallel fashion toward schools and districts, imposing centrally designed mandates and generating similarly negative responses.)

A third approach to motivating veteran staff is performance appraisal. Some districts seek more rigorous, "get-tough" evaluation procedures, while others turn to the more collegial model of clinical supervision. Neither, unfortunately, offers much hope. The former almost never works, as schools have little leverage over tenured teachers ("My board wants me to crack a whip I haven't got," as one superintendent put it); nor do its less punitive cousins, plans that try to motivate performance through career ladders and merit pay. Although these inspire periodic spasms of optimism in some quarters, their track record is dismal (for reasons we will review in Chapter Twelve), and any appeal they might offer would only be for newer recruits to education, not for the vast majority of current veterans. And despite Fullan's optimism, clinical supervision, as commonly practiced in the pressured confines of school life, has in my experience demonstrated a poor record of generating change with veteran teachers.[11] Even in the rare cases where supervisors have the time and resources and training to do it well, its salience diminishes over the years; with repetition, it lapses into ritual and loses relevance. A teacher in a small New England town, a true superstar in his school, said during a seminar on school improvement, "Every year for supervision I've had to list three new goals. After sixteen years and forty-eight goals, I'm tired of it. My only real aim is to continue being as good as I've been." When a veteran educator, gifted or not, is protected by tenure and focuses down, his supervisor's modest influence erodes even further.

In many ways this situation sums up the chronic problem in school improvement this chapter has sought to highlight: the failure to consider adequately the human resources that are at once the targets of change and its implementers. This chapter has helped, I hope, to make teachers' resistance to reform more understandable, but this perspective also complicates the task of school improvement. Since standard measures used to motivate change don't work, we need to find others that do. Later chapters will present a set of leadership initiatives that offer much more promise because they speak to the actual needs of people in schools. But it is already clear that the leading of change is extraordinarily difficult and that to accomplish it school leaders must lift their gaze beyond its structural components to focus on people. "All management is people management," says Vaill, "and all leadership is people leadership" (1989, p. 126). In the epigraph to this chapter, Schein asserts that people's acceptance of a new perspective depends much less on its intrinsic validity than on their own readiness to consider any new ideas at all. Before they can respond to a particular innovation, something must unfreeze their current thinking and perceptions and reach them in a fundamental way. For change agents, building such readiness is a key goal of people leadership. It is the ideal way to help educators accomplish the individual tasks of change; it is people leadership at its most artful. But before we explore the specifics of this art, we must look at an additional dimension of change and an additional set of problems: the readiness of schools as institutions.

Notes

1. The study of adult development traces the phases, stages, and transitions of adulthood—its central tasks and conflicts, its gender differences. The

study of career development focuses on a corresponding cycle in adults' work lives, mapping normative phases in professional careers and matching the needs of workers with the needs of organizations. Both are growing fields containing various schools of thought. For example, adult development theories divide in many directions. There are phase theories, which outline a specific sequence of age-related developmental tasks and transitions that individuals must master, and there are stage theories, which map a sequence of cognitive and psychological changes inside the individual. There are also differences about the normative development of men and women (see Erikson, 1963; Gilligan, 1982; Gould, 1978; Levinson, 1978; Miller, 1976; Neugarten, 1968; and Vaillant, 1977).

The field of career development has developed along two separate lines. The first, primarily psychological, emphasizes the internal career (one's personal development within a career; the effect on career choice and behavior of individual differences, personality, and the biological life cycle). The second, primarily sociological, emphasizes the external career (the realities and opportunities of the world of work; career paths and options within organizations; the nature of various occupations in society). See Derr and Laurent (1989, p. 454).

Some writers have reviewed the life span literature and applied it to teachers, emphasizing the school as a context for adult growth (Krupp, 1987, 1988; Levine, 1987). A career development perspective explores much of the same terrain but with a sharper focus on work behavior, the problems of change, and the potential for organizational response to staff needs. It has not been applied to schools in any depth. However, for an excellent overview of workplace issues in schools, see Susan Moore Johnson's *Teachers at Work* (1990).

2. The demographic data in this paragraph and the next are taken from studies by Emily Feistritzer (1990, 1986, and 1988). See also Diegmueller (1990, p. 10) and Mathis (1994).

3. For summaries of these and other survey results, see Farber (1991, pp. 1–2, 42–44) and Feistritzer.

4. Barry Farber has explored burnout in detail; my discussion draws on his analysis. The progression of burnout, as he describes it, is as follows: "(1) Enthusiasm and dedication give way to (2) frustration and anger in response to personal, work-related, and social stressors, which, in turn, engender (3) a sense of inconsequentiality, which leads to (4) withdrawal of commitment and then to (5) increased personal vulnerability with multiple physical (headaches, hypertension, and so on), cognitive ('they're to blame'; 'I need to take care of myself'), and emotional (irritability, sadness) symptoms, which . . .

(6) escalate until a sense of depletion and loss of caring occurs" (p. 35).

5. As social psychologist Dan McAdams (1993, pp. 195–196) points out, serious but exploratory studies of how small groups of middle-aged people underwent shifts in their life perspectives were overgeneralized and misapplied by popularizers—notably Gail Sheehy in her widely read *Passages* (1974)—even to the point of urging people to go seek such a crisis to avoid stagnation. See also Gallagher (1993, p. 51).

6. The evidence suggests that losing children can be quite difficult while they are making their transition away from home, but that once they are safely established, parents' opportunities for personal freedom, happiness, and fulfillment increase. This seems particularly true for women. I know many principals who report that some of their most dynamic, successful faculty members are women in midlife who have entered or reentered teaching after raising a family. They combine the benefits of life experience with the energy of people newly engaged in their profession. In addition, marital satisfaction often improves.

7. These are detailed by Schein (1978, pp. 36–48, 174–180) and Douglas Hall (1986, pp. 120–159). Much of this section is based on their work.

8. As part of this shift, people become more sensitive to the quality of their daily work experience. Questions like these become more important: If I'm out sick for a week, does anybody notice? If there is a problem in my family, does my principal stop by and ask how things are? Do I, in short, continue to be a meaningful person here? Again, this does not mean that people no longer wish to do a good job. It does mean that they are less purely concentrated on their output and more sensitive to the experience of their membership in their professional community.

9. Huberman divides the teaching career into four phases: (1) *survival and discovery* (the first three years) and (2) *stabilization* (years four to six), which together correspond to the entry phase of general career theory; (3) *experimentation and diversity* (years seven to eighteen), which is characterized by efforts to increase one's impact, first in the classroom itself and, often, more broadly within the school as an institution; and (4) *focusing down* (years nineteen and beyond), which involves a contraction of effort and interest, a reduction of energy and commitment.

10. It also illustrates one of the many good reasons for a faculty to include a healthy mix of age and experience levels. Schools have

always depended for their success on a high degree of exploitation—getting maximum effort for minimum compensation—and it is far easier to exploit eager, innocent, unencumbered beginners than weary, wily, overloaded veterans!

11. Many superintendents, principals, and department heads whom I respect praise clinical supervision. But in most of their schools I see little evidence of sustained, meaningful improvement—as opposed to temporary insights—among veteran teachers, except those who were already highly motivated. Of the many factors at work here, three bear special mention. First, supervision and evaluation, as Herzberg (1987, p. 112) notes, play at best a secondary role in motivating performance in any professional setting, because they are extrinsic to the job itself. Second, in education, these activities suffer from a perceived arbitrariness: we have no clear consensus about what constitutes best practice. Third, clinical supervision is labor-intensive, and there is a chronic problem in education about the "span of control"—most principals and supervisors have so many staff to oversee that they cannot engage each individual thoroughly. Traveling in scores of districts each year, I meet few teachers who report that supervision and evaluation even seem to be truly aimed at their professional growth, let alone stimulate it.

Chapter Seven

Setting: Assessing Organizational Capacity

*Teachers unquestionably can do what they do better. But . . .
what they do is largely fixed by their working conditions.*
—RICHARD ELMORE AND MILBREY MCLAUGHLIN (1988,
P. 41)

Every organization is more than the sum of its individual members'
characteristics—it has traits of its own that shape its performance
and adaptability. These traits naturally affect innovation, both
directly and, through their impact on people, indirectly. Thus what
is true of teachers is also true of schools: to need change is one thing;
to be ready for it and able to use it is something else again. Although
all organizations have a bias toward maintaining the status quo, they
can differ in the strength of this bias and in the extent of their resistance to change. A school's institutional readiness—its organizational capacity to adopt and implement an innovation—is crucial to
its success in innovating. This is our subject in this chapter.

We may approach this readiness by beginning with a corollary
to the last chapter's question about teachers: what are the traits
one would wish for in a school where innovation is to occur? Whatever the school's problems, one would hope that it would provide
an adequate setting for change—that is, that conditions in the
school would permit it to tackle its problems. A complete list of relevant conditions would be very long. I have found that the key factors fall into six contexts that shape the overall organizational
setting of a school:

- *Occupational framework:* The structure of the profession and its influences on the school—the nature of the work, the norms of practitioners, their social status and prevailing outlook
- *Politics:* The trust, consensus, and autonomy the school enjoys and its ability to maintain informed, supportive constituencies
- *History:* The school's previous experience with innovation
- *Stress:* The level of demand on the school vis-à-vis its organizational strengths
- *Finances:* The school's wherewithal to underwrite reform
- *Culture:* The supportiveness of the school's underlying ethos and shared assumptions

These contexts are not separate from one another; they are different but related dimensions of a school's organizational setting. Each plays an important role in how "changeable" a school is. In this sense, they are organizational prerequisites for reform: change faces long odds if these contexts, taken together, are too unfavorable. And unfortunately, this is too often the case.

Occupational Framework

Every organization is shaped by the larger occupational framework to which it belongs. This context influences the design, focus, and tone of the organization and the attitudes and behavior of its employees. It has four key features: the structure of the occupation and the nature of the work itself, the norms of practitioners, the social status of the profession, and its general ambience (the atmosphere and mood of the profession at large). If we focus not on the theoretical discourse about reform carried on among academics and policymakers but on the actual professional context of schooling, we see that it is uncongenial, even hostile to innovation.

To begin with, teaching, as an occupation, is especially prone to increasing people's vulnerability to stress and reducing their readiness for change, to pressing veteran practitioners toward the lower end of the growth and performance continuum rather than lifting them toward higher professional engagement and functioning. As a number of cogent observers have pointed out, teachers' work is, by its very nature, beset by unique pressures:

- *Social complexity.* Teachers participate in hundreds, even thousands of interactions per day, from the most mundane (greeting students in the corridor) to the most complex (encouraging students to reflect on challenging problems).
- *Multiplicity.* Teachers are almost always doing more than one thing at a time and must often switch rapidly between roles. They may reflect about their teaching before or after a class, but not during a class.
- *Personal involvement.* Teachers must connect personally with students to engage them in learning. This is difficult enough when pupil-teacher ratios are relatively low; it is even more so when, as in many high schools, teachers work with 150 or more students.
- *Motivational burden.* Teachers must capture and sustain students' interest and attention. In this sense, teaching is closer to acting or sales than to other professions such as surgery or law, where client motivation either doesn't matter or is easily mobilized.
- *Public nature.* Teachers are "on stage" performing in front of an audience for hours each day. Unlike many professionals, they make their mistakes in public and have virtually no private space to retreat to.
- *Unpredictability.* Teachers can never be sure that the same presentation will generate the same response from class to class or student to student. Though this makes for a certain variety, it also requires teachers to be instantly ready to modify their goals and methods.
- *Professional isolation.* Teachers' work is conducted away from peers. Though many enjoy being alone with their students, this seclusion deprives them of feedback and recognition—a key source of support, of confirmation of adequacy, and of information that can solve problems and improve performance (Jackson, 1968, pp. 9–19; Huberman, 1983, pp. 482–483; Sarason, 1971, p. 152–169).

Every profession, of course, has its own pressures, but these characteristics make teaching an unusually draining activity, one marked by a sharp disparity between giving and getting. It requires constant personal investment but provides little in the way of consistent, measurable reward. Teachers are used to this imbalance. A surprising number grow to accept it almost unthinkingly, as something that comes with the territory. But its cumulative impact over the years is wearing. These characteristics of teaching also lead, as we have seen, to a powerful impetus toward immediacy in school life, to a view of innovation that emphasizes near-term improvements rather than fundamental changes. "It's hard for our people to even listen to anything about basic redesign," a superintendent says. "My high school principal keeps insisting, 'We're dancing as fast as we can. Any more new steps and we'll fall down.'"

It's not just the inherent pressures of school life that affect the climate for change in schools. Norms for professional growth and innovation in education have never been high. The extensive professional development typical in other human service fields, such as medicine and mental health, is absent. As we have already noted in Chapter Four, despite the lip service paid to growth, much programming offered by districts, whether for general continuing education or for specific innovations, is inadequate. Most districts are essentially structured to maintain the status quo, not to stimulate their own improvement. Few have any real "developmental capacity." Few earmark significant funds for staff development, and the resources that are targeted are routinely sacrificed to other needs (Schlechty, 1990, pp. 96–97). Some states have recently moved to requiring continuing education units as a condition of maintaining teacher certification, hoping to stimulate professional development and learning. But these requirements are typically met through the very in-service offerings that inspire so little enthusiasm and promote so little growth.

Even if a district were to embark on a serious professional development plan, it is unclear what response it would meet, for surprisingly few teachers are exponents of growth. On some surveys about the importance of keeping up with trends and progress in one's field, teachers have scored well below members of most other occupations, including businesspeople (Krupp, 1988). This can be seen in its extreme form in in-service programs. And if the quality of much staff development fails to meet professional standards, so too does the participation of some teachers. A principal who is an expert on interdisciplinary curriculum and who speaks widely in schools describes this typical scenario, familiar to most staff developers: "The session is held in the auditorium, which has far more seats than there are faculty. As the teachers come in, many go straight to the back. The superintendent asks people to move to the front, but there is always a group, mostly male high school teachers, who stay back there. Before I've even been introduced or even had a chance to bore them, some of them have their newspapers out, some are correcting papers, some are dozing."

Even assuming that districts have given such teachers reason to be skeptical through years of poor programs, their response is still not just unprofessional—it is childish. They would never tolerate the same behavior from their students. Of course, these teachers are a minority (although they can be found in schools everywhere, and we shall have more about to say about them below), but there is a larger number who not only fail to challenge their disaffected colleagues but in fact behave as if education is essentially a static activity. As a teacher in a rural midwestern school told me, "You do pick up a new wrinkle now and then, but basically teaching is something you learn how to do and then you just do it." This attitude may seem shallow, especially to educators who take a far more sophisticated approach to professional development, but it is generally how most Americans see teaching: a job of some importance, but not one to be confused with brain surgery or, say, corporate finance in terms of its complexities and skill requirements.[1]

The third important factor in the professional context is social status. Every occupation provides its members a measure of social standing. As many observers have noted, the standing of teachers has declined markedly over several decades. This has meant, among other things, a deterioration in their sense of importance and nobility in their work. If teaching has never been comparatively well paid and has never been accorded a lofty status among the professions, it previously enjoyed a much higher regard than it does now. The vast majority of today's teachers have witnessed during their career a palpable erosion of parental support and public esteem. They see this reflected in myriad ways, from a sharp increase in high-level public criticism to a pronounced shift in the attitudes of parents. Most restructuring proposals emerge from studies highlighting flaws in our system of education, often with strong criticism of teachers' performance. Meanwhile, veteran teachers describe a similar change in relationships with parents, a turn away from mutual respect and cooperation and toward demands and challenges. Parents are less highly involved in their children's lives and more eager for schools to fill the void, yet they are less willing to collaborate with their schools and more critical of educators' judgment. Teachers and administrators everywhere, in both public and private schools, report a steady rise in the frequency of parents' challenging them—often sharply and condescendingly—about small details of discipline and instruction, demanding that exceptions be made for their children and believing their children's version of problems that occur at school.

How much does a loss of status and respect matter, not just in general but with respect to school improvement? How much does it affect teachers' attitudes toward reform? A great deal. As their public image and social status decline, teachers' self-esteem diminishes, too, and with it their sense of efficacy and their confidence. And as their perception of shared home-school cooperation shrinks, so does their appetite for sacrifice. In times of psychological deprivation, just as in times of economic poverty, resilience and generosity dwindle, rigidity and self-concern intensify. And when reform asks teachers to undertake the hard work of radically altering their practices and beliefs, it is asking for generosity, flexibility, and sacrifice as much as it is promising improvement, empowerment, and excitement.

The deprivation they experience, coupled with many of the life and career changes noted in Chapter Six, incline teachers more strongly toward what is sometimes called a "union mentality"—that is, a militant antimanagement posture, a to-the-minute definition of the work day, and a reflexive, legalistic opposition to virtually any innovation that might impinge on contractual agreements. This may not be an inevitable response to a sense of being taken advantage of, but it is, in my view, a natural one. Employees who have long felt underpaid and who then see their social status slipping even as demands upon them increase are more likely to adopt an aggressive, us-versus-them posture. The irony is that while this can increase teachers' muscle, it further diminishes their status. When it leads them to oppose changes in working conditions necessitated by certain reforms (say, a reduction in individual preparation periods to create more common planning time or a change in certification requirements to permit more interdisciplinary courses), it gives ammunition to their critics and leads the general public to see them as not only unprofessional but also opposed to improvement.

Reflecting these issues, in part, the ambience of the field of education—especially public education—is quite negative. As contrasted to the widespread excitement and optimism during the reform initiatives of the late 1960s and early 1970s, the mood of the 1990s, despite bright spots here and there, is decidedly less hopeful. Scarcely a school I visit, even the most dynamic and successful, is free of a sense of pressure, and in many there is a palpable sense of resentment. One has only to ask teachers to describe the important recent trends in their school to hear a litany of concerns about the issues described above and others outlined below. At major educational conferences, to hear the experts' presentations and then listen to the participants' conversation in the corridors is to be struck by a sharp disparity between the optimism and fervor of the former and the gallows humor and cynicism of the latter.

Politics

The political context in which innovation occurs exerts an important and often overlooked influence on its success. *Political* here refers first to the unity, stability, and autonomy that a school enjoys and second to its assertion of positional interests. The political context is determined by the level of trust that obtains among the participants, their degree of consensus about the school's problems, and the control and flexibility available to the school (Louis and Miles, p. 191).

Reform can only be built on a platform of trust and consensus. A sufficient level of trust within a school and between it and its community is an essential prerequisite for innovation. How much trust is sufficient? The more, the better. Trust is impossible to quantify, but its absence is unmistakable—and a strong contraindication against attempting reform, as we will see in Chapter Eleven. Trust begins with the formal leader. Although a leader's trustworthiness is not enough to guarantee successful implementation of change, its lack virtually guarantees resistance and failure, as I shall elaborate in Chapter Nine. None of us willingly follows someone we distrust, even if he proposes ideas we agree with. If faculty doubt their principal's sincerity and commitment both to change and to them, there is little point in his trying any real reform. The mistrust is a primary issue that must be resolved first.

A sufficient level of trust must also exist among faculty and between the school and the community. Because change causes confusion and conflict, provoking new tensions and reawakening old ones, staff must begin with some degree of mutual regard and respect, especially if the innovation involves extensive collaboration. Similarly, the larger school community must have reason to trust the principal and staff, particularly when change involves major restructuring, affects large numbers of students, or threatens traditional understandings (for example, by replacing a traditional credit-hours graduation requirement with a formal exhibition of competence).

Along with trust, reform requires a consensus among participants about the problems to be solved and the methods for solving them. We have already examined the need for consensus in Chapter Four in connection with resolving the inevitable conflict that proposals for change provoke. Here I make two additions. The first is to acknowledge a primary need for agreement about the problems—not yet the solutions—facing the school. Consensus about which solutions to pursue can be hard enough to achieve even when all parties agree on the problems that need attention; it is virtually impossible without such a prior accord. The second is to broaden our earlier emphasis on consensus within the school to include consensus between the school and its community.

Community begins with parents, but increasingly schools must broaden this definition to include the larger population. Years of a declining birthrate mean that in many districts barely 25 percent of citizens have children of school age, and some of these send their children to private or parochial schools. Thus the natural constituency of the public schools, the population whose immediate self-interest inclines it to support programs and funding, has become a distinct minority. Moreover, as America has become more multicultural and more fragmented by single-interest politics, it has become harder to build support for new programs, particularly if they have any potentially controversial elements or involve substantial costs. So schools must work harder to retain confidence and sustain consensus, not only among their natural constituents but also among the rest of the public. Two capacities they need are marketing, to find out what constituents think and want, and public relations, to keep constituents informed about the school's own goals and needs. Given the demographic changes just noted, these skills are likely to become ever more important.

In addition to trust and consensus, a school attempting major change needs to have a significant measure of autonomy, particularly with respect to priorities and staffing. Most restructuring reforms aim directly at the individual school. But as we have seen, most districts suffer from "simultaneous multiple improvement"—an overloaded improvement agenda. One consequence is that when an individual school does the hard work of initiating reform, it too often finds that district-level initiatives and state mandates intrude on its efforts and claim priority.

> At Redtop Elementary School the faculty, behind the dynamic leadership of a new principal, decided to devote itself to a major "read and write" campaign, concentrating on reading recovery and process writing. This was in line with district priorities on improving the literacy and self-expression of its students, 50 percent of whom came from low-income, non-English-speaking families. However, during the first year of the initiative the district hired a new assistant superintendent, who soon announced districtwide K–12 curriculum revision projects in science and math. Then the state's Department of Education challenged the district's efforts at inclusion of special needs students and threatened court action unless there were vigorous efforts (including extensive staff training) to comply with the letter of the law. Redtop soon found its own priorities set aside: money was redirected, meetings were preempted, and staff were reassigned.

Turnover and reassignment of personnel are among the greatest hazards to innovation. Of course, change agents sometimes wish for the freedom to transfer resistant staff out of their buildings, but more devastating than being stuck with recalcitrants is to lose key members. A significant measure of school-based control over staffing is essential to maintaining the impetus for innovation (Louis and Miles, p. 221). A school that lacks a locus of control can rarely become a locus for change.[2]

History

A school or district's historical track record with regard to past change efforts also influences its readiness for innovation. Many have developed what Fullan calls "an incapacity for change." Because school districts commonly adopt innovation without pursuing adequate follow-through or clearly understanding its inherent difficulties, many of their efforts seem to fail, leaving in their wake frustration, anger, guilt, and disillusionment. The more frequently this occurs, the more skeptical teachers are likely to become about the district's commitment and follow-through and the more they are likely to resist any reform, regardless of its potential (Fullan, pp. 73–74). The pattern becomes circular: inadequate implementation leads to resistance, which becomes reflexive and helps sabotage implementation of the next change, which reinforces future resistance, and so on.

When advocates of reform are reminded of this cycle, they often attribute it to failure on the part of particular individuals or institutions. Smarter people or better schools, they suggest, would avoid such errors. And very often, with the clarity of hindsight, we can indeed identify specific mistakes. But implementation problems are so common—even in projects developed by smarter people in better schools—as to suggest that something systemic, something inherent in organizational life, may be at work. Two somethings, in fact. The first is that the outcomes of an innovation are never perfect; at best they approximate the planners' expectations. As we have previously seen, there are no surgical strikes in school change. Even if it achieves its stated goals, no reform ever achieves *only* those goals, without any unanticipated consequences. As soon as it is adopted it becomes a source of uncertainty and pressure in different parts of the system (Kaufman, 1971, p. 85).

At Greenville High School, a new, integrated English–social studies curriculum for the ninth grade, developed during an expensive summer workshop, enjoyed good success. It engaged students and helped them cover more material more thoroughly. It also led to unintended stresses. The district had planned to concentrate the following year's resources on new curricula at the elementary and middle school levels, but parents of ninth graders began demanding improvements in other high school subject areas similar to what had been accomplished in the English–social studies curriculum. They persuaded the school board to scrap the earlier plan, to the dismay of elementary and middle school teachers. The following year, tenth-grade teachers, faced with students who were more advanced—and who complained of being bored and began presenting more behavior problems—found, to their great chagrin, that they had to spend much extra time modifying their curriculum "on the fly." Tension increased both within the high school and between it and the other Greenville schools.

From an outcomes point of view, this is not a worst-case scenario—parents liking a school's innovation so much that they lobby for more; teachers are being stretched to modify their courses. More commonly, the positive outcomes are less clear-cut and the negative ones more pronounced. The more numerous, stressful, and unexpected the latter, the greater the likelihood of resistance.

A second factor at work in the cycle of innovation and frustration is the organizational stability noted in Chapter Three. Since an organization's structure and culture are built to preserve the status quo, they not only resist change at the outset, they continue to do so: "After an organization has been changed even a little, it begins to freeze into its new pattern almost at once; it does not remain loosely structured and flexible. All the tendencies that inhibited change in its prior configuration promptly make themselves felt in the new one" (Kaufman, p. 68). Most large school change efforts reach only initial or partial implementation and then petrify, eventually becoming targets of future reforms. Since each round of reform creates a new set of roles, positions, and policies, the cumulative result of repeated structural change, especially in large districts, is "layering—the piling of administrative echelon upon administrative echelon in an unremitting quest for coordination, symmetry, and comprehensible order" (pp. 76–77). A classic example is New York City's tortured history of decentralization over the past century, an odyssey that has produced a kind of "fragmented centralization" with ever more central office administrators to supervise, coordinate, and gather data on the school department's various units and programs, despite periodic efforts to transfer power to the schools (Tyack, p. 172). This type of reorganization can actually make change more difficult than it was before and complicate future innovation. Though few districts face New York's complexities, many find their efforts to restructure for the future compromised by their history.

Stress

An institution's readiness to use reform is powerfully influenced by its stress level—the range and intensity of demands it faces and its corresponding ability to cope. Just as the treatment of a specific medical symptom depends in part on the patient's general health (including her ability to tolerate the added stresses of the cure itself), a school's preparedness for a certain innovation depends on its overall strength relative to the demands made upon it. Ironically, the more pressured the school, the more it may need reform—and the less it may be able to undertake it. Some schools, of course, are under far more pressure than others, but as a group, American schools, trapped between rising demands and limited resources, have become textbook cases of stress.

In everyday speech we refer to stress almost as a kind of infection that we can catch. To medical researchers, stress is internal, the reaction within an organism when the demands of the external environment tax its ability to cope (Selye, 1974, p. 14). The level of stress depends both on the severity of the demands and the strength of the coping mechanism. In the case of schools, for "demands" we can read "change." Researchers have long known that all change, positive as well as negative, requires us to learn new ways of responding to our environment and thus creates stress. For "coping ability" we can read "resources and support." Some individuals just seem to be stronger copers, more personally resourceful; researchers speak of their "psychological hardiness." Hardy or not, all individuals, in conditions of stress, benefit from interpersonal support. Research has shown that the more isolated people are, the more vulnerable they are to stress; support not only makes people feel better, it helps them think better, improving their problem-solving ability (Caplan, 1981, p. 419). The greater the gap between demands on the one hand and resources and support on the other, the greater the likelihood of stress. This formula applies not only at the most basic biological levels, such as to the white blood cells in our bodies, but also to people as individuals, as families, as groups—and as schools.

If as a nation we had deliberately sought in 1957 to devise a plan to subject schools to high levels of stress, we could have not have improved on history. I choose 1957 because it offers an excellent benchmark. It was the year the Russians launched Sputnik, the first space rocket, terrifying America and spawning a wave of educational reform and recrimination. In the intervening decades schools have contended with a relentless expansion of their tasks, both academic and nonacademic. Though the resources made available to them have also increased, they have not come close to matching the rise in expectations. Demands to restructure are unwelcome to many teachers precisely because they arrive on top of changes, planned and unplanned, that schools have not yet been able to digest, let alone master. From an outsider's perspective, it may seem that many key features of school life have resisted reform and shown remarkable stability, but from the perspective of practitioners, schools are awash in a sea of change.

The academic changes alone are stunning. There has been extraordinary growth in both the scope and sophistication of curricula. The sheer volume of what we teach to children as they move from kindergarten through twelfth grade has soared—I know veteran curriculum coordinators who insist that it has more than doubled in the past forty years. Anyone who has worked in our schools knows that nothing is ever removed from the curriculum; material is only added and compressed downward. In American history alone there are nearly four full decades to teach that didn't exist in 1957. And as course content grows larger and more dense, it often grows more sophisticated—mathematics and science have expanded beyond anyone's imagining in 1957. The radical expansion of the curriculum is epitomized for me by a math teacher who reports that during his twenty-five-year career his Geometry I textbook has been revised twice. In the process it has grown from 240 pages to 600. "But I still have to get my ninth graders through it between September and June," he explained. "So you see why I don't take any sick days."

These curriculum changes are the first part of a phenomenal rise in expectations that lies at the core of schools' current problems.

The second is the student population. For even as we demand that our schools cover more—and more complex—subject matter, we are requiring them to do so with an ever wider range of students, including more who have special difficulty with challenging material. As Schlechty points out, our schools, contrary to common perception, have never been better at their traditional task of providing a basic education, but they seem worse because they have never before been expected to serve such a "grand purpose"—to provide a full education to all children, rather than just a majority of them, and to go beyond this to teach all children higher-order thinking skills, and to go even further and help develop students' attitudes. If there appear to be more bad schools than there used to be, it is in good part because more schools are trying to teach children who, in the so-called good old days, "would have been working in factories and sweatshops" (1990, pp. xvii–xviii).

Our new accelerated expectations reflect economic realities (there are now few decent jobs for dropouts) but not pedagogical ones (we don't yet have the instructional technology, let alone the resources, to achieve the ideal academic outcome with the full range of students). This problem is further compounded by changes within students themselves: they are becoming steadily more disadvantaged and difficult to teach.[3] This shift paints a portrait of social disintegration in America, a steady abandoning of direct care and support for the young by the other institutions on which our society and successful schooling have depended—most notably the family:

- The nuclear family (two parents—one breadwinner, one homemaker—and two children) now constitutes only 7 percent of all households (in 1950, it was 60 percent). In its place has arisen the "permeable family" (two parents working, single-parent families, remarried families), which is more fluid, less stable, and far more vulnerable to outside pressures. Its central concern is work, not domesticity; its core value autonomy, not togetherness. Parents must devote ever more time to their jobs, reducing children's direct parental contact and requiring them to be independent at ever earlier ages.
- Almost 50 percent of kindergartners can now expect that their parents will divorce and that they will spend at least five years in a single-parent home.

- Twenty-five percent of children currently live with only one parent (in 1960, fewer than 10 percent did). We call them "single-parent" families, but as a grim Carnegie Corporation (1994) report notes, most are "mother-only" families, half of whom have no support from and little contact with the father. Children from these families are significantly more likely to have behavioral and academic problems, to drop out of school, to become single parents themselves, and to achieve a lower socioeconomic status than children from two-parent families, irrespective of race.
- Twenty-five percent of school-age children live below the poverty line.
- Thirty-one percent of births are to unmarried mothers (in 1950 it was 5 percent).
- Half of all babies are born with what a federal study panel deemed to be health deficiencies that put them at risk for school failure; of the twelve million children under the age of three, many are at risk of permanent harm from these deficiencies that can damage their cognitive, social, and emotional development.
- More and more students come to school ill (in many communities, visits to the school nurse are increasing at a rate of 20 percent per year) because so many working parents do not keep sick children home.[4]

The list could include many other relevant challenges. At its most dramatic, the more difficult nature of the student population has been reflected in an epidemic of violence and shootings among youth that has begun to plague many communities, especially large cities, and their schools. It has also been reflected, less violently but with equally serious implications for learning, in a trend reported by kindergarten and first-grade teachers everywhere: more and more children come to school less ready to learn. They are not less intelligent; they are less ready to be students—less able to master the basics of cooperation and concentration, less ready to listen while someone else talks, less ready to negotiate and share, less ready to work hard at teacher-designated tasks, less ready to spend time working out a problem if its answer doesn't appear at once. A compelling picture of the problem is painted by H. G. Bissinger in a portrait of a suburban Chicago high school:

It's the end of another day at Proviso West, and for Dennis Bobbe, a social studies teacher, it's not a moment too soon. He came to the school in 1966 when it was at its apex, filled with those seemingly timeless shows of spirit, the pep rallies, the sock hops, the earnest debates over war and peace. Now, it's nobody's school, all the spirit sucked dry. He finds nothing remarkable about Proviso West at all, except, perhaps, for the pathos. "They're actively resisting learning," he says of his students. "They just don't want to learn. It's not fun. It's too much effort." He pauses, and then takes a turn inward.

"Maybe it's me."

He knows they're bored to tears. He knows what their ability to analyze or do something in-depth is. He knows what the pop culture effects of television and music are, "the bing-bang-boom," as he calls it.

"I can't compete."

He caters to them, minimizing the complexity of the material and the amount. He tries to be an entertainer, even though that contradicts his whole persona—beard, soft voice, pudgy body. "Kids come in asking for a routine. A vaudeville show. Abbott and Costello. Who's on first?" He talks about United States history and he sees the glaze set in their eyes. He could lecture naked. He could lecture upside down. He could not lecture at all. Would they even notice? He's getting too old, too entrenched to grope for meaningful answers. "I am near the end of my career."

Yet he wonders what happened to the notion of the American public school as a sacred place, a vital place, a place unlike any other in the world. "What was it that peeled away? What was it that was lost?" [1994, p. 56].

Veteran teachers everywhere will recognize Dennis Bobbe's situation, or aspects of it, from their own experience. The gaps we are asking our schools to close are truly unprecedented.

All this said, I must add an important qualification. The dramatic rise in expectations that has plagued our schools cannot be blamed entirely on outside forces. Educators have contributed to their own burden. Sarason criticizes both practitioners and researchers for decades of overpromising, of embracing the growing list of new goals and targets, programs and designs and implying that these would be readily, even rapidly achievable. By contrast, the medical community has long emphasized the complexity and intractability of the conditions it is trying to cure and the inevitability of high costs and slow progress, thereby reducing public expectations—and public frustration and criticism. We believe doctors when they tell us that cancer is enormously difficult and that cures will be expensive and incremental. Education's problems are every bit as complex and intractable, and so, argues Sarason, the educational community needs to follow suit, to get off the "moral hook of promising more than it can deliver" and "increase public understanding of why the problems in schooling . . . are and will be so vexing" (1990, pp. 37–39).

Finances

However the blame is apportioned for their burgeoning responsibilities, many districts, even as they struggle to meet these obligations, are suffering the strains of fiscal decline. Near the core of any serious consideration of school improvement lies money—or, more accurately, the lack of it. For one thing, many of the educational problems that have spurred calls for reform stem from our schools' relative poverty. For another, change isn't cheap.

Beginning in the 1980s with federal budget cuts and state-level tax caps, American schools began to suffer a growing gap between the rise in expectations and the resources available to fulfill them. By the 1990s, the cumulative impact of years of tight federal funding, magnified by new rounds of state cuts, has been felt from Massachusetts to California and from Michigan to Florida, often reaching crisis proportions. Though few districts have yet suffered the celebrated fate of Alpena, Michigan, where the public schools closed months early in 1993 due to a budget shortfall, or the severe retrenchments in Chicago later that same year, all across the country, few teachers and administrators can remember when the disparity between expectations and resources was greater. (In California, ever the trendsetter, the statistics are grisly. Over the fifteen years following its adoption of the infamous Proposition 13 tax cap, it fell from fifth in the nation in per-pupil spending to forty-second. It saw its dropout rate leap to the third highest in the nation and its students' test scores sink to the very bottom).

The case that schools are, on the whole, underfunded has been made so often and so persuasively by so many experienced observers,[5] and is one I see confirmed so regularly in my own travels, that I take it as a given; for me, it requires no further proof. We are a nation that spends more on cat food than on textbooks (Houston, 1995, p. 170). Virtually all of the serious surveys, commission reports, and academic studies of American schools of the 1980s point to chronic underfunding as one major source of their performance deficits. Too much schooling is carried on in decrepit buildings in chronically dangerous surroundings with outdated textbooks, insufficient supplies, and impossible teacher-pupil ratios. Far more schooling is carried on in minimally adequate buildings in periodically dangerous surroundings with slightly less antiquated textbooks, barely sufficient supplies, and teacher-pupil ratios that are merely undesirable.[6] "Most jobs in the real world," says Sizer, "have a gap between what would be nice and what is possible. One adjusts. The tragedy for many . . . teachers is that the gap is a chasm, not crossed by reasonable and judicious adjustments" (1984, p. 20). The long-term impacts of this deprivation are ominous. A thoughtful study of workplace conditions in schools and their impact on teachers leads Susan Moore Johnson to conclude, "It is illusory to imagine that public education can be at once cheap and effective. If teachers are poorly paid, many who enter classrooms . . . will be those who cannot find jobs elsewhere. . . . If schools are not repaired and maintained to permit safe, comfortable work, good teachers will take their skills elsewhere. . . . If funds are not available for new books and equipment, if there is no budget for clerical assistance, if classes and teaching loads are large, students will suffer and teachers will continue to leave teaching" (1990, p. 333).

Over and above the need to improve the baseline support for schools is the added cost of innovation. Few schools can achieve fundamental restructuring without funds to underwrite at least three major costs: training, consultation, and transition management.[7] (These are in addition to the cost for the physical "stuff" of implementation—materials, supplies, and, depending upon the specific innovation and setting, renovations to the school's physical plant.)

The first, training, is geared both toward increasing staff members' skills and toward developing some staff members' abilities to become future sources of internal expertise (Louis and Miles, p. 251). Its costs include not only the trainers themselves but also temporary staff additions to free teachers for the training. The funding problem is already apparent. If it is fair to attribute part of the blame for ineffectual professional development to poor design by those who run schools and part of it to disaffected teachers who fail to give innovation a chance, we must also acknowledge that it usually reflects a paucity of resources. Of necessity, school districts invest much less in training than does corporate America, which routinely spends 5 percent of its managers' time on professional development and training—time that comes out of the regular work day, not out of afternoons that follow a day's work. In education, this would amount to nine or ten days per teacher per year. In most districts, the very idea—hiring each teacher for ten days during the summer or hiring a substitute for each teacher for ten days during the school year—would be laughable.

The contrast with corporate America is acute. As one who consults in the private sector as well as in schools, I am always struck by the disparity in their relative levels of support for change. From a similar vantage point, Schlechty notes that, compared to training programs for educators, those for executives have more "class," by which he means "everything from the ambiance of the meeting place to the quality of the materials to the fact that executive training sessions usually are accompanied by refreshments, which is seldom the case with teacher 'in-service.' The best teachers can expect, quite often, is a cup of coffee in a cafeteria where the custodian is cleaning up during the training session. The chairs are hard, the afternoon is late, and personal obligations await. This is not an atmosphere conducive to serious thought or feelings of self-esteem" (1990, p. 107). When I first read this passage, I thought immediately of a high school in a small, poor New England city where I used to give a lecture each year. Six times a year the faculty would gather at 3:00 in the decrepit student cafeteria, where, for two hours of mandatory staff "development," they would sit on ancient, splintery, backless stools attached to the lunch tables and listen to outsiders like me while the kitchen staff were indeed cleaning up. Each time, just before I began, the principal, acknowledging the difficulties, would lean over and whisper, "I don't care what you tell 'em, Doc, just let 'em go a bit early."

In addition to direct training for teachers, innovation usually requires the purchase of other consultation. We have seen that one reason it is hard for an organization to change itself is that its members are embedded in the status quo. It is extremely difficult for them to gain enough perspective on their own functioning to see it in its full context and to design effective alternatives. We all know our own organizations intimately, in a way that a stranger cannot, but as we saw in the concept of culture-as-prison in Chapter Three, our involvement also deprives us of perspective because we come to take certain ideas for granted and to get enmeshed in a particular way of seeing things. Consequently, when trying to change fundamental aspects of our workplace we need not only the advice of outsiders about special content areas—an expert in cooperative learning or authentic assessment, for example—but also help to gain some distance from ourselves and to see our efforts in a broader context. This is especially important when, as so often happens, reform provokes tension, conflict, and confusion among members of a faculty.

Reform's third cost center, one which in my experience is frequently—and fatally—omitted from restructuring projects, is for a formal transition management structure. Apart from the problem of perspective, another reason any stable organization has difficulty changing itself is because its regular structures can rarely be used for managing change (Beckhard and Harris, p. 74). At the most basic level, "novel allocations of time, space, funds, and authority create the need for vast amounts of information and frequent human contact—to supply new facts and ideas, to penetrate confusion and uncertainty, and to promote new forms of working together" (Mojkowski and Bamberger, 1991, p. 22). They also create needs for strong coordination and orchestration, for what Louis and Miles call "steady, active work" on such tasks as "monitoring, communicating, linking, problem finding, and coping." But the school's people are fully occupied performing their existing functions. Hence it is often necessary to create a unit to manage the change. For a serious, large-scale improvement program in a school of any significant size this requires, they suggest, the creation of a specific position (at least a half-time equivalent, if not more) for an individual who will coordinate the innovation, and the establishment of a steering group representing various key constituencies, which meets regularly to assist the coordinator (pp. 264–265). However it is composed, this team cannot work without adequate time. Its members cannot be asked to pile change management on top of all their regular tasks; they require specific released time for this new function.

Of all the complaints of teachers about the difficulties of change programs in schools, none is more frequent than "not enough time." Whether it is site-based management or authentic assessment, integrated curriculum or new technology—or, most commonly, when it is all of these and other initiatives, too—there is never enough time to support the innovation. The National Education Association (NEA) cites studies showing that, compared to teachers in America, those in China, Taiwan, Japan, and Germany routinely spend much less of their work time in charge of classes (as little as 60 percent of their total time), with the rest being devoted to planning, consulting, grading, staff development, and the like. The NEA argues that given American teachers' packed schedules, school reform, far from ameliorating conditions, "is creating one more behemoth responsibility for teachers to embrace" (1993, p. 6).

Time and support aren't cheap. Hiring consultants, trainers, and a project coordinator (Louis and Miles report that successful innovations use more than thirty days per year of external assistance); providing coverage for staff who receive training, serve on steering committees, or engage in collaboration; and purchasing new equipment and materials all cost money. The minimum start-up cost to fund a major innovation in a high school is an additional $50,000 to $100,000 per year for several years (Louis and Miles, p. 242). In large schools tackling large changes, the cost is higher. This should not be surprising. For some years now the financial press has been full of stories about companies downsizing and taking massive "restructuring charges" against their income to reflect the transitional costs of becoming more competitive. Only in schools do we consistently seek major reform on a shoestring, clinging to a futile formula for fast, cheap change: plan in the summer, implement in the fall, spend very little, measure good results by spring.

There is, of course, an opposing view to all this. Advocates of choice and voucher systems argue that we have squandered money on schools and should be able to restructure via reallocation, without increased expense (Finn, 1987, p. 63). Contrasting the rise in teachers' salaries to the decline in students' test scores (Brimelow and Spencer, 1993, p. 72), they argue that forced competition, not further funding, is the path to improved performance. Even reformers who are sympathetic to schools are upset by the waste and the recurrent fiscal scandals in the schools of major urban areas. I know many principals and teachers who are eagerly seeking to improve their schools and are dismayed by the aimless, inconsistent way their district spends large amounts of in-service money. Whether such errors would be corrected by choice and voucher programs is far from certain. The flaws in these proposals have been cogently argued in many other places and are beyond my purview here. However, having worked in one way or another in several hundred districts, I can say that I have yet to see a school, rich or poor, that could restructure itself on its existing budget.

The fiscal conservatives' challenge does serve to emphasize two key problems in the school improvement agenda. The first is some reformers' blindness to (or fudging of) funding issues: almost every restructuring initiative costs money, but almost none has a budget. Few proposals attend directly to the price of improvement. Fewer still factor into their outcome forecasts the realities of budgetary constraints. The second is schools' docile acceptance of impossible improvement plans. Whether this is a reflection of the overpromising noted above or a result of years and years of being conditioned to make do with minimal resources, many administrators and teachers have apparently gotten used to underestimating or accepting others' lowball estimates of the resources necessary to accomplish change. They regularly agree to undertake extensive reforms on bare-bones budgets rather than asking even something so mild as, "How did you think we might accomplish all that at no additional cost?"

Culture

When demands and resources are so out of balance and the setting for change is so problematic, staff morale, performance, and cohesiveness typically deteriorate. To sustain them over an extended period requires a supportive culture that maintains continuity and reaffirms the meaningfulness of work. Organizational culture, as we saw in Chapter Three, is a unique, deep structure of assumptions and beliefs that defines an organization's view of itself and its environment and shapes for its members the meaning of experience. When these assumptions and beliefs emphasize the nobility of the work, a "can-do" attitude, and a strong commitment to one another, faculty are buffered against the disillusionment and fragmentation that might otherwise overtake them. They can fashion an energizing sense of common purpose and remain connected and mutually supportive instead of becoming isolated. If the culture also supports exploration, they will be more willing to innovate, even in the face of deprivation. Despite stress, there will be something to work with.

Many schools (especially those that are better financed) show evidence of a positive underlying culture and a tradition of pride and accomplishment despite the pressures outlined in this chapter (although most of these also show evidence that years of stress are eroding this foundation). But in far too many of schools I have visited, especially urban schools that teach the most challenging students amidst the greatest shortages, the culture nurtures neither commitment, competence, nor initiative. Teachers cannot identify a sustaining mission or a set of values that unites them and drives their work. The culture is one of learned helplessness, a mixture of cynical resentment and passive resignation:

> In some schools, teachers hold low expectations and classroom routines bore children to death. School staff may complain bitterly and work to undermine each other. Parents may be overwhelmed by issues of economic and personal survival, and students may be more focused on drugs and life on the street than on books and classrooms.

> People can become as attached to mediocrity, negative symbols, and harmful rituals as they can to positive heroes, symbols of achievement, or celebratory rituals. For some, negative meaning is better than no meaning at all [Deal and Peterson, pp. 14–15].

I would argue that for *all* of us negative meaning is better than none at all. I would add that the personal issues reviewed in the preceding chapter and the organizational issues reviewed in this one combine to make negative meaning readily understandable and far too likely—as I have learned by sharing with audiences of educators the following true story about the Naysayers.

At Prospect High School, a second-floor faculty lounge is inhabited solely by a small group of older male teachers (no one else dares to enter). The group is known to itself and to everyone else as "The Naysayers"—the title appears on the door—because its members criticize anything and everything, including all current practices *and* any suggestions for improving them. At inservice presentations they show overt disinterest. At faculty meetings, they often laugh sarcastically and make derisive comments about the problems, topics, and proposals under discussion, reserving, it seems, particular scorn for suggestions made by newer, younger members of the faculty. No one challenges them. Though few in number, they hang over the faculty like a dark cloud. They are classic cases of the tendency, noted in the last chapter, of becoming attached to one's burdens: they have become wedded to theirs. They have not just settled for negative meaning, they have adopted a negative identity, living in a hostile dependence on their school. "Prospect is the place these guys love to hate," says one of their colleagues. "If things got better here, they'd be lost."

Prospect might seem an exceptional case, a natural for fostering this kind of negativity. It has long been a dingy, dispiriting, dangerous facility serving a chronically disadvantaged population in a city whose government has raised corruption and incompetence to art forms. But as I began describing the Naysayers to audiences of educators, I was at first surprised by their vigorous head-nodding and outright laughter. They knew whom I was talking about. The Naysayers, it turns out, have confederates all across the country. I have even heard them described in a National Public Radio report on a Chicago high school, where they also occupy a second-floor, male-only teachers' lounge (Glass, 1993). Naysayers are to be found in schools of all kinds, usually in small numbers but almost always with disproportionate influence—vivid proof of the power of negative cultures to resist change.

Implicit throughout this discussion is an old truth: over time, success depends crucially upon adaptability—so much so that the two are nearly synonymous. Unfortunately, the need for improvement does not nearly guarantee the capacity for it; many schools are in deep trouble in good part because they have been unable to adapt. It is thus a central irony of reform that the schools most needing change are often the ones least able to achieve it. This is hardly a welcome prospect. Nonetheless, a certain level of strength in the school as a setting is a clear prerequisite for restructuring. That the right conditions do not obtain does not mean that reform is ultimately impossible. It does mean that the school must first undertake the advance work to make itself ready, such as confronting and resolving a major trust problem or improving its political standing with important constituencies. During this time, small, individual improvements may be manageable, but major innovation is likely to fail and to damage the chances for future reform (Louis and Miles, p. 188).

We have now looked at three dimensions of change: (1) substance, the characteristics of the reforms we call restructuring; (2) staff, the readiness of the educators who are being asked to accomplish it; and (3) setting, the readiness of the schools where it is to occur. In each case we have seen that the obstacles to improvement are far greater than commonly thought. They create an unprecedented challenge for the fourth and most vital dimension of change—leadership—to which we now turn. Given its unique complexities, restructuring requires not only a new paradigm of change but also a new conceptualization of leadership, one that, ironically, tries to simplify the task of leading and that emphasizes not new techniques but old truths—truths that contain our best hope for meeting the problems I have traced and so transforming our schools.

Notes

1. For one thing, entry is easy (and so is reentry if one takes a leave), tenure means security, work days end early, vacations are frequent, and summers are free. For another, teaching has always been a field that places little emphasis on practitioners' development. Its ancient roots are in religious devotion, in service and sacrifice, not professional enhancement. In America, it was long the work of women prior to their getting married and bearing children—hardly a profession at which one would need "development."

2. A related note: few schools have designed plans to orient and support new members who arrive after a change program's inception. This increases the damage done by turnover. A scheme for bringing newcomers up to speed should be a part of any reform effort.

3. A striking example of this issue is the requirement for full inclusion of special needs students in regular classrooms. It is a microcosm of the promise and problems of American education. It can be seen as our schools at their noblest, maximizing opportunity for even the most disadvantaged. There has been some impressive success, chiefly in elementary schools and chiefly with students whose learning disabilities are relatively uncomplicated by emotional or motivational problems. But in too many schools the successes are overshadowed by a set of larger burdens, which range from overpromising and underfunding to an enormous increase in logistical complexity and requirements for teaming, among others (Evans, 1990, pp. 73–74). Inclusion also illustrates a key aspect of a broader trend in education, the shifting of responsibility for child development and student performance away from a shared school-student-parent-community partnership onto the school alone. It has increased the obligation of schools to provide or purchase an almost limitless array of academic, social, medical, and psychological services; and the rights of parents to demand these services, no matter how great the cost or how small the potential benefit to the disabled student, have grown out of control (see Rosenfeld, 1989, p. 32, and Kauffman and Hallahan, 1995).

4. See Carnegie Corporation, 1994, pp. 4–15; Hodgkinson, 1985; Moroney, 1994, p. 28; Viadero, 1993, p. 5; Usdansky, 1996, p. 4; Whitehead, 1993, pp. 47, 66. The concept of the "permeable family" is David Elkind's (Scherer, 1996, pp. 4–9).

5. See, for example, Johnson, 1990, pp. 58–79.

6. Quite apart from any question of restructuring, there is a growing issue of rebuilding: most of America's public schools were built before 1967 and will soon need repair or replacement (Schlechty, 1990, p. 77). This deterioration is most noticeable in schools in poor urban and rural areas, but it is easily found as well in apparently well-off suburbs. Reform will have to compete with renovation for scarce dollars.

7. The occasional examples of a charismatic principal and a heroic staff who make miracles out of pitiful resources are exceptional and nowhere near the norm.

Chapter Eight

Leadership: Old Paradoxes, New Promise

It is the ability of the leader to reach the souls of others in a fashion which raises human consciousness, builds meanings, and inspires human intent that is the source of power.
—WARREN BENNIS (1984, P. 70)

The economist Burton Malkiel has observed that some things in life can never be fully appreciated or understood by a virgin (1990, p. 25). This is surely true of teaching, as well: those who haven't done it can't truly appreciate its burdens and complexities—though this has rarely stopped them from criticizing teachers. For their part, teachers often feel free to disparage administrators. But if, as teachers rightly feel, teaching has its unique pressures, so too does leadership. And if, as the preceding chapters have argued, the dilemmas facing teachers are far more serious and complex than many Americans and even many educational thinkers and policymakers imagine, those facing school leaders are, in my view, even more formidable. Principals and superintendents must not only help staff contend with all the issues, both personal and professional, we have explored so far, they must cope with these issues themselves while simultaneously assuming the primary responsibility for initiating and implementing change. The challenge is immense, but it cannot be abandoned; too much depends upon it. The rest of this book is devoted to the leadership of school improvement.

Just as change is elusive, so too is leadership. Good leadership can be felt all through an organization, says Bennis: "It gives pace and energy to the work and empowers the work force." In well-led organizations people feel that they make a significant contribution, that what they do has meaning, that they are part of a team or a family, that mastery and competence matter, and that their work is exciting and challenging (1989, pp. 22–23). Morale and commitment are high even in the face of hardship. But though its impact is palpable, though most of us feel we know a good leader when we meet one, the essence of leadership remains unclear. Is it a matter of skill or charisma? Of science or art? Of politics or principle? Are its methods universally applicable or situation-specific? Are leaders born or made? Yes. Leadership appears to be all these and more. Despite thousands of empirical studies yielding hundreds of definitions of leadership, there is still no consensus about it. We still don't know conclusively what distinguishes leaders from non-leaders and strong leaders from weak ones (Bennis and Nanus, 1985, pp. 4–5).

This uncertainty has helped create a steady market for leadership fads. Because most leaders contend with an endless string of problems, many of them unexpected, they often make a quick analysis and then reach for a quick solution, selecting one that is currently popular (Bolman and Deal, p. 29). But "none of the management fads of the last twenty years—not management by objectives, diversification, Theory Z, zero-based budgeting, value chain analysis, decentralization, quality circles, 'excellence,' restructuring, portfolio management, management by walking around, matrix management, intrapreneuring, or one-minute managing—has reversed the deterioration of America's corporate competitive performance" (Hammer and Champy, p. 25). We know that leadership matters enormously, but we haven't yet been able to capture—or teach—its essence.

We also haven't learned how leadership concepts developed in noneducational spheres apply to schools. Here is the life cycle for a leadership theory:

1. It begins outside of education, developed by political scientists from studies of gifted historical figures or by management

experts from studies of gifted business leaders (no one would ever think of basing a leadership model on studies of gifted school administrators!).

2. It gains favor in corporate America and comes to be a hot concept in management writing.
3. As it nears the apex of its influence, someone decides to apply it to education, even if it has little apparent relevance to schools.
4. It grows hot in educational circles as it begins to cool in the corporate world, where it is showing hitherto unnoticed weaknesses.
5. It is often misapplied in education, either through slavish rigidity (failing to modify the model to fit schools' unique characteristics) or false clarity (adopting the form of the innovation but not its true substance).
6. Well after it has lost its cachet among business leaders, it lingers on in vestigial form in schools and schools of education, until its popularity finally subsides there, too.

At any given moment there are likely to be several theories at different stages in the cycle competing with one another. Education is littered with their corpses.[1] Our problem is to get a grasp not only on leadership but also on concepts that are relevant to schools.

But before we even get to theory, there are realities to contend with. As they confront the imperative to innovate, school leaders face many obstacles. Two are especially powerful. The first is that the business of simply maintaining schools, never mind changing them, has grown so arduous that it keeps principals and superintendents under relentless pressure, greatly reducing the energy available for anything other than tending the status quo. The tensions that are innate in leadership have acquired a new intensity, leaving too many administrators vulnerable and stressed instead of vigorous and stimulated. The second is that the assumptions underlying the practice of many leaders are inadequate to the task of innovation. Most administrators have been trained to see leadership in terms of the rational-structural paradigm we examined in Chapter One and to approach their roles in ways that actually inhibit rather than foster change. Fortunately, the strategic-systemic paradigm offers a better—and in key ways simpler—approach. Moreover, gifted thinkers have begun applying its precepts to school leadership. This chapter reviews key dilemmas confronting those who must spearhead school change and the traditional viewpoints that have dominated leadership theory and practice; the combined picture is not pretty, but it situates the dilemmas of leading school reform in their true context. From there, the chapter traces a turn in leadership thinking that holds encouraging promise for the future.

Chronic Tensions

Most of the talk and writing about organizational leadership emphasizes the new (as I have done)—new problems and the need for new solutions. Many of the current issues facing school leaders do feel exceptional and unprecedented. But they are not wholly new; they are more intense manifestations of age-old dilemmas. Leadership has always been beset by intrinsic stresses—pressures and paradoxes that are inherent in the role. Before we consider the demands of leading innovation, we will begin with a look at five of these core tensions.

Managing Versus Leading

In recent years it has become common to make a distinction between leadership and management, venerating the former at the expense of the latter. Leadership is the exercise of high-level conceptual skills and decisiveness. It is envisioning mission, developing strategy, inspiring people, and changing culture. Management, on the other hand, is making sure the bells ring on time. Managers, it is said, do things right, while leaders do the right thing (Bennis and Nanus, p. 21). I amend this distinction below, but there is undeniable truth to it: conceiving new ways to promote professional discourse among teachers via telecommunications is not only a higher-order task than, say, suppressing students' vandalism of bathrooms, it is more rewarding. The problem is that most school leaders, like most executives everywhere, have always spent far more time managing than leading. Running an organization seems to be a matter of solving an endless set of "messes" (Bolman and Deal, p. 29). Efforts to exert leadership are usually cut short by the need to manage these messes. This point lives for me in a visit to Tom Black, the new principal at Mason High School:

Tom found Mason to be very traditional, with a heavy emphasis on separate academic disciplines and teacher-centered lecturing. As he sought to move the school's structure, schedule, and orientation toward an "essential school" model he encountered significant faculty resistance. One morning we sat down to discuss these issues. Tom began elaborating his philosophy of student-centered learning and integrated curriculum, and his plan to engage the faculty in a reconsideration of the school's mission and values. Just then there was a call from the Department of Public Works. A major water main had broken, and the school would have no water for the rest of the day—no water to prepare lunch or flush toilets.

Tom called his superintendent to ask if the school should be closed. After a few minutes of discussion there was a long pause, and then Tom asked, "And you think teenagers won't take advantage of that?" The response must have been something like, "I know you'll do your best." Tom made noises of reluctant agreement. The superintendent had decided that students could not be sent home—few parents would be at home to receive them. Those who needed to use the bathroom would be transported by bus to a nearby elementary school. Tom had to announce the water cutoff over the public address system and advise all students needing to use the bathroom to report to the office for bussing. We terminated our leadership discussion so he could go manage.

Management issues are not always so blatant, but they are wearing in their repetitiveness and their intrusiveness. Studies have long shown that executives of all types tend to work "at an unrelenting pace," with their activities notable for their "brevity, variety, and discontinuity" (Mintzberg, 1989, p. 3). Long episodes of high-level conceptualization and reflection are rare. A principal in a school near Tom Black's explains that many of his brief interactions with people involve "someone wanting a piece of me. My job is more high-dreck than high-tech. It's day after day of 'Have you got a minute?' and 'Guess what just happened?'"

Resources Versus Demands

I have rarely met a leader who felt that the resources available were adequate to meet the demands of the job. I have found a sense of insufficiency ubiquitous among leaders of both private corporations and public agencies and, within each of these sectors, among leaders of both comparatively poor institutions and comparatively wealthy ones. Leaders perpetually feel caught between the requests of clients (and staff) for more resources and the realities of limited supplies. "Resources" usually comes down to "money," either directly or indirectly (more staff, more materials). But no matter how much money is available in schools, it is never enough; nor, it seems, are there ever enough people (or enough good people), enough time, enough materials, or enough space. From the perspective of an outside observer the available resources may seem more than adequate, especially compared to those of similar institutions; from an internal perspective, they rarely do.

The Paradox of Power: The Dependent Leader

What is true of resources is equally true of power: leaders rarely feel they have enough. In most organizations no one admits to having any real power: everyone feels fettered, either by internal forces or external constraints (Morgan, pp. 180–181). (In their classrooms, teachers are like leaders in this respect: they often feel that what happens is dictated more by students' behavior and response to the subject matter than by their own intentions or influence.) Most of us tend to imagine that if we could move up in the hierarchy we would acquire *real* power and then could truly effect change. Educators who seek careers in administration often do so with this in mind. They become principals in part to "make a difference," to right wrongs and correct flaws that chafed them as teachers, and to assert a vision of schooling as it should be. The first great shock awaiting them is discovering how little power they truly have.

When a teacher ascends to the principalship of a school, he immediately begins to realize how much he depends on his former colleagues. He can exert a strong sway over the character and climate of a school and the thrust of its teaching, but it is the staff who must day in and day out translate ideas into action and who, enjoying the protections of union, tenure, and tradition (academic freedom) can generally implement a principal's ideas with wide latitude. Some principals try again, moving up to become central office administrators and superintendents. But the higher a person rises, the less direct contact he has with the organization's clients and staff; the more attenuated his influence, the more subject to misinterpretation his actions become. Of course, in any direct encounter a superior is more powerful than a subordinate, but the experience of leading, especially when it comes to getting large numbers of people to change, has usually left leaders far more aware of their vulnerability than of their power.

Symbolism Versus Substance

The paradox of power has always been matched by a parallel tension between substance and symbolism. People who seek leadership positions to make a difference expect to be engaged in substantive matters of policy and purpose; but just as they find themselves surprisingly dependent, they also discover that they are often hostages to ritual. Here again, the higher the position, the further removed it is from hands-on activity and the more its occupant is confined to gestures that are primarily symbolic. At the highest levels (the presidency of the United States, for example), one spends vast amounts of time on such gestures: meeting with representatives of group A or their opponents in group B, being photographed with refugees from country C, inspecting hurricane damage. The problem here is partly that symbolism is draining—a steady diet of "showing the flag," "pressing the flesh," and "sending signals" wears on a leader—but the larger problem is that symbolism often ends up being so much more important to a leader's success than substance. A superintendent offers this example: "Last fall I spent whole weekends designing an improved curriculum development process. I was fully engaged in furthering our core educational purpose, but I wasn't at any Saturday football games. The school board raked me over the coals for not being visible and fostering school spirit." The pressure to concentrate on creating perceptions is both intense and, for many leaders, debilitating.

Isolation in a Fishbowl: The Personal Toll

The fifth chronic tension of leadership is also a paradox: being at once alone and exposed. All the old jokes about it being lonely at the top are rooted in truth. The most dramatic change in moving from a staff position into a leadership role is the loss of peers. A teacher who is promoted to principal may continue to enjoy trusting and rewarding relationships with faculty, but she is inevitably distanced from them. Becoming a leader enlarges her responsibility. Her charge is now the whole institution, not just her classroom or one department; she must engage the whole faculty, not just her close colleagues. Promotion also diminishes support. If a tornado rips the roof off the building, if a teacher dies of a sudden heart attack, if parents are concerned about a controversial curriculum topic, it is the principal or superintendent who will be called and who will have to respond. She will not always have to respond entirely alone, but she will usually have to respond first and orchestrate the response of others, who will take their cue from her. And most key leadership decisions, especially sensitive ones, are made in relative isolation. Over and over again in my consulting work with principals and superintendents I have seen the same dynamic: when they are able to gather and talk with one another about the personal burdens of their job, the stress of their isolation is sure to emerge as a powerful recurring theme.

Another strong theme is a companion problem: being constantly in the public eye, both internally (within the school) and externally (within the community). Although they are isolated, principals and superintendents have always been "on display." Indeed, they often feel their loneliness most sharply in public. Superintendent Robert Spillane of Fairfax, Virginia, says his job makes him "a celebrity of sorts. People know who you are, and they see your picture on television. . . . But the loneliness is that you're always 'on,' you're always performing as superintendent" (Jones, 1994, p. 27). In addition to being alone in a crowd, leaders must make key decisions alone—and then deal with the very public consequences of these decisions. These may involve anything from enforcing unpopular school rules about student behavior to dismissing a popular but incompetent teacher. The agony they provoke can be intense.

New Intensity

These five tensions are not new in nature; leaders have always had to contend with them. What is new is their extent and intensity. The changing nature of organizational life has exacerbated these chronic conflicts to the point of disempowering leaders and diminishing the quality of their lives. Permanent white water has overtaken and destabilized organizations of all kinds. Heavy industry, public utilities, technology, communications, financial services, the media, medicine, law, human services, philanthropy—each of these fields has undergone a revolution in structure and process; each has seen dramatic alterations in its basic assumptions and taken-for-granted practices. And so, too, has education.

These changes begin with the extraordinary increase in expectations discussed in Chapter Seven. As America has given its schools more and more to do, often enforcing the requirements with complex regulations, management tasks have multiplied and the imbalance between demands and resources has accelerated. The former problem has twin faces: legal and bureaucratic. Schools have hardly been immune to the plague of lawyers visited upon so many areas of American life. Over the past thirty years I have watched volumes on school law multiply on the bookshelves in administrators' offices. From personnel policies to students' rights, decisions once routinely left to the principal are now fraught with legal peril if he fails to observe every detail in the byzantine, often contradictory mazes of state and federal laws and regulations.

Accompanying this legal explosion has been a bureaucratic deluge. From counting empty bus seats to dotting the *i*'s and crossing the *t*'s in reports for mandated and categorical programs, administrators spend more and more time riding the audit trails. (Title I and special education are sources of particular frustration in this regard.) Together, the legal and bureaucratic requirements have created a glut of paperwork and a preoccupation with procedure that have expanded administrators' workloads and shriveled their room to maneuver and freedom to exercise their judgment. The result is a professional frustration and lack of personal fulfillment that is truly impoverishing the quality of their lives. And all this is to say nothing of how these trends keep them from trying to stay current with basic aspects of instructional leadership and promising developments in curriculum and instruction!

As noted in Chapter Seven, the imbalance between resources and demands has never been greater, with a rising tide of expectations outstripping the growth of budgets. This phenomenon is visible in communities of every socioeconomic level: resources have not kept pace with demands. Although some prefer to focus on the comparative funding disparities between wealthy and poor districts (Kozol, 1991), in my experience these disparities do not mean that wealthier schools have adequate resources to accomplish what is asked of them. I consult in school districts where the per-pupil expenditure is among the lowest in the nation and in others where it is among the highest; in neither do educators feel able to fulfill the demands made upon them. In poorly funded schools the deprivation is obvious. But deprivation is always relative, not to other schools but to the demands upon one's own school. Typically, taxpayers who are providing higher levels of funding expect even higher returns on their investment; in fact, they feel entitled to them. In the nation's premier school districts the predominant sense is not one of elegant sufficiency but of chronic anxiety about rising parental expectations and diminishing public tolerance for any shortcomings whatsoever.

Management burdens and demand-resource imbalances are difficult enough, but school administrators have also had to contend with a larger pattern of social and cultural fragmentation in America that has disempowered leaders in all sectors. In looking at teacher burnout, we saw that one cause was the dramatic social and cultural shift since the 1960s toward challenging authority and asserting individual freedom. These trends have caused serious, if not permanent damage to community, consensus, and institutional credibility in America.[2] Many Americans, it seems, can no longer imagine "a political system that would enable them to share in the governing processes and trust in its outcomes" (Greider, 1992, p. 25). This creates what Bennis sees as a kind of conspiracy against leadership. In *Why Leaders Can't Lead* he argues that when consensus was lost, institutional leadership was crippled.

> The notion of the public good, the common accord has always been at odds with traditional American individualism, but it blew apart in the explosive 1960s, when virtually every institution came under fire. . . . We questioned everyone in authority and every institution. We formed blocs of like-minded people to agitate for what we wanted and oppose what we didn't want. . . . As individual autonomy waxed, institutional autonomy waned. External forces impinged more and more on the perimeter of our institutions; the incessant concatenation of often contrary demands grew. . . . This

fragmentation, which existed in virtually every organization, marked the end not only of community, a sense of shared values and symbols, but of consensus [1989, pp. 61–62].

The result is a chronic crisis of governance, a "pervasive incapacity of organizations to cope with the expectations of their constituents" (Bennis and Nanus, p. 2).

This incapacity traces its roots not just to the impact of the 1960s emphases on individual freedom and opposition to authority but to the malignant, selfish turn that these took during the deification of selfishness, of capitalism run amok, in the 1980s, an era Cornel West summarizes as "Reagan, Rambo, and retrenchment." The much-discussed economic and political impacts of Reaganism—a widening of the gap between rich and poor, a debasing of government and the very concept of public service—were accompanied by a cultural impact equally damaging, a "spiritual impoverishment" that values "power, pleasure, and property" above other personal or civic virtues. Consequently, "public life seems barren and vacuous. And gallant efforts to reconstruct public-mindedness in a Balkanized society of proliferating identities and constituencies seem farfetched, if not futile. Even the very art of public conversation—the precious activity of communicating with fellow citizens in a spirit of mutual respect and civility—appears to fade amid the noisy backdrop of name-calling and finger-pointing in flat sound bites" (West, 1994, p. 48–49).

Leadership is difficult enough when shared values and symbols and mutual respect and civility obtain; it is nearly impossible without them. When, lacking a sense of mutual commitments, we stand ready to mistrust at a moment's notice; when, lacking a concern for the common good, we scorn compromise; when, focused on short-term gain, we replace loyalty with narrow self-interest; and when, in our entitlement and mistrust, we litigate any kind of dispute, no matter how trivial, we make leadership a more and more onerous burden. This is felt in organizations everywhere, and certainly in schools.

Although many educators and laypeople alike see schools as instruments for social change, in reality schools reflect society far more than they shape it; they are vulnerable to it far more than they influence it. Indeed, as Schlechty points out, "America's educators have had considerable success in running schools [whenever there has been] value consensus" (1990, p. 28). But when, as in the late twentieth century, there is not only no consensus but much conflict, the chronic leadership tensions of dependence, symbolism, and public criticism are magnified. And where leaders could once expect to be accorded a fair measure of respect and an assumption of good faith until they proved unworthy of these, where they could once have expected a fair measure of discretion on the part of the media and the citizenry at large, they can no longer do so.

All of these trends decrease school leaders' sense of efficacy and heighten their feelings of isolation, insecurity, and inadequacy, a reality I often think of when I read the job postings in *Education Week* or the *New York Times* ("We seek a dynamic thinker with a strategic vision for the twenty-first century"; "Opportunity to lead a richly diverse district to world-class status," and the like). I measure such enthusiastic prose against the actual lives of school leaders. Most of the principals and superintendents I know like the field they've chosen and the role they've reached—few would seriously consider doing anything else—but virtually all acknowledge that their professional lives have grown more complicated and less satisfying. The aspects of the job they most enjoy, such as working directly with teachers and students ("actually doing direct things about learning," as one superintendent put it), have been steadily diminished by the problems cited above. Diminished, too, have been family life and personal well-being, sacrifices that are rarely recompensed by a show of public appreciation or a sense of professional accomplishment. If the advertisements were candid, they would have to include something like this: "We seek a miracle worker who can do more with less, pacify rival groups, endure chronic second-guessing, tolerate low support, process large volumes of paper, and work double shifts (seventy nights a year out). You'll have carte blanche to innovate, except that you can't spend much money, replace any personnel, or upset any constituency." Of course, if the ads emphasized the wear and tear of leadership, salaries might need to double to attract applicants. "The question," says a superintendent, "is not just whether I can do it all, but whether it's worth the cost."

Attempting to do it all and to limit the costs, school leaders, like their counterparts in corporate America, have tried a variety of methods. These begin with working harder. People work longer, first informally (staying later, taking more work home, coming in on weekends and holidays) and then formally (more and more principals are now hired for a "twelve-month year" rather than on the once-common ten- or eleven-month basis). When workaholism fails to meet demands that keep expanding, people often turn to time management courses. However, for all but the truly disorganized these prove paradoxical: work expands to fit the time saved; one no sooner learns to do more in less time than one is given more to do. When time management fails, leaders try to "work smarter" by enhancing their technical knowledge and skills. Advanced degrees, conferences, and workshops proliferate, but they fail to alleviate the pressure (Vaill, 1989, pp. 5–6). At a seminar on school change, a superintendent said: "Every principal and central office administrator in our district has a doctorate—fifteen years ago not one of our predecessors did. I've quadrupled our budget for out-of-state travel and attendance at conferences. We gather voluntarily on occasional Sunday evenings to discuss leadership books and articles. You couldn't find a group that's more up on the latest thinking, but every one of us is working flat-out nonstop, and we still can't keep up with the demands." School leaders are, if not an endangered species, at least an embattled one.

If this vulnerability is due in good part to the contextual changes of recent decades and the pressures and complexities they have spawned, it is nonetheless surprising given the apparent growth in our knowledge of leadership. The field has mushroomed in recent years. Leadership seminars and management workshops do indeed abound. It would seem that we have never known so much about the subject. And yet, this expertise has failed to prevent or resolve the problems noted above. Although we might expect that leadership training would address itself to the problems outlined here, this is not the case. The reasons grow clearer when we look more closely at the actual nature of what we "know" about leadership. The theories and models that have predominated in the training of school leaders have not only failed to reduce or resolve the actual managerial problems of running schools, they offer little promise for leading innovation.

The Rational-Structural View: Leadership as Technique

For much of this century the rational-structural paradigm of organizational functioning, rooted in Taylor's scientific management and its derivatives, has dominated leadership thinking. As we saw in Chapter One, this paradigm treats organizations as rational systems that should be structured for maximum efficiency and that depend upon planning, command, coordination, and control. It treats management as a science or a technical profession rooted in research and logic, measurement and efficiency. Though few management experts or organizational leaders might now describe themselves as disciples of Taylor, the influence of scientific management remains broad, deep, and active. For example, many of the widely known systematic management programs of recent decades not only repeat specific elements of Taylorism, they are, like scientific management itself, "one best way" models of leadership. Some of these have, as noted earlier, found their way into education. Just as the principles of scientific management were to apply to all sorts of organizations, so too have these approaches presented themselves as pertinent to a wide range of institutions.

The concept of management as an applied science led naturally to the development of management as a profession and to the sustained expansion during the 1950s, 1960s, and 1970s of graduate programs in both business administration and school administration. Being a manager or executive came to mean being adept in a body of knowledge and a generic set of skills. Once versed in the proper techniques of structuring work and supervising people, leaders could apply these methods across a variety of settings—in a bank or insurance company as well as in a factory. John Sculley, CEO of Pepsi-Cola, could switch from soft drinks to technology, becoming CEO of Apple Computer. This view of management has had a profound influence on the leading of all sorts of American organizations. Even though there is little evidence to suggest that the leading of a school resembles the leading of a corporation (Pepsi and Apple probably have more in common than either does with a school), professional management, and the sources of authority on which it draws, has predominated in the preparation of school leaders.

Professional management draws on three sources of authority: bureaucratic, technical, and psychological.[3] The first stems from formal position and official power in an organization's hierarchy. It emphasizes rules and regulations, roles and expectations. It assumes that supervisors are more expert and trustworthy than staff and that accountability should be external. Its primary leadership strategy is "expect and inspect": employees are subject to direct supervision, and compliance is measured according to standards developed by the supervisor. In this and other ways it is quite close to Taylor's original tenets—have managers design the work and delineate workers' job duties; use objective methods to ensure efficiency, train staff to perform specified tasks in specified ways, and monitor and measure performance closely. It is, at its core, take-it-or-leave-it management: staff members comply with leadership directives, or else.

The second source of authority for professional management is technical. It rests on logic and research. Both the practice of the work itself—in the case of schools, teaching—and of leadership are applied sciences in which technical knowledge predominates over personal judgment and experience; objective evidence outweighs values and beliefs. Leadership based on technical authority relies on research data to shape practice in standardized ways and calls for careful monitoring and supervision. It is potentially less coercive than bureaucratic authority in that it appeals to expertise, expecting people to conform to a higher standard based on "technical rationality [and to] craft notions of . . . best educational practice" derived from research (Sergiovanni, 1991, p. 328). However, this kind of leadership can easily turn into Shaw's "brute sanity" (Chapter One), insisting that staff comply with expert prescriptions by virtue of their manifest truth.

Psychological authority—interpersonal skills and motivational techniques—is the third underpinning for professional management. It emphasizes cooperation and communication and rests on "interpersonal style, cleverness, guile, political know-how, and other forms of managerial and psychological skill" (Sergiovanni, 1991, p. 328). It presumes that while teachers and administrators have different goals, their differences can be negotiated. Teachers have legitimate needs, and the administration's targets will be better accomplished if these are met. It assumes that "what gets rewarded gets done," and its primary leadership strategy is "expect and reward": if expectations are clear, the work climate is positive; compliance is rewarded, and teachers will want to participate and go along (Sergiovanni, 1992, p. 32).

Generally, these three sources of authority are used in conjunction with one another. Many efforts to improve the running of schools, such as the effective schools movement, for example, or the instructional leadership movement, have emphasized a combination of bureaucratic, technical, and psychological authority. These different strands in the theory and practice of professional management emphasize a "list of functions" or "list of skills" approach. From studies of successful managers, researchers build an inventory of functions (planning, budgeting) or skills (supervision, conflict resolution) that are supposed to summarize the executive role (Vaill, 1989, pp. 114–115). These taxonomies usually begin with instrumental and technical competence but also include a strong emphasis on psychological authority (human resource development, interpersonal skills, and so on).[4]

The increasing emphasis on management as a generic, portable competency and on the importance of human relations skills has led to the rise of contingency theories of management. These argue that no single form of leadership is optimal for all settings. Rather, they suggest that different kinds of organizations—and different types of issues—require different kinds of management. An elementary school, for example, demands different leadership than a frontline military unit. And more importantly, they call for managers within a given setting to be able to apply a range of skills as the particular context requires (within the elementary school, different staff groups may respond best to different kinds of handling). "Situational leadership," as it is known, has gained wide popularity in management theory and training. Key to this approach are two concepts: flexibility and style. The ideal leader is seen as having a rich repertoire of problem-solving techniques and can thus respond effectively to a wide variety of people and issues. The techniques themselves are usually grouped into constellations and defined as "leadership styles." Advocates of situational leadership see leaders as preferring a predominant style based on their experience, education, and training—but also as being flexible.[5] They can learn to readily adapt their style to the requirements of different situations.

Not surprisingly, the typical school administrator is an amalgam of all these influences. Though few might claim to be practicing an applied science, most are committed to a technical view of management. They have been trained to see running a school primarily as a matter of technique, especially psychological technique. To most school leaders, "knowledge and skill about how to motivate, apply the correct leadership style, boost morale, and engineer the right interpersonal climate [is] the 'core technology' of the education administration profession" (Sergiovanni, 1992, p. 33). Just as a good teacher should have a repertoire of instructional strategies to match the learning styles of each of her students, so should an administrator, according to the beliefs of situational leadership, have a flexible inventory of leadership approaches that generate the right results from different constituents.

Situational leadership reaches its apotheosis in training programs that purport to develop management styles. Of these perhaps the most notable is the Meyers-Briggs Type Inventory (yet another leadership instrument that became popular in education as it was peaking in the private sector). Participants answer test questions and then score themselves on four major scales (extroversion-introversion, sensing-intuition, thinking-feeling, judgment-perception), from which they then sort themselves into different types and temperaments. A workshop then follows to help them learn more about their particular styles and those of the people with whom they work and develop ways to communicate better by modifying these styles.

Trying to make of school administration a kind of technology has had its benefits. It has surely helped to nourish the organizational skills required of principals and superintendents as they cope with the burgeoning complexities and procedural intricacies of school life. It has also helped create a more respectful and democratic climate in many school districts and has opened the way for administrators and teachers to solve problems more effectively. And as anyone who has ever led anything knows, leaders cannot survive without certain core techniques, both subtle and blunt. No parent in a family, no teacher in a classroom, and no principal in a school can succeed without at least periodic use of deliberate maneuvers designed to influence others' behavior. But though management-as-technique has come to be taken for granted as sound administrative practice, its flaws are significant, even for maintaining the status quo. And it offers no hopeful basis for changing schools. On the contrary, it is a key contributor to past difficulties in implementing reform and to current problems in schools.

Failed Fixes

As prominent as they are in leadership discourse and practice, the expressions of the rational-structural paradigm are simplistic and incomplete. They have exacerbated the very problems that school leaders are trying to solve, and they have proven inimical to innovation. School reform is about big leaps, radical reform, and bold experimentation. It requires commitment and performance that are above and beyond, off the chart. It needs people to extend themselves beyond their formal roles and schedules. But relying on bureaucratic and technical authority has the reverse effect. An emphasis on standardized performance—detailed job descriptions and strict monitoring of outcomes according to preset objectives, for example—can at best encourage teachers to respond as technicians following procedural scripts. A cramped, literal, unreflective outlook and attitudes like "That's not my job" (which, by many accounts, are rampant in our most demoralized urban school districts and not uncommon in many others) are often attributed to teachers themselves and to their unions, but they are fostered by bureaucratic and technical approaches to management (Morgan, p. 36).

> Two long-serving superintendents in the Ruby Ridge Public Schools came to education after careers in the military. They left a legacy of rigid command-and-control management. Every employee, including all professional staff, must punch in and out on a time clock. Teachers must sign in at professional development sessions. Curriculum guidelines for each subject area at each grade level are spelled out in meticulous detail, and teachers must complete quarterly checklists indicating the topics they have covered. Although there is no strong union presence, teachers throughout the district seem to be just going through the motions. They arrive at the last minute, leave as soon as allowed, and plod mechanically through the curriculum.

Because it encourages staff to develop narrow, rigid concepts of their work, this kind of management is inevitably "limited to achieving minimums, not maximums" (Sergiovanni, 1991, p. 49) and is antithetical to meaningful change.

At a broader level, treating leadership as a list of functions or skills simply doesn't match up with real life. In the real world, no one experiences her job as a list of functions or domains or herself as a list of competencies. The leading of any work group is a matter of a whole person in a whole environment interacting in concrete ways with other whole persons in the immediacy and unpredictability of the moment (Vaill, 1989, pp. 114). Inventories and taxonomies of leadership simply fail to capture this complexity. They miss "the whole that is greater than the sum of its parts . . . the real-world, day-to-day action" (Mojkowski and Bamberger, p. 26) of school leaders. The problem is not necessarily that the particular functions or skills are irrelevant but that leadership cannot be reduced to a list, especially in the dynamic context of a school that is undertaking reform. In addition, the lists are endless. As the complexities of organizational life multiply, experts keep enlarging the leadership catalogue: more domains, more tasks, more techniques; more to do, more to learn. The cure becomes another part of the problem, because it requires yet more from the overtaxed leader.

A related problem here concerns leadership training. There is a growing consensus that the way we prepare and renew our school leaders is grossly inadequate. The general model for leadership training for principals, as Barth points out, is as follows:

1. Find schools where pupils are achieving more than what might be predicted by their background.
2. Observe principals in those schools and find out what they are doing.
3. Identify these behaviors as "desirable traits."
4. Devise training programs to develop these traits in all principals.
5. Enlist principals in these programs.

This model, Barth suggests, is straightforward, compelling, logical— and surprisingly ineffective, in good part because conditions in one school are seldom similar to those in another (1989, pp. 246–247).

When we move beyond the everyday business of running a school to the vastly more complex work of changing it, our training and development models are even more inadequate. Even though "the skills required of restructuring administrators are not amenable to a single-day workshop or even a year-long effort" (Mojkowski and Bamberger, p. 50), we rely almost exclusively on the "Whitman Sampler" approach: one-day workshops on strategic planning, two-day institutes on systems thinking. But just as a taxonomy of skills does not capture the essence of leadership, these isolated, disconnected bits of training fail to give school leaders the tools to transform their institutions.

Probably the most important flaws in traditional approaches to leadership are found in the excessive reliance on style. Despite its apparent appeal, it ignores vital psychological realities. It can produce some success in individual encounters, but it is a weak foundation for the challenge of leading a group, especially when that group is being asked to implement sweeping change. To begin with, it offers a false simplicity: just identify the approach demanded by a situation and apply it. In reality this complicates leadership, because it requires the leader to become all things to all people, to constantly adapt his behavior to meet the styles of others. Moreover, responding to a wide range of situations in a variety of different ways necessarily entails vagueness, imprecision, and inconsistency, making leaders' true commitments hard to discern (Badaracco and Ellsworth, 1989, p. 202–205). When principals try to translate their advocacy of change into multiple "languages" to match the various styles of faculty members, they become hard to read and to count on; the clarity of their message suffers.

Even worse, leaders who base their practice on styles frequently come across not just as inconsistent but also as insincere, as trying to "manage perceptions and create impressions," as studied and calculated rather than spontaneous and genuine (Badaracco and Ellsworth, p. 202). One reason is that most of us can't pull it off; we're simply not good at switching styles. All of us are "creatures of habit, experience, and personality"; we can't "mask [our] real beliefs, values, and thinking" (p. 6) from those with whom we work closely. Few of us can routinely, naturally, and sincerely make the multiple translations, much less the personal changes, so blithely advised by Meyers-Briggs trainers like this one: "If Arthur develops his *J* [Judging] side by planning and organizing more, and if Adrienne develops her *P* [Perceiving] side by being a little more flexible and spontaneous, they'll get along just fine and have a better chance of developing their full potential" (Hemenway,

1994, pp. 16, 20). And if an elephant develops its *S* [Speed] side by being quicker on its feet, it can chase a cheetah. This kind of prescription is scarcely more practical than the horoscope advice in daily newspapers.

Another reason that situational leaders seem manipulative is because they often are; many take a skeptical, even cynical view of people. It is important to realize that the chief reason for studying styles is not just to understand others but to influence them, to extend one's repertoire of ways to affect others. We may not like to think of this as manipulation, but this is often what it amounts to. There is nothing wrong with leaders' trying to influence constituents; they would be useless if they couldn't. But when they hide these efforts in a human relations cloak, in an apparent emphasis on good communication, they inevitably and justifiably arouse suspicion. Imagine that you are having a lively discussion with your boss about an important issue when it suddenly dawns on you that he is applying a technique to you. If you are like most people, your instant response is to draw back; a gap has suddenly arisen between you. His words may not have changed, but they have now taken on a different meaning. This illustrates the critical risk of situational leadership: it damages that most precious commodity, trust (more about this in Chapter Nine).

Taken collectively, the flaws in professional management have at their core a confusion of means and ends. Organizing one's practice around how to do things instead of around what to do and why abandons the true essence of leadership and degenerates into a "managerial mystique" (Zaleznik, 1989, p. 2) that emphasizes procedure and technique—process, structure, and politics—at the expense of substance and purpose. Convinced that good methods generate good outcomes and that procedural controls overcome human inconsistencies, practitioners of this mystique end up substituting methods for outcomes and treating controls as goals. School improvement plans become surrogates for actual improvements, and leadership tactics and styles become substitutes for real purpose (Sergiovanni, 1991, p. 329). Although it is important to know how to achieve a goal, something at which sound management can help, the basis of leadership is to decide which goals are worth pursuing. In education, there has been far too little of this. Administrators have been taught to be organizational operatives rather than visionary thinkers. Too often they end up as "maintainers rather than leaders" (Louis and Miles, pp. 22–23), shrinking the potential for school improvement and innovation.

I should acknowledge that I have seen some administrative groups and school boards that were suffering from severe, basic dysfunctions benefit from learning about styles as an early, ice-breaking step on the road to conflict resolution. I also know many school administrators whom I respect who feel that they have enhanced their leadership through the study and application of situational techniques and styles. For example, many of them have enjoyed the Meyers-Briggs. They report what I think of as a jolt of validation ("Yes, I am a factual, results-oriented person; no wonder I don't get along with Fred, who depends on intuition and emotion") and a new appreciation that people have different ways of perceiving and interacting. Many say they are better able to interpret others' behavior. However, the benefits they describe are tactical rather than strategic, maneuvers to treat symptoms rather than to tackle root causes. Few can identify a deep effect of these techniques and styles on their practice (and far more importantly, neither can their staffs). To repeat, the question is not whether we have different styles or whether it is valuable to learn about them. We do, and it is. But they are not readily or permanently changeable, and basing a leadership practice on trying to do so cannot offer a meaningful, viable basis for leading change. No leadership style seminar turns an anxious, controlling principal who cannot delegate tasks into a confident, trusting principal who shares responsibility (although it may help turn him into an anxious, controlling principal who is *trying to act* confident and trusting). More importantly, no technical training makes any principal into someone who inspires people to follow him into the jungles of radical reform.

The Strategic-Systemic View: The Transformational Transformation

Fortunately, the thinking on leadership has been transformed— literally. After several decades of emphasis on science, techniques, and styles, the field took a sharp turn in the 1980s toward what came to be called transformational leadership and a new set of views nested in the paradigm I have called strategic-systemic. Strategic management, systems theory, participatory management—these and other models have changed the face of leadership. As I noted in Chapter One, they do not all fit neatly under one conceptual roof; they have differences in content and emphasis and offer different diagnoses and prescriptions. They are strategic because they concentrate on the core competence and basic direction of an organization, and they are systemic because they acknowledge the multiplicity and complexity of factors acting within and upon the organization. And most may be said to be transformational in that they seek improved performance in the name of deep, fundamental values that transcend technical competence. Though these viewpoints have enjoyed popularity recently and have become fads in the corporate management field, to my eye they offer the only real hope of improving our efforts to implement school change.

Strategic-systemic approaches to leadership emphasize substance rather than technique. They see leadership not as a science but as a craft, a unique blend of practical experience, personal skill, judgment, and intuition, all informed by training and research. Managing, like teaching, is simply too messy, complex, and unpredictable to be treated as a logical, linear activity. Although in theory it is a matter of devising goals and plans which then determine the resources used and outcomes achieved, in actuality it is often a matter of improvising, of adapting goals and outcomes to the resources available (Sergiovanni, 1991, p. 48).[6] Any craft includes technical aspects and useful tricks of the trade, but they are not the basis of its practice. Similarly, theory and research about management are not irrelevant but tend to be both too general or too specific to be useful; they are often less relevant than the judgment of the experienced practitioner (Sergiovanni, 1991, p. 326). What does guide leaders in exercising their craft are two key concepts: purpose (the pursuit of a vision for the institution based on shared values and beliefs) and followership (the enlisting of people in this effort on a basis of genuine commitment and the empowering of people throughout the organization as decision makers).

Purpose and followership form the heart of transformational leadership, a seminal concept developed by James MacGregor Burns (1979). Transformational leadership is one of two primary modes of leadership; it is best understood in contrast with the other mode, which Burns called transactional and which subsumes most of what we commonly associate with management and much of the rational-structural model I have outlined previously. Transactional leadership is based on an exchange, a bargain between people who are motivated primarily by self-interest. A good transactional leader tries to ensure that these exchanges are "governed by instrumental values such as fairness, honesty, loyalty, integrity" (Starratt, p. 7) and that the procedures are clear, evenhanded, and respect the rights and needs of all. At its most enlightened, transactional leadership achieves mutually beneficial compromises. Congress is designed to function in this way. Composed of members representing competing interests (including their own self-interest), it uses formal procedures (rules of order) and less formal traditions (seniority) to establish a level of fairness, accountability, and predictability, without which it would descend into true chaos. But transactional leadership is entrenched in the status quo and quid pro quo. It is essentially a pursuit of tactical advantage and trade-offs; it cannot lift a group above a certain level of competition and compromise and mobilize it to make fundamental, second-order change. And at its emptiest it degenerates into the maneuvering and manipulation of the managerial mystique, reducing leadership to hollow technique and ignoring a whole realm of experience that truly motivates excellence: "The management values now considered legitimate are biased toward rationality, logic, objectivity, the importance of self-interest, explicitness, individuality, and detachment. *Emphasizing* these values causes us to *neglect* emotions, the importance of group membership, sense and meaning, morality, self-sacrifice, duty, and obligation as *additional* values. . . . What we need is an expanded theoretical and operational foundation for leadership practice that will give balance to the full range of values and bases of authority . . . [a] *moral dimension in leadership* (Sergiovanni, 1992, p. xiii, emphasis in original).

This moral dimension is precisely what Burns identified as the core of transformational leadership. Motivated by such deep values as freedom, community, and justice, transformational leadership is concerned not just with what works but with what is good. It speaks to a fundamental human need to affiliate with transcendent values and overarching purposes. It "seeks to unite people in the pursuit of communal interests" (Starratt, p. 7), to raise the attitudes, values, and beliefs of organizational members from the self-centered to higher, altruistic levels. In this respect, it shares much in common with charismatic leadership.

Charisma is one of leadership's enduring mysteries. Throughout history, many famous and influential leaders seem to have possessed an intense personal magnetism and a remarkable power to influence people. Often we think of their charisma simply as the power to mesmerize others. But there is far more to it. The essential characteristic that recurs in accounts of charismatic leaders is their ability to touch people deeply, to enlist people in a cause by forging a unique and powerful bond with them. They seem to embody "some *very central* feature" of existence and the cosmos, a centrality that, coupled with a remarkable intensity, gives them extraordinary impact on people (Shils, 1965, p. 199, emphasis in original). A contemporary practitioner, the Reverend Jesse Jackson, summarizes the charismatic connection this way: "Truth, like electricity, is all around us, but we have very few conduits for it. What you do is plug the people into your socket, they give you that electricity, and you give them the heat and light" (Frady, 1991, p. 57).

In an age that glorifies technical skill, such notions are unpopular with leadership experts, most of whom dismiss charisma as idiosyncrasy or psychopathology. Some scholars, however, take an opposite approach, trying to demystify it and "operationalize" it. Jay Conger (1989, pp. 25–34) defines charisma as a process rather than a set of personal qualities. He identifies four "stages" of charismatic leadership:

1. Being sensitive to constituents' needs, seeing current problems as opportunities, and building a vision that addresses them
2. Articulating this vision in a way that simultaneously makes the status quo unacceptable and the new vision appealing
3. Establishing trust among followers through proof of sincere commitment to the vision
4. Showing the means to fulfill the vision, including the setting of their own personal example, the empowering of others, and the use of unorthodox methods

Viewed thus, charisma is quintessentially transformational. It is far more compatible than technical approaches to leadership with the pursuit of a transforming vision and the building of commitment to innovation, with risk taking and the seeking of bold innovation. Though studying Conger's four stages will not make one charismatic, each is crucial to creating a commitment to change; it is impossible to imagine an administrator successfully leading the restructuring of a school or district without attending to them in some way.[7]

This is not to say that one must be charismatic to lead change. Charisma can help, of course, but "the world is full of colorful, charismatic people," only a few of whom "are associated with sustained organizational excellence" (Vaill, 1989, p. 65). As will become clear in succeeding chapters, there are many effective ways for those of us who are not charismatic to lead innovation. But charisma underscores the profoundly personal nature of leadership—its personal roots in the leader and its personal impact on followers. "The leadership that counts," as Sergiovanni says, "is the kind that touches people differently. It taps their emotions, appeals to their values, and responds to their connections with other people" (1992, p. 120). It begins with followership.

Followership

Transformational leaders induce followers to pursue "goals that represent the values and the motivations—the wants and the needs, the aspirations and expectations—*of both leaders and followers*" (Burns, 1979, p. 19, emphasis in original). They help people "to feel their true needs so strongly, to define their values so meaningfully, that they can be moved to purposeful action" (p. 44).[8] This is essential: fundamental organizational change requires both the "tapping of existing sources of human energy and the creation of new energies" (Eden, 1990, p. 191). Reform initiatives that call for new ways of thinking about teaching and learning and new ways of relating among adults in a school community depend on real engagement, genuine investment, and extra effort on the part of teachers. It is impossible, for example, to become a true accelerated school through rote competence or by-the-book obedience. It requires the broad, active endorsement of the school community and the ongoing participation of "cadres" who plan and lead changes in the school's instruction and governance. These kinds of innovations cannot be accomplished by leadership that focuses only on "issues of style and levels of decision making" and that defines as good practices those that just aim at getting staff "to do what the leader wants and be happy about it" (Sergiovanni, 1992, p. 2). These and other innovations invite and demand high levels of staff awareness and involvement, the kind of dedication that only comes when people act purposefully—as followers rather than as subordinates, a distinction that is critical to contemporary leadership theory and to restructuring.

Subordinates do what they're told. They respond to bureaucratic authority and can, at their best, be good soldiers who respond to marching orders. They like to know what's expected and often will readily comply (although they rarely do more than what is required, and they need monitoring). They also respond to psychological authority, with their commitment to their job dependent on the rewards they receive. It is fairly easy to get most people to behave like subordinates through a combination of extrinsic rewards (promising them a favorable evaluation, a promotion, or a bonus) and pressures (threatening to report them, demote them, or fire them). However, when the rewards and pressures lose their novelty or their force, commitment and performance decline (Kouzes and Posner, 1987, pp. 26–27). So, when the leader has few of these motivators available, and when the goal is exceptional performance that depends on staff willingness and internal motivation—precisely the conditions in school reform—what then?

What is needed is followership. Followers are defined by two key characteristics: they are committed to "a purpose, principle, or person outside themselves," and they "manage themselves well" (Kelley, 1988, p. 86). A follower is an adherent, someone who subscribes to the teachings or methods of another—someone, that is, who follows a leader, but who does so because he *wants* to and who, on his own, behaves according to a compact they share. Followers are committed to "a vision of what the school . . . can become, beliefs about teaching and learning, values and standards to which they adhere, and convictions" (Sergiovanni, 1992, p. 71). This commitment makes them enthusiastic, initiative-taking participants in the pursuit of an organization's goal (Kelley 1988, p. 85). In this respect they behave more like leaders themselves than like subordinates. When people "become attached to an organization or a way of doing things as persons rather than as technicians," they come to value their work as an end in itself (Selznick, 1957, p. 28). Teaching is no longer a job but a source of personal satisfaction. In this regard, the distinction between management and leadership is that managers "get other people to do, but leaders get other people to want to do" (Kouzes and Posner, p. 27). The wanting is crucial to followership, and leaders of school restructuring must inspire it.

Sources of Transformational Authority

How does one begin? An excellent way to conceptualize this task is to think of staff as volunteers. "Assume that they are there because they want to be, not because they have to be. What would need to exist for them to want to enlist in such an organization? What would you need to do under those conditions if you wanted people to perform at high levels? What would you need to do if you wanted them to remain loyal to your organization?" (Kouzes and Posner, p. 26). Among the factors that inspire commitment and loyalty, two stand out: the leader's credibility, which we will consider in Chapter Nine, and an intrinsically rewarding work environment. Rather than "What gets rewarded gets done," we should apply a new axiom, one that helps explain why people seek to excel: "What *is* rewarding gets done" (pp. 43–44, emphasis in original). It is here that purpose becomes so vital. "People pursue excellence and strive for improvement because they believe in what they are doing" (Schlechty, 1990, p. 108). To commit oneself to sustained high-level performance requires an emotional investment in a belief, a set of values or ideas, something that gives the effort special meaning and imbues work with moral purpose. The best term for such leadership is, I think, *purposing,* which as we have seen, refers to inducing clarity and consensus about an organization's basic purposes and commitment to them. Purposing is central to building followership.

Transformational leadership that focuses on purpose and followership draws on two sources of authority that are at once deeper and higher than those on which transactional leadership rests. The first is professional authority, in the form of seasoned craft knowledge and personal expertise. It recognizes that practice is idiosyncratic and that scientific knowledge informs this practice but doesn't dictate it. It expects teachers "to respond to common socialization, accepted tenets of practice, and internalized expertise" (Sergiovanni, 1992, p. 38), much as doctors and lawyers have traditionally done. Occupations like law and medicine substitute professional, cultural, and moral influences for formal hierarchical leadership. These substitutes diminish the need for formal leadership in two ways: first, by reducing hierarchical influence, they enable change to be initiated at lower levels of the organization, where the daily decisions that affect implementation and performance are really made; second, they require staff "to act in a more professional, self-determining manner" (Weick and McDaniel, 1989, p. 344). Leaders in professional organizations focus not on programs or tight supervision but on values and results; they direct rather than control (Schlechty, 1990, p. 44). The appeal of professional authority is in many ways technical, in that it emphasizes the importance of best practice, but its expectation is that staff will be inducted into a self-motivated and self-monitoring adherence to professional standards. Its primary strategy might be summarized as "intrinsic reward" (what is rewarding gets done). Leaders try to promote a dialogue with faculty about professional values and how to translate these into standards. They give teachers both support and latitude in fulfilling them, and they expect teachers to hold one another accountable for meeting these standards (Sergiovanni, 1992, p. 38).

The second source of authority is moral. It emphasizes responsibilities "derived from widely shared values, ideas, and ideals" (p. 31). It expects teachers to respect common commitments and mutual interdependence. It relies on a "normative rationality . . . that places everyone subordinate to [these] ideas, ideals, and shared values and asks them to respond morally by doing their duty, meeting their obligations," and accepting the responsibilities of community membership (Sergiovanni, 1991, p. 328). From this perspective, people are motivated not solely by self-interest but also by emotion and belief; schools are defined by their values, beliefs, and commitments. The primary leadership strategy here is "what is good gets done." The leader works with the staff to make explicit the school's defining values and beliefs and to translate them into informal norms for performance and behavior, and he then relies on these norms to ensure fulfillment.

To provide a glimpse of these transformational dimensions of leadership in action, Sergiovanni has elaborated four stages of leadership, each linked to a level of school improvement. Though each stage comprises a distinct set of improvement strategies, in practice they can be used simultaneously for different purposes, as needed. Leadership by bartering is often found at the initiation stage of school reform. It is truly transactional, with a principal or superintendent trying to encourage interest or experimentation with change by making it worth people's while ("I'll get class sizes reduced if you'll try heterogeneous grouping"). Bartering draws on psychological authority and emphasizes skills and styles, the flexibility of the situational leader trying to create an inviting climate. It speaks to the physical, security, social, and ego needs of people at work. It stimulates a calculated response from staff, in which they remain focused on the extrinsic gain they will earn by participating. This kind of leadership can be effective when the problem is one of achieving basic competence or there is a fundamental disagreement between the leader and the staff. It can also help get things moving when there is no consensus for change. But without commonly shared goals or interests, there is virtually no basis for any kind of leadership beyond horse trading. Similarly, negotiating basic agreements on a new direction or a new set of practices merely opens the door to reform. Bartering can take a school only so far.

To move beyond routine competence and general agreement, a leader must move beyond the transactional to the transformational; she must inspire strong commitment among staff to move them to extraordinary performance. This involves building and bonding, the second and third stages of leadership. Building is often found during the period of uncertainty or "muddling through" after an innovation has been adopted and is getting under way. It draws on professional authority, and its focus is on arousing human potential, raising expectations, empowering people, and encouraging greater commitment and performance. It offers "opportunities for achievement, challenge, responsibility and recognition for accomplishment. It motivates people to work by giving them a chance to fulfill their higher-order psychological needs for esteem, competence, autonomy, and self-actualization" (Sergiovanni, 1991, p. 125). It stimulates intrinsic interest and involvement among staff because the work goals themselves become professionally rewarding.

Bonding occurs at the "transformative" or "breakthrough" stage of innovation. It draws on moral authority to lift the level of behavior and aspiration throughout the school community (Sergiovanni, 1991, p. 125–126). Sergiovanni invokes the notion of a covenant between leader and led, a shared, higher-order, fundamental agreement that all members of a community subscribe to and mutually reinforce. Everyone's involvement is not just intrinsic but also moral, based on a sense of obligation born out of commitment. This kind of leadership speaks to needs for purpose, meaning, and significance. Mutually agreed upon values, goals, and norms create a cultural core for the school and link its members in a common endeavor (pp. 124, 133).

The fourth and final stage of leadership and school improvement is banking. It occurs after transformation, as improvements become "routinized." The new purposes and practices are institutionalized in the daily structure of school life. At this point, the principal becomes a kind of steward who practices "servant leadership" (the concept is Robert Greenleaf's [1977]). He "ministers" to the school's needs, enabling others to better fulfill their responsibilities, and acts as a "high priest" by articulating and protecting the school's values (Sergiovanni, 1991, p. 126).

Two Caveats

All of this sounds lofty and inspiring. It deserves to. Transformational leadership offers perhaps the only viable route to the kinds of fundamental reforms our schools need. But two cautions are in order. First, despite the richness of its implications, it is at risk of becoming an orthodoxy, with all of the limitations of other orthodoxies that already litter the path. The danger here lies in exaggerating the necessity of being "transformationally pure," of being a True Leader rather than a mere manager. Burns, for instance, insisted that a leader could be either transactional or transformational, but not both. Yet there is evidence that many leaders function along a continuum, using both kinds of authority (Starratt, p. 10). As I have already suggested, it is a rare administrator who can avoid management altogether and devote herself exclusively to leadership; even the most farsighted leader who is highly focused on an ennobling purpose has to deal with logistics, politics, and nitty-gritty realities and employ transactional tactics and bureau-cratic authority. This means that we must revise the fashionable yet invidious distinction between leadership and management. They complement each other, and both are crucial to successful orga-nizational functioning. Good management, in other words, is vital not only to maintaining a strong school but also to improving it. The question is not one of purity but of emphasis, of moving a school toward higher levels of functioning through the use of higher-order levels of authority.

A second caution involves false clarity. Adopting the form but not the substance of an innovation is not a shortcoming unique to teachers. Administrators may adopt the framework of a new, popular management concept but implement something quite traditional:

> In Cedarville, new superintendent Bill Vincent arrived with all the latest termi-nology about strategic management. He engaged the administrative cabinet in a series of "strategy sessions," but his approach could not have been more con-ventional. Instead of emphasizing purpose, followership, and a high level of autonomy and judgment on the part of administrators, Vincent employed tra-ditional, management-by-objective implementation plans. He required each principal to list six goals for the year with a set of specific implementation steps for each, which he then insisted on reviewing with them point by point at two separate evaluation sessions per year. His notion of "strategic," rather than freeing school leaders to identify goals and implement flexibly, enslaved them, provoking anxiety, frustration, anger, and cynicism.

Other examples could be easily adduced. Systems theory, for exam-ple, is fast becoming an orthodoxy and suffers as much misguided implementation as does strategic planning. And the same is true of participatory management, as we will see in Chapter Eleven.

Clearly, then, as we contemplate the potential for transform-ing schools, modesty is in order. It is easy to embrace transforma-tion—Sergiovanni's descriptions are inspiring and conjure exciting images of what schools might become—but it is quite something else to figure out how to become transformational. To actually move an entire school from bartering to building to bonding to banking is an endeavor of unprecedented complexity. For the most part, the literature on transformational change is more enticing than helpful: the serious works combine rigor and rapture; the slick knock-offs sell gruel out of greed. The former tend toward dense theory and eloquent evocations of the "ideal leader." Their stories of transformational icons who overcame huge obstacles— Abraham Lincoln, Franklin Roosevelt, Winston Churchill, Ghandi—are stirring. But these figures, whatever their transformational genius, also had clear external enemies who presented threats that commanded attention, simplified issues, and temporarily unified diverse constituencies. And they weren't trying to change schools! As for the thin books with thin ideas, they dilute theory to pabulum and make prescriptions that are so broad as to be empty or so situation-specific as to be useless.

Given our present knowledge and current circumstances, then, we must expect transformation to be rare, not routine. And yet, its appeal is obviously compelling. The question is not whether we should try to foster this kind of leadership in schools but how: How do school leaders build purpose and followership? How do they inspire commitment in others? Transformational leadership is the only kind that can hope to accomplish the reform so many schools need in the face of the problems so many schools endure, the only kind whose underlying premises fit the kinds of change restructuring calls for. And thankfully, it is the only kind that can simplify the lives of administrators, the only kind that seeks improvement not by multiplying technical tasks but by concentrating on an essential core. It this core to which we now turn.

Notes

1. A recent example is Total Quality Management (TQM). As its popularity began to accelerate in educational circles, articles began to appear in business journals pointing out that it was not a panacea, after all. Among other things, TQM demands a high level of staff cooperation, which can dissipate quickly when tight budgets threaten job security. And some of its key concepts, such as "zero defects," are simply not relevant to schools.
2. In books such as *Habits of the Heart* (Bellah and others, 1985), *The Culture of Narcissism* (Lasch, 1979), and *The Culture of Complaint* (Hughes, 1993), social critics have pressed this case and provoked much discussion, but they haven't stemmed the tide they decry.

3. In this discussion of leadership authority and elsewhere throughout this chapter I am greatly indebted to Sergiovanni's insightful work (1991, 1992).

4. A recent example is a manual, *Principals for Our Changing Schools* (National Policy Board for Educational Administration, 1993), that appears to have been developed in classic list-of-functions fashion. Its creators began with both a "task analysis of the principalship," results of which were reviewed by focus groups of administrators, and a "conceptual model and 'Taxonomy of Standards'" developed by academics. It then integrated the two sets of outcomes, had this composite reviewed by industrial psychologists and then refined by other experts, and ultimately produced a model of the principalship that divides it into twenty-one domains (pp. 18–25). States have followed suit. Massachusetts, for example, proposed new evaluation procedures identifying six general "principles of effective administrative leadership," covering twenty-seven different areas reflected in ninety-two "descriptors" of ideal behaviors and skills (Massachusetts Department of Education, 1995).

5. Perhaps the best-known advocates of situational leadership are Hersey and Blanchard (1988), in *Management of Organizational Behavior.*

6. Two leading exponents of this view are Donald Schön (1984) and Henry Mintzberg (1989). To Schön, a manager is a craftsman practicing an art "that cannot be reduced to explicit rules and theories" and that "reveals itself in . . . situations of uncertainty, instability, and uniqueness" (pp. 36, 41). Mintzberg contrasts the planning of strategy, a decidedly rational matter of systematic analysis, with the crafting of strategy, which calls on "traditional skill, dedication . . . mastery of detail . . . involvement, a feeling of intimacy and harmony with the materials at hand" and is the product of experience and commitment (p. 26).

7. For example, we have already seen in Chapter Four that to be "unfrozen" people must be dissatisfied with the status quo and find the change desirable and feasible.

8. Burns began by asking how we exert influence as a leader, a central question with many dimensions. Three are relevant here. The first is personal. We must decide *"whether we are really trying to lead anyone but ourselves, and what part of ourselves, and where, and for what purposes."* There is a vast difference between simply trying to secure our own advancement and trying to achieve a social good, but leadership always begins "by clarifying within ourselves our own personal goal." The second is *"whom* are we seeking to lead?" We must *"define our potential followers, not in the manipulative sense of how to persuade them to our own ends*

. . . but in terms of mutuality. " This is not a matter of simply identifying target groups to persuade, but of identifying the "aspirations, values, and goals that are to be mobilized" within these groups. The third is "where are we seeking to go?" Though this answer seems obvious when we have immediate objectives in front of us, Burns was among the earliest writers to recognize that goals themselves are changed by the initial and intermediate steps we take to achieve them, that targets are "transformed as more followers become involved," and that conflict inevitably arises and affects outcomes. He insisted that *"the ultimate test of practical leadership is the realization of intended, real change that meets people's enduring needs. "* Finally, Burns asked "how do we overcome obstacles to realizing our goals?" Here his primary emphasis was on "recognizing the motivations of potential followers in all their fullness and complexity" (pp. 460–461, emphasis in original).

Part Three

Leading Innovation

Chapter Nine

The Authentic Leader

The true force that attracts others is the force of the heart.
—JAMES KOUZES AND BARRY POSNER (1987, P. 125)

Transformation begins with trust. Trust is the essential link between leader and led, vital to people's job satisfaction and loyalty, vital to followership. It is doubly important when organizations are seeking rapid improvement, which requires exceptional effort and competence, and doubly again to organizations like schools that offer few extrinsic motivators (money, status, power). And it is as fragile as it is precious; once damaged, it is nearly impossible to repair. When we have come to distrust people, either because they have lied to us or deceived us or let us down too often, we tend to stay suspicious of them, resisting their influence and discounting efforts they may make to reform themselves. In work groups, the more people doubt one another, the more they "ignore, disguise, and distort facts, ideas, conclusions, and feelings that [might] increase their vulnerability to others" (Kouzes and Posner, p. 147), increasing the likelihood of misunderstanding. Imagine two schools that are virtual clones, identical in faculty, administration, student body, community, budget, and physical plant, identical even in their problems and in the improvements they are undertaking. Now introduce a single difference: the principal in the first school is distrusted by the faculty. An abyss opens. Despite their resemblance, they are disparate institutions, different in climate, morale, energy level, and responsiveness to innovation. The contrast in the scope and complexity of the tasks confronting their two principals is vast.

Clearly, then, school leaders seeking change need to begin by thinking of what will inspire trust among their constituents. The answer is direct: we admire leaders who are honest, fair, competent, and forward-looking. Although these qualities seem so obvious that they are easy to gloss over, they are the basis of trust (Kouzes and Posner, pp. 16, 21). (Imagine how our national cynicism about politics would change if we found our elected officials to be honest, fair, and competent, not to mention forward-looking.) For "honest" we may read "consistent." Consistency is the lifeblood of trust. People who do what they say they will do—meet their commitments, keep their promises—are trustworthy; those who don't, aren't. Most of us prefer to be led by someone we can count on, even when we disagree with him, than someone we agree with but who frequently shifts his position (Bennis, 1989, p. 21).

Innovation can't live without trust, but it needs more than trust—it needs confidence. We cannot have confidence in those we distrust, but we do not necessarily have confidence in all those we trust. Some people whose sincerity and honesty are beyond reproach lack the capacity to translate their goals into reality. They may have lofty ideals, and even fulfill them in their personal lives, but be unable to communicate clearly to others or be inept at handling daily events. Their heart, as we say, is in the right place, but they lack something that makes us follow them. To transform schools, principals and superintendents must inspire such confidence along with trust.

The key to both is authenticity. Leaders who are followed are authentic; that is, they are distinguished not by their techniques or styles but by their integrity and their savvy. Integrity is a fundamental consistency between personal beliefs, organizational aims, and working behavior. It is increasingly clear that leadership rests on values, that commitment among constituents can only be mobilized by leaders who themselves have strong commitments, who preach what they believe and practice what they preach.[1] But they must also know what they're doing. Savvy is practical competence, a hard-to-quantify cluster of qualities that includes craft knowledge, life experience, native intelligence, common sense, intuition, courage, and the capacity to "handle things." Most of us seek in a leader this combination of genuineness and effectiveness. It makes him authentic, a credible resource who inspires trust and confidence, someone worth following into the uncertainties of change.

This chapter explores the concept of authentic leadership, its roots and its implications for practice. It sketches authenticity's essentials—integrity and savvy—and describes a process for discovering one's own authentic core, a process that highlights the personal, idiosyncratic nature of leadership. From this flow three consequences: that there are many ways to excel as a leader; that we must recast our notions of vision and strategy; and, most important of all, that effective leadership rests on a set of strategic biases (introduced here and elaborated in succeeding chapters) that simplify leadership and make transformation possible.

Integrity: Character in Action

Integrity is a fundamental consistency between one's values, goals, and actions. At the simplest level it means standing for something, having a significant commitment and exemplifying this commitment in your behavior. Leaders who have no strong values and no aspirations for their school may provide a dull consistency, but this is not something we would confuse with integrity. Even if they manage daily details adequately, they inspire no special motivation or attachment that enhances performance or makes being part of the school valuable. They are, at best, maintaining, not leading. Followership is not just impossible under their administration, it is irrelevant.

In a different way, leaders who do claim to stand for something but whose goals and actions are not aligned with their stated values also lack integrity. Those who profess aspirations that do not truly matter to them are easily seen through. When a principal dutifully introduces a district priority that she herself does not share, the discrepancy between her announced aims and her underlying beliefs will be apparent to all who know her well, even if she tries to muster up sincerity. Her falseness will ultimately be as evident as if she were adopting a style that is not her own. Similarly, when leaders do not model the values they assert or the goals they proclaim—when a superintendent announces "respect for others" as a district goal but treats staff disrespectfully—they breed cynicism and resistance. The problem of inconsistency is so wide-spread that it needs little elaboration, except to note that it can occur unconsciously. A leader may be sincere about his goal and unaware that his behavior is contradictory. Cedarville superinten-dent Bill Vincent (Chapter Eight) was seen by his principals in this way. In such cases, the leader may seem "out of it" and incompe-tent more than cynical or manipulative, but he will still invite dis-respect and resistance instead of followership.

Integrity can take many forms. Let us begin with two examples:

Jane Carroll, principal of Worthington High School, is a strong believer in "challenge." A triathlon competitor and ardent chess player, she values self-discipline and perseverance. She is overt about rewarding students and faculty who demonstrate these qualities: "Effort matters far more than talent—for teachers as well as students. Success comes from striving. As Aristotle said, 'Excellence is not an act, but a habit.' " Jane leads the school with a firm hand and engages herself in aspects of curriculum, assessment, and staff develop-ment that in many schools have more teacher involvement and control. Some faculty find her "cold," others "elitist and controlling," but she enjoys wide support, even among most of these critics, because her commitments are so clear, because she holds herself to them as firmly as she holds others to them, and because they have come to embody the school's pursuit of excellence. "She drives everyone hard," says a teacher, "but she sets the example, and we all feel the end result is an exceptional school."

Tom Russell, the principal of Jackson Elementary School, believes in individ-ual development. He reveres Thoreau and sees school as a place where every-one, child and adult, should grow at their own pace through rich opportunities and the freedom to explore, not through pressure to produce. Jackson has comparatively few rules and requirements. Tom rarely issues an order, he tol-erates others disagreeing with him, and he gives the faculty wide latitude to decide policy, even if this involves heated arguments. He is unhurried in his style but unwavering in his focus. Each year he meets with each student and each staff member (including custodians and secretaries) to talk about their growth, interests, and ideas for the school. Some teachers have found Jackson too "chaotic" and left; some who have remained find Tom too "unstructured." But most agree with the teacher who says, "This guy lives what he believes: growth, support, respect. Because of him, Jackson really nurtures people."

Few of the principals I know would want to be Jane or Tom. They might endorse qualities of each but would find both at least a bit extreme. I cite Jane and Tom here as exemplars not of the perfect principal but of integrity. For both of them, values, goals, and actions are congruent.

(Before going further, an important note: it is impossible to address the ethical dimensions of leadership that are a primary focus of this chapter without using terms that have been poisoned by politics. In the 1990s in America, *values* and *basic values* are among a constellation of terms that have been appropriated by various political groups and reduced to code words for particular viewpoints. But all of us see certain values—fairness, for example—as "basic," even if we define these values differently. There is no other way to describe them. I use all such phrases and all such words as *moral* in this primary, generic way, not to refer to a particular political or religious agenda.)

Values and personal integrity come first. At the deepest level, the values of authentic leaders are characterized by three things: personal ethics, vision, and belief in others (Badaracco and Ellsworth, p. 100). A firm set of personal ethical standards is a hallmark of most successful leaders. Over and over in the research literature, portraits of exceptional leaders describe people with unusually high standards, commitments they keep with a self-discipline that can seem excessive, even fanatical: "Outstanding leaders have sources of inner direction." They may not be terribly religious, but their beliefs give them a sturdy guide for their long-range planning and their routine problem solving (p. 100). Whatever the specific content of their views, honesty and fairness tend to be among their chief tenets. It is not that authentic leaders necessarily preach honesty and fairness as specific virtues, but they demonstrate them through the sincerity of their commitments. This is the basis of trust and loyalty in any group.

Leaders with strong values translate these into organizational vision. Like Jane and Tom, they typically hold the same standards for their school as for themselves. "Challenge and Excellence" might well serve as the motto both for Jane and for Worthington, "Freedom to Grow" for Tom and Jackson. Such commitments are important; they are crucial to followership because they provide the larger purpose that gives work direction and meaning. Leaders like Jane and Tom are able to communicate very clearly a definite notion of their school and its potential. (I will have more to say about vision below and will explore it further in Chapter Ten.)

Leaders with values and vision tend to believe that other people have the potential to be motivated by the same commitments, not just by narrow self-interest (financial gain, personal power). Though their beliefs are different, neither Jane nor Tom base their leadership on maneuvering or manipulating people through special incentives, political trade-offs, and the like. They have faith that everyone can respond, can benefit from the opportunity the school provides, can fulfill the vision in their own personal ways. This faith may take many forms—Tom offers a chance to blossom, Jane a challenge to excel—but in one way or another it conveys a confidence in the potential of people.

These same three qualities—ethics, vision, belief in others— that are central in the personal beliefs of authentic leaders are reflected in their organizational goals. By "goals" I mean both the kind of institution the leader seeks to build and the improvements he seeks to implement. Leaders with strong personal ethics who exemplify honesty and fairness generally reflect these in a meritocratic approach to management; they want competence to be rewarded. They expect high ethical standards to prevail throughout and believe that when in doubt about a decision or a problem, everyone should behave in accordance with the school's fundamental values. They acknowledge those who observe and fulfill these values, basing recognition on "what you do, not on who you are or who you know," as Jane says. At the same time, they expect members of the organization to come to share the same basic values and goals, and they are usually unambiguous and unembarrassed about this. Authentic school leaders do not necessarily champion a "my way or the highway" philosophy, but they are unwilling to sacrifice their priorities and goals, and when necessary they will challenge those who can't or won't come along. This can sometimes seem harsh and unfeeling, but for many leaders with integrity this approach is simply axiomatic: "buying in" is ultimately a basic condition of organizational membership. A case in point is this high school principal:

Last year we pushed our restructuring up a big notch: we converted to a block schedule, four 90-minute periods per day, so we could really start implementing an integrated curriculum and in-depth teaching. We'd spent a full year debating it and most people were on board, but six were still strongly opposed. They were angry and terrified at having to face kids for that long and at having to change the curriculum they'd taught for twenty years and start collaborating with other teachers. I met with each. I made it clear that we needed absolutely everyone to be truly committed, that we had finally reached the rock and the hard place; it was "in or out." They were going to be miserable if they stayed. Thanks to a special agreement with the union, we had the option of transferring people. I offered to find each their first choice of another high school in the city if they wished. No hard feelings, no shame, no blame. Four chose to leave. I worked like a maniac, and I got all of them the schools they wanted. It wasn't all happy, but they are happier, and we've made much more progress.

In a similar way, authentic leaders embrace programs or projects that reflect their values and institutional goals. They concentrate on what matters to them, again without embarrassment. They have definite notions of what is important, and they pay attention to these targets. The principal above is committed to the essential schools philosophy, which to him means "real depth learning," and the conviction that "nothing is more important than making our classrooms places where kids and teachers deeply explore challenging, important ideas. Everything else is subordinate to that."

As this principal's example indicates, integrity requires action, behavior that embodies values. Indeed, it is chiefly through consistent beliefs and goals expressed in consistent actions that we perceive a leader's integrity. The importance of setting the example, of leaders' modeling what they value, is one of the most frequently repeated themes in leadership writing. Authentic leaders translate their beliefs and values into concrete actions at a fundamental level:

Anthony Cortez became a superintendent reluctantly. After years as a teacher and then principal at Clayville Middle School, he filled in as acting superintendent and was offered the permanent position because he was so universally admired. His hesitation was simple: "I like kids. I like being around them.

Everything a school does depends on community, which means that kids know they are known: they're missed when they're absent, they're appreciated for their uniqueness, they're helped when they need it, and they're held accountable to do their part. That can't happen unless the adults like the kids and are with the kids." He delegates large amounts of his "paper and policy work" and usually averages at least three school visits—"a real visit, not a sail-through"—per week (he sometimes reads to children in the elementary schools). When he urges Clayville teachers to "reach out to kids, invest in them, know them," his credibility is absolute; his actions have always spoken for him.

When the late Henry Scattergood retired as headmaster at the Germantown Friends School in Philadelphia, a colleague wrote, "His virtues are as simple and uncomplicated as they are rare. They originate in the quality of creating in others a loyalty and affection, and even sometimes a goodness, by being himself, a man of perfect honesty, integrity, and goodness. He does not merely advise virtue, he creates it in others by offering its example and practice. . . . It is the simple yet exceptional use of character in action" (Nicholson, 1995, citing Sharpless). Whether it is challenging thoroughly resistant staff or staying close to students or spending large amounts of time on the job—or exemplifying virtue—authentic leaders embody character in action: they don't just say, they do.

Savvy

In discussing integrity, I have already been referring to "authentic leaders"; but although integrity is the chief defining characteristic of authenticity, it is not the only one. Authenticity also demands savvy, a practical, problem-solving wisdom that enables leaders to make things happen. Savvy subsumes an array of qualities, ranging from knowledge of one's field to having a good "nose" for institutional problems.[2] It includes intangibles like knowing what constitutes a good solution to a dilemma, knowing "what to do and when to do it" (Sergiovanni, 1992, p. 15). These and related qualities are sometimes called "craft knowledge" and are in good part a product of professional experience, learned skills that come with years of practice. But to me, savvy also includes native strengths, basic aspects of temperament, personality, and intelligence that are reflected in qualities like common sense and empathic sensitivity (being able to "read" people), courage and assertiveness, and resilience. These, coupled with craft knowledge, establish a leader's bona fides. In my experience, educators will rarely follow leaders unless they seem to "know their stuff"—not the tricks of leadership but the realities of school life.

Educators want leaders who know education, who are current and well versed without falling victim to fads, but they especially want leaders who are "one of us," who can still see education from a teacher's point of view and are attuned to the real world of classrooms, students, and parents. And they also want leaders who offer proof or promise of being able to "make things happen," whether this means fixing problems, finding resources, or handling people. These traits build a basic platform without which a leader lacks presence and clout and is not taken seriously:

> Jim Colby became a superintendent after a brief stint as a math teacher and then many years as a district business manager (he was never a principal). A devout convert to Total Quality Management, he failed to make it work in two different districts. In both, principals and teachers felt that his goals were formulaic and empty and his expectations unrealistic, that he didn't really understand teaching itself or the running of a school, and that he couldn't manage people. Principals especially felt that he never grasped the daily dilemmas of school life, the intricacies and politics of translating ideas into action. In the words of one, "Jim was a hard worker, but basically out of it. He just didn't have it, and he just didn't get it. You couldn't respect him."

If Jim had been charismatic, one of his districts might have made a temporary exception for him. There are gifted visionaries who can truly inspire others by the power of their ideas, the force of their eloquence, and the depth of their conviction, even though they have little practical aptitude and little grasp of the nitty-gritty. People will sometimes exempt such a leader from the "savvy requirement" (especially if there is a good second-in-command who handles the details), but they will not do so indefinitely and especially not as innovation proceeds from early optimism to actual implementation, with its inevitable obstacles.

Becoming Authentic

Let us say, then, that authenticity is ideal. How does one achieve it? The question is paradoxical. Just as genuineness can't be artificially manufactured—it simply *is*—neither can authenticity: it can't be generated; it can only be discovered. (A person cannot *act* authentic.) Still, one may fairly ask, "How do I get there?" The answer leads us again, as did our discussion of charisma in the preceding chapter, to the personal nature and roots of leadership.

It also leads first to a blunt truth: not everyone can. Despite the popularity of technical notions of leadership, most of us believe that good leaders must have the "right stuff," the right personal qualities to lead, and that these, like savvy or charisma, are to some extent innate: you either have what it takes or you don't. Most of us react to leaders in this way in our daily experience. But this view is not just folk wisdom—experience and research confirm that leadership requires a definite aptitude (Drucker, 1986, p. 159). For example, a study of identical twins who were raised apart concluded that leadership is a trait "strongly determined by heredity" (Goleman, 1986, pp. C1–C2). A study of leaders who achieved significant change in their organizations highlighted the importance of temperament and predisposition and suggested that the impulse and capacity to lead stem largely from innate talents and early childhood experience (Gibbons, 1986). Other research emphasizes that successful leaders tend to be psychologically hardy (Chapter Seven). They are resourceful and resilient. Compared to less successful peers in equally stressful jobs, they are more resistant to illness and experience both a greater sense of control over events and of positive challenge in their work (Maddi and Kobasa, 1984, p. 31). Unmistakably, they have what it takes.

The right stuff, like charisma, is a concept that might seem to suggest that there is little point in trying to teach leadership (a notion widely deplored by those who see leadership as a matter of technique and therefore teachable). But it leads to three less extreme and very practical implications. The first is that *some* central aspects of leadership are innate and unteachable and that not everyone has all the necessary potential, which means that some people will always lead better than others and that some are simply ill-suited for the task. As ordinary as this seems, it is routinely ignored in discussions of preparing school administrators to lead change. To expect that every leader can become authentic or transformational is foolish. The second is to underscore the importance of hardiness: to be effective, leaders must demonstrate and foster it. We don't follow the timid, the indecisive, and those who avoid problems, and we rarely stay committed to causes that distress us (Kouzes and Posner, p. 68).

The third and most important implication is that leadership begins at one's center: *authentic leaders build their practice outward from their core commitments rather than inward from a management text.* In addition to their craft knowledge, all administrators have basic philosophies of leading, of school functioning, and of human nature, philosophies that are deeply rooted in their personal history and professional experience. These philosophies guide their behavior, but they usually remain tacit. They are the true source of their integrity. They include basic assumptions about human nature, group behavior, and the roots of excellence. "Like a geological deposit," they accumulate during years of experience in life and work. Although few leaders pause to spell out their philosophies explicitly, "these deep assumptions influence almost everything they do" (Badaracco and Ellsworth, p. 7). Sergiovanni echoes this view when he speaks of an administrator's "known and unknown theories of practice . . . bundles of beliefs and assumptions about how schools and school systems work, authority, leadership, the purposes of schooling, the role of competition, the nature of human nature, and other issues and concerns." These constitute what he calls "mindscapes," frames of reference that, though rarely thought about, are powerful forces that drive one's practice (1991, pp. 10–12).

A leader's philosophy remains tacit in part because none of us can be fully in touch with the entire range of our knowledge, perception, feeling, and skill. At any given moment, our reservoir of expertise is larger than we can encompass, our wellspring of inspiration deeper than we can fully tap. But it also stays hidden—even unconscious—because it is buried and discouraged by formal leadership theory taught in graduate administration courses and disseminated in leadership books. The received wisdom in the field, which emphasizes techniques and styles, encourages school leaders to overlook their personal philosophies and the "hard-earned insights" of their craft knowledge, with the result that they end up drawing upon a tiny portion of their potential (Bolman and Deal, p. 37).[3] Uncovering this wisdom is the key to becoming authentic.

The Testimonial: What Do You Stand For?

There may be many routes to accomplishing that uncovering of wisdom. I prefer to begin this way: Imagine that your colleagues and friends have decided to honor you at a testimonial dinner, simply because they respect and love you so much. The meal is over, you have already been "roasted" and toasted, and speakers have lavishly praised your skills. Now, your closest colleague, who knows you best, is to offer the final tribute. This person will move the focus away from your competence to your commitment, summarizing what you stand for: the essential principle or core value, the fundamental belief deep inside you that drives your work as an educator and a leader. What will he or she say? (Note: it cannot be something like "He likes people" or "She has always stood for change," unless just liking people or change for its own sake is truly your highest value, the thing you care about most—in which case it would not have earned you a testimonial! The goal is to find out what lies below these kinds of characteristics.)

The task is simple but not necessarily easy. It usually involves talking about values that are at once ordinary and complex, plain and profound. In taking several thousand educators through this exercise, I have found that many tend to begin at a relatively superficial level, describing skills, attributes, or very general beliefs. But when they are encouraged to persevere and to talk to each other in greater depth, their answers gravitate toward values that are much deeper and often disarmingly simple, what one principal called "apple pie and motherhood" values. "I feel corny and sentimental saying this stuff," he said, "but it's all true."

The kinds of "stuff" superintendents and principals and teachers say can lead in many directions. (At one seminar, a principal whose core belief was "everything you do in life should be fun" was seated next to a colleague whose deepest commitment was to "live in the light of Christ.") But frequently the answers cluster around two broad headings, which I summarize as "equity" and "excellence." Most educators share a heartfelt commitment to students and to the development of their full potential, but they differ in their emphasis. Some, like Tom Russell, stress the importance of opportunity, fairness, diversity, and community. They are likely to believe that "all children can learn," which often means to them a commitment to special outreach and compensatory opportunities for children who are disadvantaged. Others, like Jane Carroll, emphasize goals, challenge, responsibility, and striving. They are more likely to speak of "excellence" and "standards," of bringing out the best in children by measuring them against high benchmarks. Most educators share both values to some degree, although differences of emphasis can lead to significant differences in the kinds of schools they develop.

"What do you stand for?" is an excellent point of departure for exploring one's own philosophy of schooling and school leadership, but there are three other questions that I have also found to be useful:

1. *How do I define my role as a leader?* Am I at heart a mover, someone who redesigns and reshapes, who tolerates—even enjoys—the friction that change can cause? Or am I a maintainer, someone who prefers to keep things running smoothly, who may occasionally modify or enhance things but who is by nature more inclined to accept things as they are? One's preference will of course be affected by the specific situation—a new principal at a school will see his task differently if he finds its programs and teachers weak than if he finds them strong—but by philosophy and temperament every administrator is more drawn in one direction than the other. As they reflect on their conception of their role, some see themselves as active promoters of change, others don't (Fullan, 1991, p. 167). It is important to be clear about this.

2. *What inspires the best in staff?* Is performance enhanced when a leader actively shapes the work of staff members, or is it best when they are given wide latitude? Should they be free to work as individual artisans, or should they be linked in close collaborative groups? There is a famous distinction in human resource theory between three views of human motivation and performance. Theory X holds that people are basically lazy and unambitious, that they need and want to be led; managers must direct and control their work (as with Taylorism and the "expect and inspect" model

of management). Theory Y holds that people can be relied upon to show motivation, self-control, and self-direction, provided that essential human needs for safety, independence, and status are met by the workplace (McGregor, 1960, pp. 35–36). Theory Z places maximum emphasis on human potential, calling for higher levels of trust and for egalitarian work relationships and participatory decision making involving stakeholders at all levels (Ouchi, 1981, p. 110). Here again, though local conditions will influence one's preference, each individual school leader will have a primary predisposition.

3.   *What are my strengths?* An excellent way to clarify one's basic philosophy is to identify one's particular skills and abilities and the parts of one's role that are most rewarding. A tremendous amount of leadership training and school improvement work concentrates on correcting defects. Indeed, ruminating about problems and trying to overcome them consumes vast quantities of educators' time and energy. But a person trying to discover her core beliefs and values does far better to start with her strengths, the parts of herself that she feels best about in the exercise of her profession. It is there that the essence of what matters to her is to be found. Trying to articulate this essence is not only informative, it can be hugely satisfying. I love to see superintendents and principals as they describe where in their work they feel most competent and alive; their faces light up, their enthusiasm is infectious. "When I think about what I love about my work and what I do best, it's helping kids learn important lessons about life," said one principal. "And I realize that this is actually a commitment: nurturing them into healthy growth. I feel it's sacred, and it's also something I really know I can do."

There are a range of related inquiries that can help a leader flesh out the details of his personal leadership landscape. Among them are, How well do I understand the school and its community? How solid is my relationship with my constituents? Where do I think the school ought to be headed? How should the school be governed? How prepared am I to handle the school's problems? How can I improve my ability to advance the school? If he dares, he can even ask himself, Am I the right one to be leading right now?[4]

Where Does It Come From?

The corollary to these "What do you stand for?" questions is, "Where does it come from?" Whatever the answer to the first question, whether it points to equity or excellence or some other set of beliefs, its origin is almost always personal—deeply personal, both in how strongly it is believed and in how old it is. At heart people's philosophies tend to be "dogmatic," in the original sense of the term, notes Nisbet: "The springs of human action, will, and ambition lie for the most part in beliefs about universe, world, society, and man which defy rational calculations and differ greatly from . . . instincts. These springs lie in what we call dogmas. That word comes from Greek roots with the literal meaning of 'seems-good.'" As Cardinal Newman said, "Men will die for a dogma who will not even stir for a conclusion" (1980, pp. 8–9). I don't ask educators whether they will die for what they stand for, but there is little doubt of the depth of their conviction when they speak of the "seems-goods" that matter most to them.

When I ask about the origins of their philosophy, people invariably point to their experience—their experience as an adult, as an educator, and as a student, and primarily to their early experience growing up. Few think of their courses in graduate school. In fact, the actual behavior of administrators has relatively little to do with their formal training. "They [bring] *themselves* with them to graduate school . . . and they [take] themselves back to their schools . . . knowing some new things, perhaps, but still basically themselves (Blumberg, 1989, pp. 19–20, emphasis in original). The study of management contributes to what they know (and to their espoused values) but has a modest impact on how they act. Administration, after all, mostly involves not the application of theory and data but the "idiosyncratic use of the self in interactive work situations" (p. 183), and people start learning about using themselves in such situations early on in life. Basic ways of thinking, feeling, and behaving that shape one's approach to problems and one's perspective on the world begin early in childhood in the framework of the family, and they are firmly established long before one becomes an administrator (pp. 191–192). "The philosophy which is so important in each of us," as William James said, "is not a technical matter."

I am used to hearing teachers, principals, and superintendents confirm the nontechnical nature of their philosophy. Their stories are often quite wonderful, providing fascinating glimpses into the personal roots of leadership. One such account was offered by Lawrence Briggs, a high school principal, who explained his philosophy this way:

> I can tell you why equity is so important to me. Up through fourth grade our schools were segregated. In fifth grade we all got to go to what had been the white school. On the first day the teacher asked who wanted to perform for the class on the flutaphone. All the white children raised their hands—they had all had flutaphone lessons and music classes; we hadn't had either. I made up my mind I was going to learn to play. I found a woman to teach me and was $17 in debt to her before my parents even knew I was taking lessons. After Christmas, when the teacher asked again, I raised my hand and kept it up until she finally called on me. I stood up and played my song. Nobody is going to tell me that a kid in my school can't do something.

Lawrence is a man of imposing personal presence: big, outgoing, articulate, witty, confident. He would not, I think, claim to be the least directive, most participatory of leaders. But he enjoyed strong support among his faculty, students, and parents—in good part, I believe, because of his authenticity. Lawrence's unmistakable commitment to students—his belief in their potential and in the importance of giving them the opportunity to succeed—makes what we might call "graduate school sense": it is intellectually sound; it would readily find professional, theoretical, and research support. But its roots are far deeper, far more personal; his commitment is in his bones, and it reaches people at a level that is both immediate and fundamental.

Many Ways to Excel

Lawrence Briggs's example, and those of Jane Carroll and Tom Russell, all illustrate that authentic leadership is highly personal and therefore can take many forms, depending upon the specific commitments of particular school leaders. "Personal" here does not mean arbitrary or whimsical but individual. All leaders whose practice is rooted in deep values and strong beliefs will resemble each other in some important ways, no matter how different their philosophies. But they will also differ according to the content of their beliefs and their preferred ways of operating. Authenticity helps to reveal a wonderful, liberating fact of leadership life: there are many ways to excel.

Most leadership research has been conducted in "low-performing systems"—organizations in trouble. It generally attributes their problems in motivation, morale, communication, trust, and performance to the way a leader is working and assumes that a change in approach or style will correct things (Vaill, 1984, p. 102). But when we look at high-performing systems—successful organizations—we find that leadership style is rarely a determining factor in their performance; in fact, we find a wide range of styles among their leaders: "There are tyrants whose almost maniacal commitment to achieving the system's purposes makes one think that they'd be locked up. . . . There are warm, laid-back parent figures who hardly seem to be doing anything at all, until one looks a little more closely. There are technocrats . . . and dreamers. . . . Some are rah-rah optimists and others are dour critics who express their love for the system by enumerating its imperfections" (p. 102).

I know thriving, vital, high-achieving schools that are led by easygoing, democratic authority delegators and by demanding, strict perfectionists; by creative, roll-with-the-punches improvisers and by obsessive, keep-me-posted worriers; by eloquent, expansive preachers and by quiet, modest doers. Research has shown that principals who were successful change agents all fulfilled four key roles (resource provider, instructional resource, communicator, visible presence) but did so in very different ways. Some were "strong, aggressive, fearless," others "quiet, nurturing, supportive" (Fullan, 1991, p. 158). In stark contrast to situational leaders and practitioners of styles, the most successful leaders "are not human chameleons, but . . . people of distinctive personalities who behave consistently in accordance with that personality" (Badaracco and Ellsworth, p. 208). Their greatest assets are "their own passions for the organization and its mission and their own common sense when it comes to getting the most out of the people they have. Their unwillingness to turn themselves inside out to conform to some behavioral scientist's theory is remarkable" (Vaill, 1989, p. 19).

The corollary of "many ways to excel" is "every way has its weakness." Authentic leaders have shortcomings; they are usually aware of them, but they tend to emphasize their strengths and to find sufficient nourishment in their sense of themselves. One of the greatest flaws in style-based leadership theories is the assumption that one might somehow acquire and apply only the strengths of each particular style, that one might become a composite of stylistic virtues. In fact, every way of leading, like every way of being, has deficits as well as advantages, and these are inextricably linked. Principals with a genuine commitment to a participatory process can show remarkable patience and sensitivity but be poor at asserting themselves, at setting limits on those who abuse the process, and at taking firm action in a crisis. Superintendents with a take-charge capacity and an ability to tolerate conflict can demonstrate impressive courage and perseverance but ride roughshod over people, make enemies where they don't need to, and be ineffective at compromising when it is necessary. As I have already suggested, authentic leaders tend to be unapologetic about the inevitable downsides of being true to themselves. A superintendent I have known for years sometimes says, with both pride and resignation, "Like Popeye in the old cartoons, 'I am what I am.' I know what I want and what I'm good at. I also know what I'm not so good at, and I try to stick with my strengths." The authentic leader who is aware of her basic inclinations, including her limitations, is already better equipped to compensate for the latter but is unlikely to dwell on them.

Philosophy, Vision, and Strategy: What Do I Want?

To see authenticity as profoundly personal is to recast many of the premises that have come to be taken for granted about leadership and organizations, chief among them vision and strategy. In scarcely more than a decade these concepts have become ubiquitous in leadership theory, practice, and parlance. Like mission, culture, and change, they have become buzzwords. They are widely and correctly trumpeted as vital to leading innovation and are almost as widely misunderstood. Vision is seen as a product of rational planning, as deriving from a careful appraisal of the external environment (a company does a market survey, a school does a needs assessment). In fact, successful change agents rarely operate in this way. Largely overlooked in all the enthusiasm for vision is that it typically derives from "a personal and imaginative creativity that [transcends] analysis" (Badaracco and Ellsworth, p. 101). In charting an organizational course, successful leaders rely on processes that are more intuitive and holistic than ordered and intellectual, more qualitative than quantitative (Mintzberg, p. 52). Though they are typically adept at gauging needs and identifying markets, the way they meet needs and approach markets is their own: they construct their vision out of their own philosophy and commitment, their own experience and judgment, their own interests and strengths. In education, such leaders have a mental model of what they want for their school, and they trust their own assessment of the school against that model.

To misunderstand this personal source of vision is to misunderstand the origins of strategy. When, as it all too often does, strategic planning begins by identifying external goals and then moves on to analyzing internal strengths, it puts the cart before the horse. To capture its core mission—how it will relate to its environment—a group must first understand its own strengths (Schein, 1985, p. 55). Over my years of consulting in schools I have been repeatedly struck by how often successful new programs grow out of the conviction or interest of an individual principal or a small group of leaders rather than out of a formal planned change process.

The highly personal nature of vision is central to its success. The value of a vision is not just to clarify goals and plot a strategy but to inspire followers. To change, people must be "moved." This requires not just an idea but an advocate. Change begins not just with a goal but with a leader who communicates it, enlisting the organization's members in the pursuit of a compelling agenda. The leader's own commitment to the agenda is crucial to its adoption by followers:

> The greatest inhibitor to enlisting others in a common vision is lack of personal conviction. There is absolutely no way that you can, over the long term, convince others to share a dream if you are not convinced of it yourself. . . . The most inspirational moments are marked by genuineness. Somehow we all are able to spot a lack of

sincerity in others. We detect it in their voices, we observe it in their
eyes, we notice it in their posture. We each have a sixth sense for
deceit. . . . So there is a very fundamental question that a leader
must ask before attempting to enlist others: "What do I want?"
[Kouzes and Posner, pp. 124–125].

A fundamental question, indeed. Character in action is always vital
to leadership, but it is especially vital when innovation is under way:
the leader must change first—or at least very early. The leader, that
is, must not just advocate but exemplify the change before asking
staff to do so. Why should anyone take an initiative seriously if the
leader doesn't? Yet it is astonishing how often innovation is
imposed on schools without administrators' support and how
rarely administrators are accorded—or take—the time and freedom to think through what they want, to identify their own commitment or at least develop a commitment in response to an
external priority forced upon them.

This lapse could not be more counterproductive, because
although the need for leaders to commit themselves to change
applies universally, it is critical in schools, where veteran teachers
have seen many highly touted reforms fizzle and have watched
many administrators depart before their priorities reached fruition.
These teachers are naturally suspicious, sensitive to signs of hy-
pocrisy, and inclined to hold back, waiting for proof that for once
the administration means what it says and will really persevere. This
proof is most crucially needed from the principal.

Principals are widely seen as indispensable to innovation. No
reform effort, however worthy, survives a principal's indifference
or opposition. He is the leader closest to the action, the operational chief of the unit that must accomplish the change. His
involvement legitimates the effort, giving it an official imprimatur
that carries symbolic weight and confirms that staff should take it
seriously. And he is often best suited to secure the whole array of
supports, from the material to the spiritual, that implementation
demands. Research on the principal's role generally finds that
schools where innovation succeeds are led by principals who are
true Renaissance people: they do everything well. They demonstrate strong knowledge of and commitment to the innovation, but
they approach faculty in a collaborative spirit, fostering open com-

munication. They demand high standards, but they offer high levels of emotional support. They hold staff accountable, but they provide strong assistance. They run good meetings, but they reduce the burden of administrative details. The only problem is that there are apparently so few of them.

This should come as no surprise. Most principals are untrained for leading change. They have been socialized to be maintainers, not encouraged to be what I call authentic. Risk taking, despite the theoretical vogue it enjoys among academics who write about school reform, has always been—and remains—rare in schools. Almost everything one learns as a principal reinforces the old congressional saw: to get along, go along. After all, principals face the classic double dilemma of middle managers everywhere: they are given more responsibility than authority (even without reform initiatives, they are assigned more than they can accomplish), and their success requires maintaining positive connections not just with their superiors but also with their staff (they have little to gain from challenging people too sharply). And when they are asked to lead projects they did not choose or develop and may not fully grasp or endorse, they are likely to be ambivalent, especially when these projects require them to change their own roles and become active in areas, such as pedagogy, where previous improvement schemes have met with little success (Fullan, p. 152).

All of which underscores the necessity for principals to be able to work through their concerns and doubts, to make change meaningful to themselves, to clarify their own commitments. This means that those above principals—superintendents, school boards, state officials—must remember the importance of allowing time for a district's whole administrative team, especially its principals, to thrash out questions of values and goals as these relate to specific programmatic changes. (It also means that teachers who press for reform on their own must realize the importance of bringing the principal along early and, if this fails, the unlikelihood of achieving schoolwide success.) And what is true for principals is true for other key leaders. All those who have responsibility for an innovation need a chance to get on board before it is adopted, to ask themselves "what do I (or we) want," and then to stay on board, to revisit their answers periodically during its implementation. These steps take time, to be sure, but to skip them is a false economy that reduces "vision" and "strategy" to empty shells and leaders to deceivers of their constituents.

Authenticity in Action: Strategic Biases for Change

Thus far I have concentrated on leadership's overarching concerns and underlying beliefs. But making change in a school is not just a matter of the high and the deep. What about the daily dilemmas of transition, the issues small and large where policy turns into action and change must actually be accomplished? Authenticity would be little more than a nice ideal if it offered no help with these. Clarifying one's philosophy does not automatically make one savvy any more than it makes one charismatic; it does not create the wisdom that comes from experience, say, or provide the gift of empathic sensitivity. But it does wonderfully enrich one's ability to make decisions and solve problems: it makes one, in the best sense of the word, biased.

Spelling out their basic assumptions and discovering their authentic core helps leaders develop strategic biases for action to guide their work and shape the implementation of change. This notion of bias I take from Badaracco and Ellsworth, who suggest that leaders are far more likely to excel if they approach problems with certain prejudices, that is, "with preconceived biases toward handling them in certain ways" (pp. 3–4).[5] As used here, *bias* refers to a general way of thinking and acting, a predisposition that guides decision making and problem solving. It is the natural outgrowth of authenticity: a reliance on biases represents not bigotry or smallmindedness but "a quest for integrity, an effort that is at once moral, philosophical, and practical," one that seeks "coherence among a [leader's] daily actions, personal values, and [organizational] aims" (pp. 3–4). Its advantage is that it simplifies leadership, accents its essentials. Instead of long lists of "cookie-cutter approaches devised to fit all situations," which overlook the complexity and disorder of real life (p. 8), the concept of bias leads to a small set of guiding principles that help a school leader direct change according to the larger purposes that motivate his work (and do so in a way that maximizes followership by modeling consistency).

Which guiding principles? Having a philosophy does not by itself guarantee effectiveness. Not all biases are equally apt. We need to know which action orientations on the part of a leader foster change. From the organizational research literature and from my own work with schools that are implementing significant reform, four stand out as essential: clarity and focus, participation without paralysis, recognition, and confrontation. None of them is novel, and none is an arcane orientation accessible only to the gifted. They represent a new look at old truths, a reemphasizing of basics about human nature and school life that we have always known but have too often strayed from. But, as the following chapters will show, when viewed through the lens of authenticity, each of these biases acquires a new and practical emphasis.

Notes

1. The centrality of integrity to leadership has been explored by a number of writers, notably Kouzes and Posner and, with exceptional clarity, Badaracco and Ellsworth. This chapter and several that follow draw on both, but especially Badaracco and Ellsworth's excellent book *Leadership and the Quest for Integrity* (1989).
2. Arthur Blumberg (1989, pp. 55–69) offers a good summary of what it means for a school leader to have a good "nose" for the job.
3. For example, many leadership trainers have adopted Argyris's well-known distinction (1976) between "espoused theories," the premises leaders profess to hold and to use as guides for their practice, and "theories-in-use," the real beliefs and assumptions they actually rely on. It is common for the two to be quite discrepant but for people to be unaware of this discrepancy. Argyris proposed that leaders should be taught to modify their theories-in-use to make them more congruent with their espoused values, a proposal widely accepted in leadership training programs. Recently, strategic theorists, led prominently by Vaill, have begun challenging this view. Vaill argues that there are "many subtle modes and mixes of competency" in leaders' actual practice and that their private, personal theories contain much more wisdom than academics realize (1989, p. 35).
4. These questions are adapted from Kouzes and Posner, pp. 298–299.
5. Badaracco and Ellsworth use *prejudice* instead of *bias*. Several of the biases I advocate in the following chapters (notably "confrontation" in Chapter Thirteen) correspond closely to theirs and owe a debt to them, but they also draw upon different sources (including, among others, Bolman and Deal) and focus on schools and innovation, not, as Badaracco and Ellsworth's do, on corporations and general leadership.

Chapter Ten

Clarity and Focus: The Power of Concentration

When do my best results come? Always when I zero in.
—SUPERINTENDENT

Authentic leaders' practice is marked by a primary bias toward *clarity* and *focus*. I have already used these terms in Chapter Five to describe a chief dimension of the substance of any reform, arguing that for an innovation to succeed both its essential components and its relative priority must be evident to its key participants. Here, clarity and focus describe the most basic predisposition of authentic leaders: they know what they want, and they pursue it. They have strong convictions about how things ought to be, they concentrate tenaciously on a few key goals, they prefer directness and specificity in their dealings with constituents about these goals, and they exemplify their commitment in their behavior. This bias helps them solve one of the thorniest problems in leadership—vision—avoiding the empty ritual that predominates in schools and building instead a real sense of purpose. It also helps them reduce resistance and make reform meaningful for people by providing continuity in the values they champion and the example they set.

Vision Again: The Hearts and Bellies Test

I have written about vision several times in this book, and each time with ambivalence, because the topic is at once so important and yet has become so tiresome to so many in schools. One need only say to an audience of educators, "Let's talk about vision" to start a small epidemic of sighing, coughing, fidgeting, and eye rolling. As I suggested in Chapter Nine, vision has become a buzzword. One would be hard pressed to find a leadership book or seminar that fails to emphasize it or a company or a school that has not adopted something it calls a vision or a mission or a set of core values. Virtually every leadership expert would agree that clarity of purpose is essential to organizational success. I, too, have asserted that (1) a shared vision is crucial to innovation, because it helps make organizational membership and work itself meaningful and thus inspires followership, and (2) the roots of vision are deeply personal, and a leader's own commitment to a vision is vital to its adoption by followers. But if vision has become so prominent and popular because it is so significant, it is nonetheless worshipped with far more fervor than understanding. In fact, almost nowhere in organizational life is there a wider gap between precept and practice. It is a gap that a bias toward clarity and focus exposes and closes.

The vision problem begins with the fact that the term is used loosely, along with *mission* and *core values,* to describe closely related phenomena. Many experts insist on a distinction: mission refers to basic purpose, vision to future direction, and core values to underlying beliefs and guiding principles. Technically these constructs are different, but any effort to define one touches quickly on the others. All three are part of the overall dimension of purposing, the "continuous stream" of leadership actions that fosters "clarity, consensus, and commitment regarding the organization's basic purposes." The problem in schools, as in other organizations, is not that leaders use the terms imprecisely but that they fail to "purpose," to induce true clarity, consensus, and commitment through a continuous stream of actions.

What matters most about a vision is how much it matters. A vision's main function is to inspire people and to concentrate their efforts on the pursuit of a meaningful common agenda. This is how it engenders followership and invigorates performance and why its personal impact, not just its intellectual content, is so important. As IBM chairman Louis Gerstner says, it is "not something you do by writing memos. You've got to appeal to people's emotions. They've got to buy in with their hearts and their bellies, not just their minds" (Lohr, 1994, p. 1). But despite the hundreds of thousands of staff hours schools have devoted to developing vision statements, the evidence of teacher buy-in is minuscule. Though almost every school I visit has a mission or vision statement, a scant handful have one that meets the hearts-and-bellies test. In fact, it is hard to find a school where all faculty members can even cite the vision, let alone one where it shapes their practice. To read the actual documents is to see why: most make the spirit sag, not the pulse quicken. Far too much of the vision in schools is blurred and clogged instead of insightful and inspiring. Among the common failings of school vision statements are the following:

- *Length.* Statements that run to three, four, even five pages. No one can grasp, let alone be motivated by, a vision statement that is longer than a few lines.
- *Fragmentation.* Simultaneous multiple improvement—a series of discrete objectives (such as "Our students will value diversity"), each elaborated in detail (often with sublists of "descriptors" such as "A student opposes the exclusion of another student from a group activity").
- *Impracticality.* Aims so unrealistic as to spark cynicism instead of hope (the absurd pretensions of Goals 2000 that we would achieve "world-class standards" in a few short years).
- *Clichés.* A cascade of slogans and currently popular catchwords ("Our school is a community where every member respects the uniqueness of every other, where efficacy flourishes and students realize their full potential and prepare for the challenge of a changing future").[1]

Other problems could be added, but these four recur with such dismaying frequency, and in schools of all kinds, that they raise questions not just about implementation—errors in the way particular schools go about vision building—but also about the value of the effort itself.

The vogue for vision building, it turns out, rests on a foundation that is largely hypothetical. It is one thing to say that in most successful organizations members share a clear common vision, which is true, but quite another to suggest that this stems primarily from direct vision-building work, which is not. Vision is the result of a whole range of actions (a "continuous stream") by leaders, with direct discussion about it being but one component (and as we shall see, not the most important one). Moreover, the enthusiastic accounts of formal vision-building exercises that glut the management literature offer mostly idealized portraits of how the process should work. In real organizational life, successful formal vision building is quite rare; it is a process so complex and sophisticated that it exceeds the capacity of most organizations and certainly most schools (Fullan, p. 83).

Obstacles to Formal Vision Building

To be done right, formal vision work demands at least three essential requirements: lots of staff time (and hence money), exceptional leadership skills, and a clear, focused agenda. It is time-intensive. A one-day workshop or a series of monthly faculty meetings are simply insufficient. They don't provide nearly enough opportunity and continuity for people to sort out their own individual commitments and then hammer out their differences, especially if these differences are sharp. (If a staff does not already share a baseline of common priorities, it may be unable to approach the development of a joint vision that all can embrace—unless it first undertakes some preliminary steps to begin bridging its basic gaps, further increasing the requirements of time and leadership sophistication). At some point an extended off-site retreat away from the press of daily work is almost always necessary (and, in the business world, routine). But no school can close for several days during the school year, and few can even afford to rent a comfortable meeting place, let alone hire their full faculty for a summer retreat. A common way they make do is to designate a small core of teachers who meet extensively to draft a vision or a mission and bring it back to the larger school community for discussion and approval. This can prove a rich experience for the group, whose members may develop a strong allegiance to the vision, but it usually generates much less commitment among the majority who are left in a passive role until near the end of the process when there is some collective discussion prior to a formal vote to adopt the vision. When the faculty is large, this problem is magnified. But it occurs even in small schools.

> One August, I sat with the administrators of an independent school that was reviewing its previous year and planning future priorities. Ellen, the school head, kept referring to "implementing our core values as a school," values recommended by a representative team and adopted by faculty vote in June. The other administrators had little to say about these, except to refer vaguely to "Ellen's values." Eventually, when asked about this, they admitted they thought the values mattered little to the teachers, who had been too tired in June to consider them seriously and had seen the exercise as Ellen's project and little more than "intellectual decoration." This perception was confirmed when Ellen raised it with the faculty at their first meeting in September. To her chagrin, few teachers could recall the specifics of the list they had adopted.

I have met many principals and superintendents who, like Ellen, are puzzled by their faculty's continuing failure to observe "commitments" that won apparent endorsement after this kind of representative vision building.

Even if time and resources are adequate, successful formal vision building also demands exceptional leadership. It is not just a matter of setting goals and selling symbols; it is fundamentally cultural. It means getting a group to examine its "deepest assumptions about the nature of reality and its own identity in relation to its environment" (Schein, 1985, p. 325). We have already seen in Chapter Three how tightly people cling to these assumptions and are enmeshed in them. No matter how clear a principal is about her own commitments, to lead people to engage in such high levels of reflection demands rare personal gifts, among them "extraordinary insight into thoughts and feelings that are normally taken for granted and therefore not articulated," and the ability to "step outside one's culture even as one continues to live within it" (p. 325). It also requires a tolerance for conflict. We have seen that values have an emotional charge and that it is painful to have them challenged. Despite the rosy glow that attends much of the writing on vision, serious attempts to define a school's purpose often involve a lot of unfreezing, and this causes loss and provokes resentment—especially if a faculty has long seen itself as successful. The flak can be fierce.

In this regard, authentic leaders in schools, particularly public schools, are caught in a special bind: they may have strong convictions, but they have weak leverage. In the corporate world, change agents frequently adopt what Schein calls a "strong vision" approach. The chief executive spells out a definite picture of where the organization must go and how it must get there. This is the instance of the take-charge, turnaround leader, the heroic transformer who, by sheer force of will, compels change. He sets the course and makes the case, inspires and encourages, goads and insists, and, where these fail, fires and hires. In many ways, this approach is a natural fit for authentic leaders with clear priorities. But in education it is rarely possible.

The norm in schools is collaborative vision building. The principal may begin by asserting that the status quo must be altered and outcomes improved; he then seeks to engage the faculty in deciding how to accomplish this. This is a longer, slower approach that can potentially lead to a stronger consensus, but it requires persuasion, negotiation, compromise—and patience. It is in keeping with the educational trend toward empowerment and participation, but it also reflects realities that limit administrators' freedom, such as teacher tenure. To build a truly shared vision in a school, a principal faces the tough task of having to enlist almost everyone, including those who disagree with her irreconcilably (people who in a corporate setting would be replaced). For a leader who knows what she stands for and has strong convictions, this can be enormously frustrating.

As these problems illustrate, extensive formal vision work does not offer school leaders the keys to the kingdom of improvement. On the contrary, it risks repeating the managerial mystique, the preoccupation with technique that substitutes an emphasis on improvement *processes* for actual improvements. In this regard, it is useful to return briefly to a concept older and simpler than vision: the motto. To inspire, to reach the heart and the belly as well as the mind, requires a vivid, memorable image that touches people, sets a standard to guide and inspire them, yet leaves them room to develop their own understanding of that standard (Handy, p. 135). This is just what a good motto does. It is short enough to be remembered, and direct without being so literal that it limits the imagination. Like good poetry, it resonates; it is both clear and allusive:

When Ken West arrived at Pueblo Elementary School they already had a "Credo," a "statement of philosophy" that Ken found sound but long-winded ("two pages of small print that no one paid any attention to"). Ken eventually called a meeting of faculty and the PTA and told them "we need to reduce the Credo to its essence, something that really epitomizes us and inspires us." After many meetings, "we really coalesced around the phrase 'Every child a promise.' It lit us up." The school board objected that it didn't specify any goals, so Pueblo created what Ken calls "a three-bullet list about literacy, love of learning, and citizenship." "But," he says, "we organize our goals and programs under the concept of 'The Promise.' We use it so broadly in our discussions, from curriculum to discipline, that we kid each other about it ('Is that a Pueblo Promise with a capital P?'), but it's what all of us here relate to."

At its most effective, a motto serves not as a blueprint but as a touchstone. It becomes part of the school's culture and rituals, invoked ceremonially by leaders and often satirized affectionately by students and teachers. "I think of our motto," says the head of an independent school, "sometimes as an anchor (it keeps us grounded) and sometimes as an umbrella (it shelters us, and what we do has to fit under it)."

Once, of course, it was common for colleges and schools to adopt a motto, often in Latin, to express their fundamental purpose or values. One could make a case that schools today need fewer vision statements and more mottoes. But to try to reduce the typical school vision to a motto would be both comical and sad. Given the simultaneous multiple improvement to which they are subjected and the overpromising to which they are prone, the result would have to be something like *Nunquam negamus* ("We never say no") or perhaps *Omnia omnibus* ("All things to all people"). When I suggested these to an audience of principals, one responded, "I don't know the Latin, but in my district it would be, 'You name it, we start it.' We never get to finish anything, but we tackle everything." The room erupted in the laughter of recognition.

I am not calling for a wave of motto building or for motto-training workshops for leaders, or even for abandoning the concept of vision. I am calling for an end to the notion that we can motivate exceptional effort and performance merely by cramming a bloated improvement agenda through a faddish planning process. To truly "purpose," to forge the commitment and consensus vital to school

improvement, demands an approach to leading that emphasizes—
at a fundamental level and on a consistent, sustained basis—a
defined, sustained sense of meaning and direction.[2] This emerges
not primarily from workshops, committees, or votes but from continuous daily work on actual improvement efforts (Louis and Miles,
p. 226)—and especially from the clarity and focus the leader brings
to this work. A leader shapes a school's values and purposes chiefly
through what she attends to and what she models.

Clarity

Studies of high-performing systems show that their leaders provide
direction that is clear, strong, and unambivalent (not dictatorial,
but definite), that although leadership style may vary among such
organizations, within each it tends to be remarkably consistent
(Vaill, 1984, p. 86). This clarity brings many advantages. The first
is to foster trust, the sine qua non of leadership. When leaders are
consistent, straightforward, and firm, staff find them reliable and
predictable. They know what is expected and what to expect; they
know how people are to behave and how performance is to be
measured. High levels of trust raise confidence and competence
and make the workplace more compatible, which in turn makes
people more likely to cooperate and better able to tolerate stress
(Kouzes and Posner, p. 193).

Clarity also fosters commitment and garners attention. Goals
cannot be shared unless they are understood—none of us can
invest in a vision we don't grasp—and a consistent, lucid formula
tion of goals and their rationale over time creates clarity throughout an organization about its broad purposes and immediate
objectives (Badaracco and Ellsworth, p. 119). As I suggested in
Chapter Four, when faced with change, people need to know why,
what, and how: why they must change, to what, and how the change
will be accomplished. They need to grasp for themselves the necessity of changing (or at least grasp their leaders' perception of the
necessity). The leader must make the case for change, clarifying
"where we are and why we can't stay here." This requires a clear,
candid, forceful diagnosis of the issues the school is encountering—
changes in the environment, problems in performance—and of the
risks of inaction. From this emerges a course for change, a vision of

"what we need to become" (Hammer and Champy, pp. 149–150). In a strong vision scenario, the leader not only makes the case but plots the course and announces it. In a collaborative model, he engages the staff in plotting the course.

In either case, formal discussions about vision and mission can play a helpful role, provided they truly engage everyone. But the best school leaders I know tend to have little interest in these and a vivid dislike of long lists of objectives. They tend to prefer "inspirational themes" as guides for change (Louis and Miles, p. 213). The principal of an urban high school describes such a theme:

> When I first got here everything was bad—attendance, behavior, academics. I decided we'd tackle them in that order but that we'd organize our efforts under a simple heading: "You can make a difference." I worked to convince the faculty that they could succeed with these kids and that we had to convince the kids that they, too, could succeed. We began with attendance. Our message was "We want you in school." We called parents, sent them postcards about attendance, and had individual teachers follow up with each kid or a parent after each absence. Attendance improved. The second year we started on behavior—just some basics about courtesy, language, some more consistency about how we handled discipline and so on. Now we're ready to start on achievement.

This principal could have tried to frame a formal vision and spell out its underlying components ("be here," "behave," "work hard"). But, as he says, "the needs were obvious, we had no time or money for workshops, and we had to start. The theme made sense. Plus, getting started gives you momentum."

Once the why, what, and how are clear, staff carry "pictures in their heads which are strikingly congruent" (Vaill, 1984, pp. 86–87). As one teacher in an elementary school affiliated with James Comer's network of community schools (1980) said to me, "We know why we're here, what we're really doing, and what's special about how we do it." This helps to get and keep people's attention. It helps them center on key tasks, make consistent decisions, and uphold basic agreements and performance standards (Badaracco and Ellsworth, pp. 113, 120). Commitment and attention unleash energy and intensity. People feel strongly about the pictures in their head and keep after them vigorously. This in turn brings the benefits of clarity full circle, reinforcing the leader's own confidence and willingness to give staff leeway, because it lessens the likelihood of deviation and dysfunction—risks that are always present when staff have broad autonomy, as teachers do.

A predisposition toward clarity reflects an approach to leadership that is primarily directive, rather than an emphasis on situational flexibility or bottom-up democracy. It does not oppose democratic participation, but it assumes that the leader's vision is "the magnetic north that sets the compass course" (Kouzes and Posner, p. 20), that the leader must be at the forefront of framing the change and making it comprehensible. This kind of presence by a leader provides a basic confidence for staff and helps concentrate their effort and attention. These are essential in any organization, but especially schools, where the potential for false clarity is high because the goals of improvement initiatives are often broad, diffuse, and multifaceted (and hence hard to understand) and because reformers, while confident about the roots of current school problems, are often unsure about the steps they are inventing to address these problems (Mojkowski and Bamberger, p. 34). I shall have more to say about participation in Chapter Eleven. Here I can note that the ultimate goal of clarity is a shared, community-wide consensus about values and goals, but that this almost always begins from the top, or very near it; it rarely wells up from below.

What does a predisposition toward clarity mean in practice? It means that a principal will not rely on general preaching but will prefer specific statements of purpose and exemplify this preference in concrete ways:

> Tim White was enthusiastic when his district adopted a new elementary mathematics curriculum emphasizing student inquiry and hands-on manipulatives. He held special meetings with his faculty to review the rationale for the change. He took the full training course along with them. Three months into the conversion, when the PTA made its annual "enrichment gifts" ($75 for each classroom, traditionally spent as the teacher wished), several faculty put in orders for the old math workbooks they had long used. Tim called them in to ask how these materials would advance the new goals. They were taken aback, especially when Tim said he couldn't sign their purchase orders until he could "see the link." This led to a serious, difficult, but ultimately constructive discussion of the teachers' hesitations and misunderstandings about the new math program.

It also means providing candid feedback about performance:

> Shirley Wetherbee led her middle school faculty on a year-long discussion of ways to combine more challenging curricula with more student involvement in learning. Seventh-grade social studies teachers sought, and Shirley found, funding for a summer workshop to revamp their American History course. The following fall, Shirley was chagrined to find the teachers had become paragons of false clarity ("They had all the jargon about critical thinking and student-centeredness, but they were having kids memorize the Declaration of Independence"). When she met with them, though she tried to begin tactfully and to recognize their effort, Shirley was explicit about her concerns. She reviewed the school's new goals and cited specific ways the content and pedagogy she had seen failed to reflect these. She listened to the teachers' protestations and then reiterated her main themes, buttressed by further concrete examples. She insisted that the teachers modify some course content and reduce their emphasis on lecture and memorization, offered them her personal help and that of the district's curriculum coordinator, and set a date for them to report on their efforts.

Lest these brief examples mislead, it is important to note two things clarity does not mean: rigidity or abrasiveness. Authentic leaders may be persistent, but they are not blind. They will override any bias because of significant external events or institutional realities (if, say, repeated budget cuts make the pursuit of a priority impossible), but never lightly, and rarely out of personal politics (letting a teacher evade an important requirement just to reduce friction). Nor does being clear and specific entail rudeness, harshness, condescension, or taking away a teacher's discretion. Tim began by asking the teachers to tell him about their request, not by blasting them. Shirley was firm in her demands (and could not hide her disappointment), but she kept her emphasis on performance—the curriculum and student activity—not on personalities.

Focus: One at a Time

Clarity's corollary is focus. One might theoretically be clear about a long roster of goals, but the longer the roster, the harder it is to understand, let alone fulfill. Authentic leaders follow Peter

Drucker's famous advice to concentrate their efforts on a few important areas "where superior performance produces outstanding results" (1976, p. 24). This wisdom has been consistently confirmed over the past two decades: effective leaders target their energies, centering their time and effort on a short list of key issues, even if this means ignoring others. Like Tim and Shirley, they are focused on their goals, and by actively communicating their judgments about what is important, they bring focus to staff behavior. This is vital, because in every organization there are always many problems that need fixing, many projects competing for attention. Successful leaders "are not distracted by this cacophony. They know what few things are important, and in their statements and actions they make these priorities known" (Vaill, 1984, p. 96). In truth, these leaders *decide* what few things are important. The important things are not inevitable, written in the stars and discernible only to a leader with special insight. They are chosen by a leader and then pursued with a vigor and skill that brings success and makes their importance ultimately seem inevitable—and the leader visionary.

A predisposition toward focus, then, recognizes that no matter how desirable an innovation, implementers must decide its comparative importance, the priority it will receive relative to other initiatives. Because few people can accomplish more than one significant change at a time, choosing where to concentrate one's efforts is crucial—especially for educators, who are pressed to enact so many changes. Even if the choice results from a collegial, collaborative process rather than being imposed from the top, it will require a pilot to monitor progress and keep people on course. If superintendents are not definite about which program or which constituency has top priority, principals' daily decisions in their schools will not show a consistent direction. Similarly, if principals are not definite, teachers' daily decisions in their classrooms will also fail to show a consistent direction. "He who would do good to another," said William Blake, "must do it in minute particulars."

What does focus mean in practice? It means something as elementary as it is rare: pursuing one major change at a time per person and per work group. The prospects for improving schools would leap exponentially if this simple premise were adopted.

"One at a time" is the rule of thumb in the private sector: an innovation with six components will have six separate teams, and each particular work group will concentrate on only one. This does not mean innovation must be narrow. Far from it—reform may be wide-ranging and multifaceted. But the more complex the project, the clearer and more compatible its priorities must be and the more its elements must fit coherently under one conceptual roof and in combination make sense to those who must implement it. If it has multiple dimensions, individuals must not be expected to master all of them at once. The Coalition of Essential Schools, for example, bases its secondary school reform on nine "common principles" that combine into a coherent, comprehensive program. But these principles involve curriculum, pedagogy, assessment, governance, and structure, and they can only be accomplished in stages over a period of years. And they need to be unhindered by other unrelated initiatives. The more the project aims at deep, thorough, cultural change, the fewer companions and competitors it must have. School improvement cannot succeed as an endless string of add-ons.

When I recommend focus to educators, most agree readily—they know the futility of the bloated improvement agenda better than anyone—but they cannot imagine how they might even begin to press seriously for it. Teacher audiences ask, "Do you recommend this to administrators?" Administrative audiences ask, "Do you recommend this to school boards and state officials?" And given the forces arrayed against focus—the legislative and regulatory mandates, the diverse reform constituencies, the political and legal advocacy of special interest groups—their doubt is understandable. I have already acknowledged that innovation triage is hard. There are, however, at least three practical ways school leaders can push for focus.

The first is to accentuate the positive, to advocate strongly and proactively with the relevant constituencies for purposes one values rather than against those one doesn't. In this way authentic leaders tend to control the terms of debate, because they assert their key themes over and over. In their interest and enthusiasm, in the intensity of their own concentration, they often fulfill Winston Churchill's definition of a fanatic ("one who won't change his mind and can't change the subject"). Being so positively focused on their goals, they emphasize not just the external rationale of the effort but also its intrinsic rewards—how exciting, how promising, even how enjoyable it is. This creates interest and invites participation (Kouzes and Posner, pp. 227–228). Because of this and because they frame their goals in terms of fundamental, enduring commitments (see below), they are better able to keep their own priorities in the forefront of everyone's attention. In the same way, they enact the principle that an organization's mission and strategy begin with its strengths, not its deficits or the apparent needs of its "market." To solve most problems, a school needs to draw on its talents, and it will achieve greater success sooner by actively seeking to maximize what it does well.

The second builds upon Schlechty's observation that good leaders ask not just, "What needs to be done that is not being done now?" but also, "What [can we] quit doing so we can do what we need to do?" (1990, p. 106). When pressured from above into simultaneous multiple improvement, an authentic leader will at least ask this second question, confronting—civilly (gently, even)—the lack of focus. Thus, when faced with a demand to do something new, one asks, "And what shall we stop doing?" When the answer is "Nothing. We want you to add this to the list," one asks, "How did you think we might do that?" When the answer is "I know you'll be creative," one replies, "Actually, I think that will interfere with our ability to fulfill our existing commitments. Where should we concentrate?" When this fails to produce a change of heart and the new demand is imposed, one does one's best. Then, at year's end, when the criticism is "You didn't accomplish the new priority," one doesn't apologize, one agrees: "Yes, that's right. As I feared, our agenda is too full. I think we need to target our top priority and really go after it."

If there is little hope of paring down the agenda, a remaining option is to stretch out time lines of individual items, especially for recurrent improvement projects (such as curriculum upgrades). In a progressive rural district, a newly appointed elementary curriculum coordinator, remembering her own frustration as a fifth-grade teacher, helped bring focus to her new role in this way:

For years we had been on an annual cycle of curriculum review. We'd be implementing the new science units we planned last year but also be having to plan the math changes for next year. We never had a year to debug or consolidate. We were racing ever faster on a treadmill, and our product was shoddy. I shifted us to a three-year cycle for each major subject: plan science in year one, implement and troubleshoot it in year two, confirm it in year three. We're developing much better material, and people feel much more confident and fulfilled.

There are probably few restructuring projects that couldn't benefit from having their time lines extended. Even modest extensions can enhance the quality of outcomes—and build a case for focusing reform.

Continuity

Clarity and focus, by improving vision, can reduce the resistance innovation normally provokes, especially when they emphasize continuity. Continuity is essential because change causes so much loss. We have already seen that people are usually ready to respond to the case for reform only after they have been unfrozen—that is, when they are distressed because disconfirming data has caused them to acknowledge problems in their performance. When the magnitude of the disconfirmation and its attendant change is great enough, it disrupts the meaningfulness of experience, arousing a deep existential anxiety. It threatens people's ontological security, their fundamental confidence about the nature of things, the very way they understand the world and their attachments to people and ideals. It also challenges their competence, as old practices must usually be abandoned before new ones have been confidently mastered. Unfortunately, as we noted, innovators too often treat the actual adaptations required as a simple matter of substitution, whereas grief resolves itself through a much more complex process of reformulation. To adapt successfully, people must be helped to see how purposes and attachments and skills that are threatened by change can be reworked in the context of their own experience (Marris, p. 158). It is here that an authentic leader can play a crucial role, serving as the transitional object that helps people over this difficult gap.

Transitional object is a term used by psychotherapists to designate the pacifier, teddy bear, or blanket that helps a small child make the transition from dependence toward independence (and, by extension, the objects that in later life serve a similar purpose). These objects, which carry the ambience of a nurturing mother, are a source of essential comfort and security—of continuity—to toddlers as they move away from their primary dependence on their parents. Because attachment is so central to our security as children, it becomes permanently embedded "in the meaning of safety and reward for the rest of our lives" (Marris, p. ix). So, too, adults—especially at times of change—seek transitional objects, though these are usually people rather than things. A therapist, for example, may become a focus of a patient's intense attachment as he struggles to let go of dysfunctional patterns of behavior and try relating to people in new ways. For adults as for children, confidence to experiment is linked to security of attachment. It comes "from this underlying trust. . . . We become sure of ourselves if we trust that the moral order, the knowledge and abilities to which we were introduced by those we needed to love will continue to reward us with secure attachments" (p. ix).

To bear loss and invest in new ways of behaving, to move from bereavement toward commitment, to abandon old competencies and try new ones, people need help to modify their patterns of understanding and attachment, to graft new perceptions and priorities onto the roots of older ones. They almost always need a person—a leader—to embody the change and create the bridge between the old and the new, to help them relinquish what they hold dear so they can move on. But this can never be forced. "To make [new] dreams apparent to others and to align people with them," says Bennis, requires not just "mere explanation or clarification but the creation of meaning" (1989, pp. 20–21).[3] A vital function of an authentic leader's vision is to do just this and, in the process, to provide the psychological safety that permits people to take the risk of trying new competencies. It is best accomplished when the leader's vision overtly emphasizes continuity, making change more familiar by linking the future to the past and emphasizing existing strengths.

When leaders can explain change in clear, focused terms and connect innovation to long-standing values that matter to constituents, reaffirming wherever possible the school's traditional principles and qualities, they help staff link the new with the old and bear the uncertainties and losses of change. This means framing change so that it maintains some connection with previous routines. One doesn't try to sell reform strictly on the basis of its technical merits or its newness; neither helps people find meaning in change, and the latter can make it seem a dangerous, unpredictable Pandora's box. Rather, one helps people to see change and its losses as part of an expectable, inevitable sequence of events, so that they may begin to retie "past, present and future together again with rewoven strands of meaning" (Marris, p. 21). One shows them how reform grows from, reflects, or connects to their abiding commitments. The less the new practices resemble the old ones, the more vital this linkage. A leader's clear focus on a vision or a theme can support people through a difficult transition by helping them to understand the new goal in terms of their enduring interests. Two outstanding examples, a century apart, are offered by Abraham Lincoln and Martin Luther King, Jr.

Lincoln ran for the presidency opposed to the spread of slavery but also opposed to its immediate abolition. His primary commitment was to preserve the Union. The Union began to disintegrate even before his inauguration, and he focused his entire presidency on restoring it. During his tenure, after much ambivalence, he finally decided to issue the Emancipation Proclamation and then to free all slaves. Caught between conservatives who found him too radical and abolitionists who found him too cautious, he constantly framed his actions in terms that resonated with all of his constituents: "union" and "freedom." Lincoln, who once remarked, "I have never had a feeling politically that did not spring from the sentiments embodied in the Declaration of Independence" (Basler, 1953, p. 240), pursued change—war and emancipation—in the name of deep fundamental values that he shared with most of his countrymen. Even as he led the nation through its most violent, life-threatening upheaval, he saw and presented his effort as extending and fulfilling its core commitments.

A century later, also rallying the nation on behalf of civil rights, King offered another classic piece of authentic leadership. In his famous "I have a dream" speech, using widely known phrases from the Bible, from old spirituals, from "America, the Beautiful" and "My County 'tis of Thee," and from the Declaration of Independence, he linked the case for racial equality with the deepest, most basic American aspirations and values. Both Lincoln and King illustrate that leadership ultimately involves an ability to define the reality of others (Morgan, 1986, p. 176)—not that a leader forces a definition on people or tries to manipulate them, but that he reaches them in a way that helps them see the new in terms of the enduring, to preserve continuity while fostering change.

One need not be a Lincoln or a King to accomplish this; one can do very well by being a marketer rather than just a salesman. To oversimplify, where selling presses a product or service on customers and aims to help them find it important, marketing asks customers what they find important and tries to design a product or service accordingly. Marketing has come to be seen as a fundamental approach to innovation. Organizations do best not only when they attend to the satisfaction of their external customers but also when staff who must cooperate see each other as "internal customers," with interests and work needs that must be fulfilled. Bringing this marketing emphasis to school improvement, Schlechty defines as a "customer for change" everyone "whose support is needed to bring the desired change to fruition." Teachers are primary customers. If they are to invest their time, energy, support, creativity, and insight, they must be able to expect in return something they value (1990, p. 84). Hence, simply selling change as a solution to current problems is likely to create resistance. After all, "present problems have their locus in current reality, and we are all part of that reality." People are unlikely to embrace change that demeans them and forces them to "confess prior sins." So, educational leaders, as they market improvements, must consider how these innovations will serve or threaten the critical values of teachers (and of other constituencies). They need to ask themselves how a proposed change, without betraying its integrity, can be implemented in such a way as to maximize the values it serves and minimize those it threatens, and how it can elevate teachers' professional self-esteem and feelings of worth (p. 89).[4]

A key ingredient in this effort is to build on strengths in the staff and in the school; it is an essential part of the continuity message. Not only will a school need to draw on its strengths to solve its problems, it will usually achieve greater success sooner by actively seeking to maximize what it does well. And having strengths acknowledged—even those that are no longer relevant—can reduce people's antagonism to change. Members of a school community will find it easier to face up to problems if their leader reaffirms their competence. Schematized, the continuity message would be something like this:

> At our school, we have always believed in Z and we have always been especially good at pursuing Z in two ways, A and B. Now, because of a set of changes [in the world around us, in our own resources, in what we have come to know about how students learn, etc.] we need to pursue Z in different ways. We also need to expand our goals to include Y. As we do so, A will continue to be vital, but B, though it has been important and we have done it well, must change to C, and we must add D to our strengths. These changes will be challenging, but if we concentrate on our commitments and draw on our skills, we can do it.

When a principal or superintendent can frame innovation in this way, it can greatly reduce resistance and help a school community reach a consensus for change.

This message will be important not only for teachers but also for parents and the general public. I noted in Chapter Seven the need for districts, in light of the declining proportion of voters who have children of school age and hence a natural interest in education and its support, to reach out, to create a more informed public. I also noted that few school districts are expert at marketing and public relations, at building community awareness. These are complex tasks in their own right; they are not just a matter of "selling" change but of helping people understand the true strengths and real needs of the schools. As they seek the approval and financial support of the general public, districts will have an easier time if their message provides continuity amidst change.

Example

Good preaching and good marketing serve change powerfully, but they are not enough. Practicing what one preaches is also essential. The best transitional object is one who embodies the change he seeks. I have already said that authenticity, by definition, involves integrity in action, that leading by example is not only an ideal way to inculcate values and purposes but an essential one, that the leader must change first if others are to follow:

> [Moses] persuaded the children of Israel [to] go forward toward a land of milk and honey when all they could see around them was sand. One man couldn't force a whole people to set off into the desert; he had to inspire them with his vision. He also set a personal example. When they arrived at the Red Sea, Moses said, "Here's the plan. We're going to march into the sea, and the Lord will part the waters, and we'll walk through on dry land." His followers looked at the Red Sea and said to him, "You first." He went, and they followed. Being out front when the risk presents itself is part of leadership [Hammer and Champy, p. 105].

When a leader is out in front (and following through), when his behavior exemplifies the change he advocates, he not only speaks with the special credibility of the exemplar, he offers people a literal personification of continuity, a way to picture themselves accomplishing the change.

Reflecting on the example one sets is always instructive. Leaders can ask themselves directly, "What do my actions tell people about my true values and goals? Do they confirm what I believe and what I preach?" This can help an administrator gain some perspective, but it is hard to view oneself from the balcony when one is actually performing in the play onstage. None of us can have complete self-perspective and are fully aware of our impact on others. To complete the picture leaders would need to pose the questions to their constituents, conducting a kind of market survey about themselves. This is not always practicable, but when it is, the results can be surprisingly informative:

> When Carl Jamison asked the staff at his elementary school what they most noticed about his actual behavior, he was astonished that they immediately thought of the cafeteria. The teachers commented on his "perfect attendance" (he would almost never agree to hold meetings at lunchtime), his involvement (he moved actively from table to table, chatting and joking with students, intervening early in disputes, occasionally calling the room to order to make special commendations of students or groups for particular accomplishments), and his pleasure (he obviously enjoyed himself). Carl realized that

they were right. "I've always preached personalization. I want teachers to really connect with students. It's just crucial to me. I guess the cafeteria is a key place where I stay in touch myself. And to be honest, even though I'm forty-five I still like hanging out with the kids at lunch."

As Carl discovered, one of the best measures leaders can use to gauge the example they set is to consider how they spend their time. Leaders who inspire followers care passionately about their goals; they are intense and they persevere—a combination that can be magnetic. Their intensity may be quiet rather than noisy, but it is almost always exemplified in their investment of extraordinary amounts of time. Authentic leaders accrue on the job large amounts of both "microtime" (their hourly, daily presence on the job) and "macrotime" (that is, they tend to stay in their jobs for a long while) (Vaill, 1989, pp. 94–95). Both send clear messages to followers, confirming the leader's commitment and setting a standard for others to emulate.

At the micro level, of course, most leaders feel they are prisoners, not masters, of time, always at someone else's beck and call. But this is never fully true. We may feel perpetually trapped by other people's demands, and our schedule may in fact be under heavy pressure, but there are always some choices, some chances to do some things differently and to do other things that are neither prescribed nor prohibited. Faced with two simultaneous meetings, we attend one and not the other, or if we attend both, we choose one first or stay at one longer. (I know principals who dutifully voice their support for inclusion programs but who never attend meetings about special needs students.) Given a brief half hour of freedom during the day, we make a choice about how to fill it. How any leader spends her time, especially discretionary time, communicates a powerful message. "It is in this area of choices that the opportunities for excellence exist" (Sergiovanni, 1991, p. 24).

At the macro level, when staff believe a leader will stay put to see an innovation through, confidence and energy are enhanced—and the ante is raised. Though vital to leading innovation in any organization, macrotime is particularly important in schools, where the carousel of reform and the transience of administrators have bred such doubt among teachers about support for reform initiatives. It may take considerable time and considerable repetition for teachers to believe a principal or superintendent means to stay, but when they come to believe it, it makes a difference to all. Those who had hoped "this too shall pass" need to reconsider the merits of their passive (or active) resistance. Those who find the change appealing are encouraged to invest their own time and energy, even when the going gets rough:

> When Jim Wood, as a new principal, led his high school in a restructuring along the lines of an "essential school," there was virulent opposition from right-wing conservatives and Christian fundamentalists. As the furor intensified, fed by false charges and much misinformation, Jim found faculty resolve beginning to waver. He realized that, among their other fears, teachers also weren't sure of his commitment, anticipating that he, like other administrators they had known, might seek calmer pastures elsewhere, leaving them to face their critics unsupported. He gathered them and said, "I'm not going anywhere. I'm not going off to get my doctorate and become a superintendent. I've just bought a house here, and I'm staying as the principal here. I'm going to see this through with you."

All too often, talented principals and superintendents don't make Jim Wood's choice to stay. The promising reform projects that have died in the wake of their departures are too numerous and too discouraging to count.

I began this chapter on a note of ambivalence, then proceeded to argue the importance of being definite, unambiguous, and specific. I conclude it by sounding the same two themes. Having criticized rational-structural reformers in Chapter One for relying on "brute sanity," I do not wish to repeat the same fallacy: just because something seems self-evident and useful to an observer doesn't make its adoption easy for a practitioner. There is no doubt that a bias toward clarity and focus swims against the cultural current that socializes administrators to be passive maintainers and against the political current that espouses simultaneous multiple improvement. It calls for courage—"not the valor of grand, heroic acts, but determination and honesty practiced daily in . . . small situations and familiar dilemmas . . . the courage to do and say what one believes to be right, rather than what is convenient, familiar, or popular; the courage to act on one's vision" (Badaracco and Ellsworth, p. 201).

This can certainly entail some risk. And yet, the real risk of the bias is the awful price of avoiding it: disabling change, disempowering the leader. Institutionally, it is essential to the creation of meaningful purpose, the mobilizing of commitment to improvement, and the adoption of achievable agendas. Practically, it helps leaders concentrate on a general pattern of behavior rather than a series of maneuvers, it frees them to express their priorities in their own ways, it invites them to look for "opportunities for excellence" where they can make a real difference, and it opens the path to followership through setting an example. It thus offers the great gift of leverage, simplifying school leaders' tasks even as it enhances their power to inspire.

Notes

1. I keep a collection of egregious vision documents. The most stunning covers both sides of an eleven- by seventeen-inch page, much of it in tiny type, and lists a vision, a mission, eighteen values, three sets of goals (sixteen for students, eleven for staff and administrators, five for the community), and action plans for four years, with up to eighteen items per year.
2. An excellent example is Carl Glickman's call for schools to adopt a single overarching goal: to prepare students to be productive citizens of a democracy. Besting other nations in math or science, teaching basic skills or critical thinking—these are "subgoals of the larger, single goal of public education. When these subgoals are treated as primary goals, they lead to fragmentation, vulnerability, and despair as schools try to be all things to all people" (1993, p. 8).
3. Alexander Herzen, the Russian revolutionary, said, "You can waken men only by dreaming their dreams more clearly than they can dream them themselves" (Mortimer, 1982, p. 243).
4. The less possible this seems, the greater the need to delay implementation and seek ways to "prepare the situation for the change" (Schlechty, 1990, p. 85).

Chapter Eleven

Participation—
Without Paralysis

*The paradox of getting more done by freeing up teachers to
decide what they will do, rather than putting pressure on
them to perform, is based on a universal human truth.
Leadership which taps the creativity of those who are at the
center of the project . . . will always do better than
leadership that uses its authority.*
—HAROLD HOWE, II (1994B, P. 40)

*But I'm through with the purity, with endless committees
and endless debates about process. I still want people
involved—I love this faculty and I seek its voice all the
time—but I'm the "Head." I provide the starting point
and the framework.*
—HEADMASTER

School improvement is embedded in an ethos of empowerment
and collegiality. The second wave of the restructuring movement
has concentrated not just on redesigning curriculum and instruction but on realigning roles and relationships to unleash teachers'
energy and influence and enhance their professional cooperation
and support. To fulfill these priorities, administrators are to practice participatory leadership. They are to relinquish conventional
uses of power and politics and nurture instead shared governance
and collegial interaction. This reflects a larger trend in leadership
thinking, a strong emphasis on community and on "servant leadership," the leader as a steward of a self-motivating, self-managing

community.[1] Take-charge bosses, no-nonsense autocrats, wily manipulators—all are in disrepute. In the balance between top-down and bottom-up leadership, the bottom, it seems, is up.

The prospect of a committed, empowered, collegial community served by an enlightened leader is exciting. It has obvious congruence with important concepts we have explored, such as followership. Its appeal spans the political spectrum, exemplifying American values of freedom and self-determination on the one hand and community and democracy on the other. Understandably, the schools where it really happens are exceptional, exhilarating places to work. But they are few and far between. The participatory-collegial ideal is, like formal vision building, beyond the capacity of most schools and based on assumptions that overlook key psychological and organizational realities. Participation is extremely complex. It can embroil schools in controversy, exhaust participants, and hamper efforts to reform instructional programs. Collegiality more often falls flat, failing to excite much interest and commitment. Here again, as with so much in education, the question is how—or how fully—a noble ideal can be realized.

Authentic leaders endorse the ideal, but not slavishly. They want to optimize collective involvement and professional community, but not at the expense of their core commitments. They will not sacrifice substance for process, clarity and focus for a management modality. They do not abandon traditional authority; they use it judiciously, building involvement as they can in a variety of informal as well as formal ways but asserting themselves as they must. They provide a binary leadership that is both top-down and bottom-up. In this way they avoid the pitfalls that can turn empowerment and collaboration into quagmires, and they help school communities deepen the commitment on which improvement depends.

Participation and Collegiality

Most educational reformers see traditional school leadership, epitomized by the administrative bureaucracy, as disenfranchising teachers (and ultimately students and parents), forcing them into conformity and isolation, depriving the school of their wisdom and creativity, and denying them the chance for professional growth. The proposed solutions generally emphasize the notion of the school as a community: a democratic community governed by its members, an intellectual community of lifelong learners, and in some cases a moral community sharing a covenant of values. They also emphasize individual potential, the notion that all teachers have the potential to be leaders (Barth, 1990, pp. 144–145). The individual voice is empowered, not suppressed, but as a respectful, contributing part of a harmonious, reflective, self-renewing choir. Rather than following specific rules and administrative decrees, teachers should "work together to examine the challenges they face, and then decide—as a team of thoughtful, committed professionals—how best to proceed" (Lee, Smith, and Croninger, 1995, p. 2).

To accomplish this transformation, traditional management is to be replaced by shared governance and traditional teacher isolation by collaboration and collegiality. The first is reflected in a rising trend toward site-based management (SBM). Power devolves to the individual school, and teachers play active, leading roles in governance (the preferred mode for which is consensus); in turn, they share power with students in classrooms, encouraging them to be active, engaged learners. The second is expressed in collaborative structures in which teachers work together (observing one another's classes, team teaching, designing interdisciplinary curriculum) and reflect on their work together (participating in study groups, peer coaching groups, and so on), drawing on and contributing to the knowledge base in their field.

The vogue for participation rests on three core beliefs: rightness, effectiveness, and transfer. For many, treating teachers as clock-punching, do-what-you're-told hourly laborers and isolating them from one another and from intellectual engagement in their discipline are simply wrong. Shared governance and a culture of collaboration and collegiality are The Right Things, especially for an institution like a school, which should encourage democratic virtues and high standards of performance. For others, the chief argument for participation is that it simply works better, improving decision making and performance (Schlechty, 1990, p. 52). There is almost universal agreement that organizations that draw on the knowledge of their staff make more informed choices and enjoy higher levels of productivity and morale due to people's increased sense of control and accountability. When it comes to innovation, participation is a primary path to commitment: people are much more likely to invest themselves in something they help shape. And, importantly, many reformers posit a transfer effect from school practice to classroom practice. Teachers who are empowered to help make decisions about their school will structure their classrooms to empower students in the learning process, encouraging students to take greater responsibility for their own education.

The rationale for making schools not just collectively governed but truly collegial places is that it will enrich not only the quality of teachers' work lives but also their classroom practice. Collegiality denotes a collaborative work culture in which teachers talk regularly and seriously about their practice, observe one another's work, jointly design and evaluate curriculum, and teach one another what they know about their craft. Anyone who has been part of a such a process, or anyone who has seen first-rate teachers engage in reflective practice together, knows its power and excitement. Opportunities to collaborate and to build knowledge can enhance job satisfaction and performance. At their best, they help schools create a self-reflective, self-renewing capacity as learning organizations. For these and other reasons, shared governance and collegiality have become enshrined as twin ideals in school improvement.

To many, these ideals are both right and full of potential for transforming schools. To me, they are compelling—as ideals. But as implemented in most of the schools I know, they fall short of their promise so consistently and in such predictable ways that they require reconsideration. The problems they encounter may be grouped under two headings. The first is resistance—few teachers, it seems, want to be fully empowered and collegial; for many, these goals involve changes that swim against the tide of life and career. The second is complexity—these are very sophisticated innovations that demand far more of participants than their advocates acknowledge.

Resistance

Whatever its rightness, shared governance draws more skepticism and opposition than enthusiasm from teachers. Sarason (1990, pp. 63–64) describes a typical example, a joint effort by the superintendent and the head of the teachers' union in an urban district to empower the district's high school faculty. Teachers would be free to make any changes they wanted—within budget limits—to improve their schools, which had many problems that could be addressed without additional funds. Their early enthusiasm quickly deteriorated. They soon announced that they did not believe they would really be allowed to do what they wanted; they were sure their recommendations would be overruled or dismissed, and they wanted to withdraw from the project. This is both an old story (in the late 1960s I encountered it trying to help reform the teaching of English in my high school) and a very current one (in the 1990s I have met hundreds of principals and teachers who are dismayed by how many faculty become hesitant or resistant when offered a real voice in change). This opposition is often magnified when empowerment includes parents and the community, especially in schools where teachers feel blamed by the public and parents for students' deteriorating performance and behavior and, at the same time, believe parents are providing too little care and discipline for their children and too little support for the school. In such situations, site-based management can actually increase alienation by intensifying teachers' belief "that they are [being] manipulated by administrators who do not understand the circumstances of their work" (Louis and Miles, p. 195).

Efforts to enhance collaboration and collegiality provoke apathy more than resistance; they just rarely get very far. Teachers generally aren't hotly opposed so much as disinterested. Many don't volunteer for peer coaching or team teaching projects, or for study groups. They do object to plans that would reduce their individual preparation periods to permit more collaborative planning time (this can cause strong opposition if forcibly imposed). And even in schools where teaming is an integral part of life, many teachers participate passively, attending meetings but essentially just going through the motions. "Our collegiality train has left the station," says a principal of a middle school, "but it has many cabooses." Teachers' relations with one another are mostly marked by congeniality (being pleasant) but not collegiality (serious professional interaction). Though collegiality's benefits are "obvious, logical, and compelling," it is "the least common form of relationship among adults in schools," observes Barth (1989, pp. 229–230).

Collaborative efforts are ever fragile—hard to start, hard to sustain. The entrenched norms that prevail among teachers remain those of autonomy and privacy, "not open exchange, cooperation, and growth" (Johnson, 1990, p. 179).

Teachers' resistance to building a participatory community may be understood in many ways. Some observers attribute it to years of demoralization and enforced passivity in badly run schools or to cynicism from past reforms that defaulted on promises of empowerment. Sarason's union president ascribed it to fear. His teachers were afraid that if they used their new power and things went badly, they would be "clobbered" (1990, pp. 63–64). I think all of these apply, but the primary issue is that, for large numbers of teachers, participation and collaboration oppose the tendencies of the life and career cycles.

Whatever they promise, shared governance and collaboration always mean more work—and more complex work, and more work with other adults rather than with students. They require greater investment in the workplace and higher levels of sophisticated adult interaction. Many teachers welcome neither. To begin with, these initiatives almost always come as add-ons to existing workloads: governance meetings occur in the evenings or, occasionally, before or after school; team teaching requires not just performing together but extensive preplanning and debriefing. But I have rarely encountered a school that has significantly reduced teaching loads to compensate for these added demands. Many veteran teachers feel this as a particular burden: more work at school is precisely what they don't want. Developmentally, many of them are inclined away from broader job involvement and toward the narrowing of professional priorities ("focusing down") and the pursuit of personal interests, as described in Chapter Six.

There is also the truth that many teachers, regardless of age, prefer to work with children than with adults. Most report that their success and satisfaction come chiefly from their dealings with students, as Dan Lortie (1975) pointed out long ago and as anyone who talks to teachers today can ascertain. They often see colleagues, administrators, and parents as potential intruders and hindrances. Even faculty who are gifted with students can be unhappy and awkward with adults. Two of the best teachers my children ever had were fabulous to watch in a classroom but incapable of looking a parent in the eye during a conference. And I recall a wise and talented special educator speaking wistfully about her school's conversion from pull-out services to inclusion: "I see the rationale," she said, "and I believe it's good for students. But now I spend hours and hours coordinating with other adults. I went into this field to work with students. I *miss* my kids."

In this connection, there is a related—and largely overlooked—reason that collective interaction doesn't always fit well for teachers: the career they have chosen is not just student-centered, it is an idiosyncratic craft. By its very nature—its immediacy, its unpredictability, its social complexity (Chapter Seven)—teaching is in many ways an inherently individualistic occupation. In many respects, a teacher is an "independent artisan," an autonomous tinkerer, an intellectual craftsman who uses whatever he can find in his workshop to solve the problems presented by the project he is working on. He is not a deliverer of highly scripted, linear instructional sequences but a skillful, adaptive improviser (Huberman, 1993, p. 16).[2] Much of what any teacher does is highly personal, and over time every teacher develops a unique instructional repertoire, a set of personal, artful, but often tacit assumptions and responses.

This means that technical communication among teachers is more difficult, less necessary, in some ways even less appropriate than it might seem. It is more difficult because two people can teach the same curriculum to similar students but operate in vastly different ways on vastly different assumptions that are hard to explain, let alone bridge. It is less necessary because in the most basic practical terms, schools can easily function as a set of independent workshops (quite unlike hospitals, for example, which literally cannot operate without close linkage among staff). And it is less appropriate because the separateness and "professional egalitarianism" that incline teachers to keep to themselves is routine among artisans. "Noninterference with the core work of others constitutes a sign of professional respect," while asking for assistance can seem a sign of weakness and offering unsolicited help a sign of arrogance (p. 29).

Complexity

Participation and collegiality may ultimately improve a school's effectiveness, but they are very difficult to achieve. They ask of people a remarkable sophistication and commitment, a fundamental shift in roles and perspective that is hard for any workforce to develop, especially if it must maintain its traditional functions and master other innovations at the same time. In the first place, simply giving power to those unused to it is no panacea, as Sarason's example illustrates. When the level of trust or readiness is low, trying to initiate change through extensive participation is not only futile, it can exacerbate tensions. There is usually much preliminary work to be done to create a climate in which empowerment and participation can start. And even when teachers do embrace opportunities for governance, the complexities have barely begun.

Few teachers have had any practice at making major institutional decisions, let alone at being held accountable beyond their immediate classroom. It is unreasonable to expect them to become instantly adept at it. Top-down autocrats have their blind spots, but so do bottom-up staff who have had little exposure to the big picture of governing an entire school. Converting to consensual decision making is slow and intricate work, second-order change at its most challenging. It means, among other things, "making rules for making rules" (Aronstein and DeBenedictis, 1992, p. 134). This requires a skill for managing group dynamics that teachers may employ deftly with students but much less easily with one another. (To refocus a class whose discussion gets loud and lost is one thing—the teacher is, after all, the clear authority—but to do this with a group of peers requires of everyone a shift of perspective that is far from automatic.)

Chief among the necessary rules and skills are those for resolving conflict, something at which educators, on the whole, lack aptitude and experience. As we will see in Chapter Thirteen, schools observe strong traditions of conflict avoidance. Teachers rarely engage in the open expression and negotiation of conflict with colleagues and leaders. Many advocates of teacher empowerment and shared governance tend to imagine that creating participatory structures will generate harmonious, trouble-free decision making; they make little provision for preparing people to resolve conflict. Or they believe that what discord does arise can be handled through constructive, nonconfrontational methods of bargaining. Both assumptions are false.

Early on I noted that from a political perspective conflict is a routine feature of organizational life. When resources and money and opportunities for advancement are scarce, when people compete for jobs and titles, when groups compete over power and policy, conflict is natural. To some extent, every organization is an arena where significant competing views naturally confront one another and must be worked out (Bolman and Deal, p. 387). When reform threatens to upset the organizational status quo and the distribution of resources and power, conflict intensifies. In this regard I also noted that though advocates of change generally champion it in rational terms as better, more effective, and so on, there is always a political dimension to their claims. With change, as with so much in life, where you stand depends on where you sit. As we saw, the claims may always be questioned: Better and more effective for whom? At what cost? A newly created, self-governing group is rarely skilled at negotiating such differences.

To the extent that they do acknowledge the potential for conflict, proponents of participation tend to rely on optimistic, noncompetitive approaches—"win-win" bargaining, as it has come to be called. Unlike the traditional, competitive "win-lose" stance typical of labor negotiations and political maneuvering, win-win negotiation offers strategies for settling differences cooperatively through good faith bartering based on enlightened self-interest. Disputants ask, "How can we all benefit and build long-term mutual advantage?" rather than, "How can I win this immediate fight at all costs?" The best known example of this approach is that advocated by Fisher and Ury. They criticize traditional "positional bargaining," in which each side stakes out a position and then makes concessions to reach an agreement, as inefficient and as overlooking the potential for solutions that could better benefit both sides. They recommend "principled bargaining," which separates the people from the problem (avoids personalities, tackles issues on their merits); focuses on interests, not positions (keeps larger overarching goals in sight, rather than getting locked into specific positions); invents options for mutual gain (makes extra effort to seek solutions that benefit everyone); and insists on objective criteria (agrees on an independent standard to measure outcomes and procedures) (1981, pp. 3–11).

This approach offers a genuine basis for both mutually advantageous negotiation and for resolving differences in a comprehensive, forward-looking way. It is a kind of enlightened behavior that appeals to higher-order communitarian aspirations. It fits well not only with the values of empowerment and democracy but with the concepts of stewardship and servant leadership; one can only recommend it. However, it does have sharp limitations. It applies more readily to clearly demarcated differences—an expiring union contract, for example—than to less clear-cut ones, such as whether a new teaching method or curriculum is worth adopting. It requires large amounts of time, which in many schools is the scarcest of commodities. More importantly, it overlooks some realities of human behavior—including some of its baser aspects, such as selfishness—and requires a unique set of circumstances: mutual good faith; a rational, self-observing perspective (the ability to get outside oneself); and a broad, farsighted definition of self-interest by all concerned. It also demands a sufficient degree of common purpose. If faculty members hold sharply conflicting views about their primary roles and educational goals, they can rarely collaboratively design a process for resolving them. And, of course, reform initiatives emphasizing participation usually do accompany major programmatic changes that are themselves challenging or controversial (authentic assessment, say, or heterogeneous grouping) and thus divide faculty. This creates two simultaneous tasks that require highly sophisticated skills to master: changing program and changing process. Either alone is a large undertaking; together they are enormous. False steps, frustration, and conflict are inevitable.

Quite apart from governance, trying to build collaborative structures and opportunities makes its own addition to the complexity of school life. Team teaching can be a bad fit for many educators—especially those who run highly interactive classes—not just because of its extra time demands but because it requires modifications to each partner's idiosyncratic craft (Huberman, 1993, p. 18). At a different level, successful collaboration can exacerbate staff turnover problems. Interdisciplinary teaming can be an excellent way to enrich teachers' professional stimulation and classroom practice, but it makes turnover more upsetting. In a traditional, unteamed school, the loss of a teacher may have little impact on the daily experience of colleagues. But when a member of a closeknit unit leaves, it disrupts colleagues' daily work with one another and their teaching and can provoke real anger and grief, which then cloud the entry of the teacher who fills the vacancy. The closer the team's ties, the less welcome the newcomer and the longer it takes her to learn the ropes, earn acceptance, and become a contributor.

Group dynamics are always at play in any school, but efforts at empowerment make people more aware of them, sometimes to the point of "processitis" (my term for a preoccupation with procedure and interaction that affects many self-governing groups). It occurs when process concerns dominate a faculty's attention so much that they impede rather than improve performance outcomes. Processitis can be a defense mechanism, a displacement, as when a staff that is deadlocked or scattered over a substantive issue ("Shall we detrack our school?") retreats into procedural considerations—the fairness of the decision process, the representativeness of a committee, and so on. It can also stem from simple incompetence, such as when a group lacks the conceptual strength to make rules for making rules. It gets lost in abstractions or it can't function at a sufficiently abstract level, and it never agrees how to conduct its business.

A third cause is, ironically, positive. Learning about and talking candidly with one another about group dynamics and interpersonal interactions can be very exciting and involving. It opens whole new vistas for some teachers, inviting them to rethink the functioning of their school and reexamine their personal relationships, creating new connections and intimacy infused with the excitement of discovery. Whatever the cause, when procedural issues repeatedly sidetrack programmatic issues, dysfunction and demoralization loom. Here is a near-worst-case scenario:

> Smithson Middle School was to embark upon shared governance in a first year of restructuring and use this process to overhaul its course offerings and tracking system. The faculty decided that for decision making to be truly democratic, the chairing of meetings should rotate among all teachers. This proved disastrous, for their leadership skills varied widely and the program changes sparked fierce disputes of a kind beyond their experience and capacity to manage. Some teachers were too timid to maintain basic order during heated discussions, while others used the chair as a pulpit. After much controversy, the faculty agreed to have a single moderator, but they could not decide whether to vote on candidates or seek a consensus choice. They eventually elected the school psychologist, who was fascinated by the group's dynamics. She injected into their discussions many personal "interpretations" about individuals'

power needs and gender biases, which derailed whole discussions, inflamed some teachers, and ultimately led to a "meltdown session," with some faculty refusing to attend any more meetings. It took until April to agree on a new moderator and a few basic ground rules for debates and decisions. The faculty finally returned to the curriculum and grouping issues, but since the school year was nearly over there was not enough time to design and implement any changes. These had to be tabled for consideration the following year.

This kind of processitis also illustrates another complication of shared governance: how much leeway can be allowed for dysfunction and bad decisions when a group is developing its decision-making capacity? In Smithson's case, the development of new, challenging courses was the cornerstone of the district's response to a public outcry over declining test scores. Privately, the principal fumed that the teachers were "fiddling while Rome is burning; our community wants to see us taking action for students." But she was reluctant to seem "disempowering or manipulative" by overriding their fledgling efforts.

In addition to improving decisions and increasing faculty engagement, empowerment supposedly produces similar benefits in classrooms. A faculty that makes its voice heard will, in theory, begin to encourage the voices of students. They will make classes more active and students more assertive, encouraging them to be more responsible for their own learning. Unfortunately, this appears to be a fallacy. Studies suggest that most schools that have new politics still have old pedagogy, that engaging teachers in governance leads them to concentrate on governance but not necessarily change their classrooms.[3] Whatever its merits, participation simply doesn't concentrate in any direct way on instruction. In fact, it is such novel, complex, draining, time-consuming work that it can interfere with teachers' ability even to be in their classrooms, let alone to plan and implement new curricula and new ways of teaching. And as we saw in Chapter Five, the basic assumptions about instruction held by teachers and administrators are deeply ingrained and remarkably persistent. They are rooted in the deepest bedrock of schooling, its most unconscious, taken-for-granted level, one that shared decision making in and of itself simply doesn't reach.

All of this makes the rush to site-based management—especially the rush by states to mandate it—seem another misapplied quick-fix fad. True SBM is an indigenous, grassroots phenomenon; an institution's members design their own model for governance or, *on their own,* adopt someone else's model. What some states now have instead is the oxymoron of centrally mandated grassroots involvement: a compulsory, procedure-ridden template for SBM that, paradoxically, orders schools to be autonomous according to prescribed procedures.[4] This contradiction is further compounded when SBM is grafted onto an otherwise heavily structured state reform scheme that dictates curriculum, methods, assessment, grouping, length of school year, professional development, and evaluation. It delegates to the schools, as Sizer notes, "everything except the very heart of the matter"; the state retains control over the school's "intellectual agenda" (1995, p. 79). Real decentralization would hold schools accountable for results but not dictate their methods. So long as external authorities still compel detailed procedural compliance, we have only decorative (and disingenuous) decentralization—the old top-down fist in a new bottom-up glove.

Similarly, the keen interest in collaborative culture, though appealing, overlooks a fundamental advantage of teachers' isolation: autonomy. It turns out that, contrary to much educational rhetoric, collaboration and autonomy cannot be reduced to a simple good-versus-bad dichotomy (Fullan, 1991, p. 136). Separateness has its costs, but it offers the benefits of freedom, benefits so rewarding that they have created an "ecosystem" among teachers that is exceptionally "complex, coherent, and resilient" with an "awesome capacity to wait out and wear out reformers" (Huberman, 1993, p. 44). A truly collaborative culture cannot be implemented simply by structuring interactive opportunities and work arrangements. These may help such a culture ultimately develop, though often they lead to contrived collegiality in which teachers are put through collaborative paces that have little impact and wither away. But they work, at best, very slowly, and only as part of a larger sustained context that nurtures higher levels of mutual support and permits people to develop truly meaningful relationships rather than artificial connections—and only under a strong leader.

Binary Leadership

As hard as it is to foster participation and collegiality, it does happen. There are schools where governance is genuinely shared and faculty are meaningfully engaged in substantive collaboration. These schools differ in many respects, but the ones I visit all have a similar feel about them, an unusual combination of easiness and intensity that is almost palpable when you enter. Their style is informal, but their staff and students are highly involved in their work. Classrooms and hallways seem to buzz with activity—but purposeful, not frantic activity. At meetings, there tends to be more humor and candor and less "administrivia" than in other schools. The overall tone is upbeat. And there is always a powerful principal, someone with passion and presence (that is, someone with conviction and confidence, not necessarily flamboyance), someone who seems competent enough to make *any* system of governance work. In most cases, this principal was one of the cocreators of the school's shared-decision-making and collaborative efforts. Some are more charismatic than others, some are better organized, some hold more firmly a "first among equals" status. But I have never known, and cannot imagine, a school in which empowerment and participation flourish over time without a strong principal.

There is really no surprise here—except perhaps that some school reform advocates should have defined participatory leadership in such a narrow way: top-down is bad, bottom-up is good. Most leadership experts agree that this dichotomy is, if not false, exaggerated. Both kinds of leadership are essential. Participation and collaboration bring definite benefits, both as ends in themselves and as a means of improving performance. But so, too, does the exercise of executive initiative. That those who are to implement change should be involved in its design does not mean that innovation must start at the bottom. Rather, true participatory leadership is "binary" (Thomson, 1991, p. 26); it enables ideas to move both up and down the organization.

Authentic leaders believe in this kind of leadership. That is, they believe in participation but not processitis; in collaboration but not forced, false collegiality. They expect to play a primary role in shaping change, and they see empowerment as a later outcome, not a starting condition. As participation grows, they are flexible but clear about decision making. They seek an optimal, not a maximal, level of involvement, often relying more on informal methods than formal procedures and structures. They know that change often requires power and pressure; that it means responsibility, not license; and that it needs a framework that they must provide.

There are many reasons authentic leaders nurture and assert their influence. At an immediate, personal level, they enjoy doing so. In the same way that good teachers like to teach, good leaders like to lead—not to control people so much as to make things happen. Authentic leadership is "follow me" leadership in its best sense; one can't attract followers if one doesn't enjoy leading. Indeed, one of the few rewards that make all administrators' management headaches worthwhile is what one superintendent calls "the charge" he gets out of leading. "I complain about my burdens like everyone else," he says, "but I love solving problems, and I especially love being able to help other people solve problems."

Authentic leaders don't simply have a generic enjoyment of problem solving, they have specific problems they want to solve. They preserve their positional power in part because they have philosophical commitments they will not abandon. Though their vision of schooling frequently includes an emphasis on empowerment and collaboration, it usually concentrates first on programs (instruction, curriculum) and on results for students. What matters most for students is that faculty are focused on the same goals, take collective responsibility for achieving these, and coordinate their instructional efforts (Newmann and Wehlage, 1995, p. 30). Though shared governance seems an ideal vehicle for achieving these conditions, it is not the only one that can do so. (In many parochial schools, for example, leadership is hierarchical yet teachers are devoted, are treated respectfully, and pursue a common purpose—and the students do well.) Good leaders stay focused on substantive outcomes and are prepared to use their influence to achieve them.

Just as leaders need and like to lead, organizations need and like to be led—not bossed, led. There is a whole range of essential functions—practical, managerial, ceremonial, and cultural—that require a chief. In this sense, leadership is a role, not a person. Every school, even the most egalitarian, needs a "head," someone to focus it, tend it, represent it, speak for it—someone to do for the school some of what a teacher does for a class. Communicating vision, monitoring outcomes, resolving conflicts—much research confirms that it takes a leader to do these things (Thomson, p. 26). Most of us have at some time been part of an organization with weak or incompetent leadership that fails to fulfill these tasks and have seen how it drains energy, creates distractions, permits dysfunctions, damages pride, and inhibits performance. Without a sufficient level of authenticity—integrity and savvy—at the top, the issue of empowering staff is irrelevant. So is innovation.

Authentic leaders know that change depends quintessentially on them. Though ideas must be able to flow throughout an organization, major change almost never wells up from the bottom. It begins near the top (and if not, it almost never takes hold without strong backing from the top). And just as it doesn't well up from below, so it doesn't begin with broad involvement and consensus. It typically starts with a key leader and a small core of people who care strongly about a particular solution to a problem. It spreads from there, but not smoothly or rapidly. For the reasons I have outlined earlier in this chapter and throughout this book, the development of widespread teacher ownership of change is usually very slow. Participation and empowerment begin after—not before—the change process starts. In the early stages of change they can be counterproductive, especially if they involve "elaborate needs assessments, endless committee and task force debates" that devour energy and time but produce confusion and alienation. In this view, participation develops during implementation as part of "a very long process of mobilization and meaning" (Fullan, pp. 62–63).

As this process unfolds, the need for pressure and support requires the assertion of executive influence. Since change requires unfreezing and disconfirmation, the challenging of deep assumptions and the raising of appropriate guilt and anxiety, it demands someone with the power to get and keep people's attention. If major innovation is merely offered as a suggestion or left as a voluntary initiative, it generally fails. The implementation of districtwide innovations, for example, tends to be more successful when the superintendent's authority, not teachers' autonomy, is the prominent moving force (Fullan, pp. 74–75). And, as we have seen, it is insufficient simply to wait for changes in belief to produce changes in behavior; one must often insist on some of the latter as a way to foster some of the former. (I treasure a relevant anecdote: implementing a controversial new policy, a corporate executive was asked by a disgruntled staff member, "Do you think you own our souls?" "No," he replied, "but we do rent your behavior."[5])

Nor is it just at the outset that pressure and support are needed. Hesitation and resistance are not one-time issues that, once addressed, vanish. They are likely to recur whenever change ratchets up another notch. They may be less intense and more brief, but they return. Staff who had a difficult time with the earlier improvements anticipate renewed trouble; newcomers who didn't live through the early changes don't know what to expect and have all the anxiety of novices. At such moments there is no substitute for an authentic leader's assertiveness and encouragement. As a gifted, experienced high school principal noted, even though he had a strong core of teachers who had been actively engaged in school change work for years, he still needed to give an extra push now and then, especially when enlarging the innovation: "Sometimes people hesitate and worry: can we go the next step? Can we really try a major change in our system of assessment or our graduation requirements or our schedule? A principal needs to say, 'Yes, we can.' "). At other times, the leader needs to slow things down. In Chicago I met principals committed to the city's decentralizing reforms who had discovered that many teachers, unused to any role in governance, became anxious, doubtful, even paralyzed when given a voice in scheduling, curriculum, and teaming. Only when principals slowed the pace of change, framed choices more extensively, and provided greater guidance did some teachers began to respond more confidently and effectively.

For these and other reasons, authentic leaders develop and maintain their capacity to apply top-down influence, but they do so sparingly. They steadily try to reduce obstacles that limit their access and influence throughout the organization, and yet they use their power judiciously (Badaracco and Ellsworth, p. 135). The simplistic dichotomy must be modified to "bottom-up as possible, top-down as necessary."

Optimal Participation

None of this means that authentic leaders don't want to empower teachers or the larger school community to the greatest extent possible. They know that this is vital to strengthening a school. But while authenticity respects process, it is results-oriented, and effective leaders are biased toward participation without paralysis, not toward procedural perfection at the risk of programmatic entropy. Left to themselves, they seek an optimal, not a maximal level of participation. How much is optimal? It depends on the leader, the school and district, the staff and community, the resources, and the improvement agenda. The best administrators I know seek to involve people wherever they can, but as noted in Chapter Five, their primary goal during innovation is a critical mass of active, committed participants, not universal support. They accept the realities that some hard-core resisters will never change, that the purely democratic school community is an unattainable ideal, and that many classroom improvements do not need, and cannot wait for, full participatory consensus. They start where they find interest or opportunity and build from there, looking to invite and encourage and include as they go.

There are many ways to build optimal participation. I have seen six that are especially useful. The first is clarity about decision making. Some authentic leaders attend more overtly to governance issues than others, but all inevitably operate using a range of decision-making processes, with some matters involving high levels of participation and others very little. At one extreme the leader has full control, decides alone, and simply announces the decision. At the other extreme staff have wide latitude to decide things on their own. In between are options that move from more leader-centered to more participatory: the leader presents a tentative decision, subject to change based upon staff input; the leader offers a range of options and lets staff choose; the leader presents a problem and solicits suggestions, and so on (Tannenbaum and Schmidt, 1991, p. 27). Among the array of choices that must be made in schools, there are many that can be handled truly democratically and others that cannot. It is being able "to decide who needs to be involved and when" that distinguishes great participatory leaders (Schlechty, 1990, p. 102). What makes them effective—and avoids much processitis—is that they are consistently clear with staff about *who* is making *which* decisions and *how*. What they offer is not pure parity, but clarity.

Changes that alter governance or affect relationships between subgroups in a school especially need clarity. Schools like Smithson that move to site-based management must address an array of issues about how decisions will be made (rules for making rules), both in the ultimate SBM plan they devise *and* during the transition while they are devising the plan. As they were at Smithson, confusion and mistrust about governance are among the largest sources of distress and cynicism during innovation and a prime contributor to processitis. Here is an example of a school that made effective use of a formal decision-making continuum to overcome these issues:

The Greystone Elementary School had long been a successful, close-knit institution. Over several years, external factors (a rapid enrollment increase that caused severe overcrowding, a sharp rise in the number of "inclusion" students with severe special needs, and the adoption of an extensive districtwide restructuring plan) significantly raised stress levels within the faculty. Teachers felt growing uncertainty about the school's future, the district's priorities, and their own potential to affect decisions. The principal gathered them at a summer retreat, where they discussed these issues and their own priorities. One outcome was to list key problems and, creating a decision-making continuum, decide which kinds of decisions would be the principal's alone, which would be hers to make with their advice, which would be "fully democratic," and so on. They also agreed that in the future the principal would determine which kind of decision-making process would apply to issues but that staff had the right to question this in a faculty meeting.

I know only a handful of principals and superintendents who have made direct use of a schema like this, but all the authentic leaders I know communicate clearly with their constituents about which kind of decision is which and are willing to discuss seriously with them any request for a stronger voice.

A second path to effective participation without paralysis is through informal outreach rather than formal structure. Authentic leaders often dislike official committees and procedural purity— they tend not to form a lot of groups who are empowered to make formal recommendations. But they are more likely than most to observe a standing "open door" policy and to be actively available and respectfully attentive to teachers and other constituents:

> Joan Blackwell has led several schools through significant, highly successful reform initiatives. During these she has faced a number of meetings of parents over the years where controversy has arisen about school policies and reforms. She has always made it a practice not to create committees and task forces and not to extend public meetings past their scheduled times, thus reserving her right to consult with her faculty and to make decisions. But she makes absolutely certain that people are heard: "I restate key points people make at meetings to be sure I've got them right. If there are still hands waving at the end, I distribute cards and ask people to write their questions or concerns. They each get a call or note back from me that same week. I'm frank when I can't do what they're asking, but they know they've been heard respectfully."

Of course, Joan and other authentic leaders don't just wait for meetings or visitors; they make frequent outreach on their own. They initiate their own asking, listening, and acknowledging. Of Tom Russell, the principal of Jackson Elementary School (Chapter Nine), a teacher said, "He seeks you out, and when you talk to him he's all yours. You can see that he hears and he cares. That makes it easier to trust him when he has a new idea." Teachers are so starved for this kind of support (and for recognition, of which more is discussed in the next chapter) that it is astonishing, and sad—and vital to innovation—how grateful they are for the smallest acknowledgment.

A third way to optimize participation is to seek informal opportunities for staff to assume leadership roles. Any organization is stronger when it has a "density" of leadership rather than a single gifted chief (March, 1984, p. 29). And a good chief seeks to develop strong leadership wherever possible. This can be done during innovation by establishing a transition management team, of the kind recommended in Chapter Seven, to oversee the project, keep communication lines open, and troubleshoot problems. It can also be done on an ad hoc basis. As people come forward with problems, the leader and the team have repeated choices to solve the problems themselves or to delegate this to others. One superintendent has what she describes as "my four-question ritual."

When a staff member comes to her with a problem, she always asks four things: " 'What's your core concern? What do you want for an outcome? What have you tried so far? What do you think you're going to do?' Only then do I ask if there is some way I can help." This leader has learned to use problems as opportunities to empower staff. She is aware that this could keep people from coming to her for fear of being assigned more than they can do, and she guards against this. "I delegate freely wherever I can, but I don't force people, and I don't just dump work on them. We discuss the resources and backing they'll need, and I make sure I provide them."

A fourth way to foster participation and collaboration is to be flexible about the implementation of improvement plans. Leaders must be willing to adapt their original design as more people invest themselves in it and as unexpected conditions and developments challenge it. All participants need to make change their own, to find their own meaning in it, if they are to adapt. This requires reformers to do much listening as well as explaining and to keep negotiating and modifying their plans long past the point where they would like to be finished (Marris, p. 156). (As we have seen, intensely committed advocates who refuse to amend their designs inspire resistance, not followership.) Being flexible does not mean abandoning key commitments, but it can mean altering the order of key priorities, and it definitely means being willing to modify time lines.

A fifth and particularly powerful way that authentic leaders enrich meaningful participation is by facing up to the inevitable conflict change causes. It is not just that friction and disagreement are inevitable during change but that they create opportunities for growth and community building. A crucial part of fostering followership is to address major sources of conflict and work them through so that they no longer inhibit innovation. Few school administrators, perhaps, think of conflict as a way to improve the implementation of change, let alone enhance participation and improve collegial relationships, but it is. The impulse of rejection is an essential part of adaptation. We must work and rework our way through this impulse in order to come to terms with loss and begin to accept change. Much of the resistance and friction during innovation is ultimately in the service of adjusting to new realities. The implementation process, therefore, must permit this impulse to express itself, and leaders must anticipate and even at times encourage it (Marris, p. 155):

> Due to rising enrollment, dilapidated buildings, and budget cuts, a regional school district decided to merge its two junior high schools and its senior high school into a single new facility. Parents and teachers at all the schools were deeply distressed. A joint committee, formed to plan a smooth transition, fell to arguing in its first meeting about what the new school should be named. Superintendent Ben Smiley debated whether to cut off this arguing, but he decided the anger needed to be flushed out. At the second meeting, he asked them each to say what they found most difficult about the merger. This yielded much complaint about insensitivity by the administration and school board. He then acknowledged what a loss the merger was for everyone and asked what they most feared about it, which put people in touch with their emotional connections to the existing schools. By the third meeting, the storm of anger and sadness had begun to wane, and Ben engaged the group in thinking about how to preserve the best of each school. The group returned to the name issue, but ultimately agreed on a "hyphenated mouthful" that kept some part of each school's original name. They then went on to plan a successful merger.

To many leaders, Ben's approach is counterintuitive and dangerous. They fear that permitting people to complain or argue risks spreading a kind of negativistic infection. But, as Ben knew, if leaders try to suppress conflict, it goes underground, where it toughens, lasts longer, and does more damage to innovation.

Ben Smiley, Joan Blackwell, and Tom Russell, like other authentic leaders, don't oversell their changes. They advocate, but they listen, and they show their strength by being able to tolerate resistance and friction. Watching and learning from them and others like them, I have come to believe strongly in the value of a sixth vehicle for empowerment, collaboration, and for the overall management of innovation. I recommend that leaders in any organization that is innovating devote periodic staff meetings to taking the pulse of change. "How are we doing?" is the question. Regular business is suspended, and the meeting is given over to a checkup on progress and to looking ahead. To be successful, these meetings must observe four rules:

1. They must be scheduled into the calendar in advance (there is rarely time to arrange them once the year has begun).
2. There must be no penalty for sincere problem finding—no one should risk censure or retribution for voicing a genuine concern.
3. The leader must not be obligated to take action on a concern, only to understand it.
4. The meeting should review successes as well as problems.

These sessions can test a leader's strength of character, because they invite bad news, especially when the change is large and demanding. In fact, many principals and superintendents can't imagine subjecting themselves to the risk, fearing that they will open a Pandora's box of complaints that, openly expressed, will inflame resistance and undo innovation. When they hesitate, I ask them to think specifically about what they fear. If their worst-case scenario might actually come to pass—if, say, the faculty hates the change or the leader so much that the meeting might overflow with anger and opposition—then the change is already in terrible trouble and most unlikely to succeed. Squelching such opposition only drives it underground and delays the chance to resolve it. Having the meeting might not save the project, but avoiding it surely will not.

In most cases, especially when there are some significant staff concerns, these meetings offer a wonderful opportunity for the leader to gather feedback and empower people, reduce resistance and reinforce collegiality, and build momentum for change. Exploring people's concerns permits them to ventilate feelings and fears and clarify misperceptions that can otherwise disable innovation. Some issues will be legitimate; responding to them will improve implementation and enhance people's sense of efficacy, that they can affect the change. Some will be repetitious grief (they may sound to the leader more like whining); but surfacing them makes it easier for people to feel considered and appreciated and, as Joan Blackwell rightly observes, harder for them to resist and sabotage. And in every meeting, time is set aside to ask about what is going well, to celebrate successes (large or small), to raise the level of recognition (our subject in the next chapter). Doing all of this publicly as an entire group, where everyone can hear and be heard, not only emphasizes the participatory nature of the change, it is an example of collegiality in action, modeled by the leader.

A Baby, Not a Delivery

When my wife and I were expecting our first child, we attended a childbirth course in which one of the mothers-to-be was preoccupied with having an absolutely pure, natural delivery. No surgery, no medication. At each class she would pepper the nurse in charge with questions about the risks of various procedures and anesthetics. After several weeks of this, the nurse finally said, gently but firmly, "Look, we're not having a delivery, we're having a baby. If you need some help to have a healthy baby, you need some help." This is the authentic participation message. The goal is a healthy school improvement outcome, not a picture-perfect process. A good process usually produces a good outcome, and ignoring process can surely damage the outcome—but so, too, does getting lost in process.

A key point in this regard is that empowerment's true target is not teachers or any other constituency, but the school. Empowerment does not mean license; it refers to obligation and duty and accountability. It does not free people to do whatever they please, but to make sensible decisions that embody the school's values (Sergiovanni, 1991, p. 137). Empowerment, participation—these concepts make sense only within a framework of shared meaning and commitment that both contains members of the school community and permits them to grow. Ideally the maintenance and modification of this framework comes to be a broadly shared task, but if this happens at all, it is only as an ultimate result. It is a late outcome, not an early condition. To achieve it requires an authentic leader to take the primary role in both shaping the framework and nurturing the capacity of others to help shape it.

Notes

1. This trend in the leadership literature treats power "as a problem to be solved rather than as a natural and basic phenomenon in organizations" and essentially seeks to translate it into "optimistic and domesticated forms such as 'empowerment' . . . or 'power in the service of

others'" (Bolman and Deal, pp. 178–179). In education, Sergiovanni (1992, 1993) and Barth (1990) are eloquent advocates of servant leadership and communitarian goals.

2. Goals are often determined by which materials are available, not the other way around, and "outcomes become goals as often as goals determine outcomes" (Sergiovanni, 1991, p. 48).

3. See Taylor and Teddlie (1992) and Weiss (1992).

4. Typically, each school must form a council, adhering to rules about representative membership, leadership, frequency of meetings, and so on. The council must then generate an annual school improvement plan covering specified topic areas.

5. I have heard this attributed to several different leaders but cannot find the original source.

Chapter Twelve

Recognition: Reversing the Golden Rule

To create and sustain for children the conditions for productive growth without those conditions existing for educators is virtually impossible.
—SEYMOUR SARASON (1990, P. 147)

Most of the measures that would markedly improve America's schools, such as a reduction in teacher-pupil ratios to permit classes of teachable size throughout the nation, are expensive. One is not. The single best low-cost, high-leverage way to improve performance, morale, and the climate for change is to dramatically increase the levels of meaningful recognition for—and among—educators. As I use it here, *recognition* refers to praise or positive feedback, but also to validation, to acknowledging and affirming a truth about a person or a situation. Fortunately, the bias of authentic leaders is toward meritocratic recognition—not toward bland feel-goodism or easy, empty praise but toward measures that confirm effort and achievement in ways that have real meaning for members of the school community and that make their experience of membership more rewarding.

Deprivation and the Double Standard

Recognition is widely seen by scholars and practitioners in many fields as being essential to job satisfaction, motivation, and performance. It undergirds the experience of success and confirms the adequacy of performance. It "reinforces learning, encourages continued effort, and produces positive feelings, self-esteem, and self-confidence" (Eden, p. 171), as well as enhancing communication and trust and raising one's expectations for one's future performance. Vital to sustaining ordinary, baseline competence, it becomes even more important when seeking extraordinary performance and during any kind of innovation. Both of these always mean doing more, never less—especially at first—and they threaten competence, patterns of relating, even the meaning of work itself. The more profound and far-reaching an innovation and the more pressure, anxiety, and uncertainty it involves, the greater the need for recognition. When demand rises, support must rise proportionately or else stress will. Without feedback confirming that what they are doing is important and telling them how adequately they are doing it, people have great difficulty developing a sense of efficacy, of genuine accomplishment, of making a meaningful difference. This is true even in corporate and industrial settings that offer workers concrete measures of success such as sales figures and production totals. It is especially true in those, like education, that don't.

All of this is so widely acknowledged that it should hardly bear repeating—especially with regard to education, where there is so much focus on student self-esteem. Decades of developmental research on the link between students' estimates of self-worth and efficacy and their academic performance have helped replace "spare the rod and spoil the child" with an emphasis on encouragement, praise, and positive reinforcement. But most schools live by a flagrant double standard: their preoccupation with self-esteem extends only to students. They shower recognition on pupils but deny it to adults. A teacher who chronically refused to acknowledge student effort and performance would deserve dismissal, not just for being unfair but also for damaging students' confidence and well-being and with it their motivation, perseverance, and performance. Yet this is precisely the condition most teachers in most schools endure (and inflict on one another). Even as they distribute praise and acknowledgment liberally to their charges, they themselves do without.

Few aspects of American education are more pathetic than the thin ribbon of recognition that flows—trickles—toward and among educators. Each year at large educational conferences, I ask audiences how many of them come from a school or district where there is any kind of formal recognition—even something as nominal as a pin for twenty-five years of service or a Teacher of the Year award. It is rare that one-third of those attending raise their hands. The examples of recognition reported by this minority generally vary between meager and pitiful, the most common being retirement ceremonies (often a tea held late in the afternoon—at nap time—and sparsely attended); PTA-sponsored appreciation events (typically a breakfast or lunch), which, if not exactly a form of charity, are no substitute for true professional recognition; and Teacher of the Month and Teacher of the Year awards, which generally inspire indifference and dislike due to their apparent arbitrariness and the necessity of beating out one's colleagues to win. When I ask about informal recognition, people mention notes from administrators, comments from parents, visits by former students who return years later to say thanks, and the like. These can be quite meaningful and very moving to teachers, but their chief characteristic is their rarity.

These audiences are not a scientific sample, but their accounts are quite uniform and confirm my daily experience of twenty-five years. During this time I have had the chance to make one-day visits and presentations to hundreds of schools and also to consult regularly over many years in several dozen, meeting with staff and administrators on a weekly or monthly basis about a wide variety of issues. Both kinds of work have taught me to assume that any educator I meet has gone at least a week and most likely a month without receiving—or giving to a colleague—a genuine professional compliment (that is, a piece of specific performance-related feedback based on personal knowledge and conveying informed appreciation of effort or results).

The sources of this deprivation are multiple, as we have already seen in chapters Six and Seven. Some are external (rising demands for achievement in the face of diminishing student readiness, a precipitous drop in status and in public appreciation and respect for educators); some are historical (education's roots as a calling marked by sacrifice, its history as mostly women's work); some are inherent in the nature of teaching (its complexity, uncertainty, motivational drain, and isolation); and some are developmental (midlife and midcareer concerns, focusing down, taking one another for granted). Together they spell starvation, leaving teachers grateful for the tiniest scraps of validation, even inadvertent:

> When Kathy Constanza became a special education administrator, she was appalled at the practices her predecessor had tolerated. She launched an aggressive set of reforms, terminating three programs, reducing and reassigning staff, and rewriting job descriptions. All of this caused great stress. Eventually she was ready to challenge staff about their poor drafting of students' educational plans. She introduced her new requirements by saying, "I know all this has been hard on you, but I have one more task." The next day, June Wilson, a staff member, sought Kathy out to thank her, saying, "That was so nice when you said you know it's been hard on us. It felt good to have you acknowledge it." Four others, on their own, followed suit.
>
> At a later department meeting I attended, Kathy reported her surprise at these reactions. She hadn't realized how scarce recognition must have been for an off-hand comment to draw so much response. June, a big, blunt woman, fixed her with a wry smile. "Look at it this way," she said. "We're incredibly hard up."

Hard up, indeed. Across America, we are turning to educators who feel chronically overpressured and underthanked and are asking them to change, to do more and to do it differently and better—quickly.

Kinds of Recognition

Given that levels of recognition must be raised, what is the best way to do this? As we have just seen, recognition can be formal or informal, public or private. It can be directed toward individuals or groups. The key questions about recognition in any school are whether it emphasizes intrinsic or extrinsic rewards and whether it flows in one direction only (top-down) or laterally, as well. There is a strong consensus among leadership experts about the value of intrinsic rewards and the liabilities of extrinsic rewards in motivating exceptional performance. Perhaps the best-known research in this area comes from Frederick Herzberg (1987). His famous theory of job satisfaction distinguishes between two types of factors, hygienic and motivators. The former are aspects extrinsic to the job, such as policy and administration, supervision, working conditions, salary, and relationships with peers, among others. If an organization handles these badly, people will be dissatisfied and perform badly. Attending to them is essential and will reduce dissatisfaction, but it will not generate satisfaction or stimulate personal investment in work; it won't inspire commitment to an organization's basic purpose or encourage extra effort or exceptional performance. A teacher who hates teaching may reduce his absenteeism if good attendance is tied to higher pay, but he will not love teaching more or involve himself more fervently in school improvement. Therefore, relying heavily on extrinsic rewards limits a school's ability to excel (Kouzes and Posner, p. 45).

To raise the ceiling rather than just reinforce the floor, one must attend to the motivators. These are characteristics intrinsic to the job, such as achievement, recognition, the work itself, responsibility, and advancement (Herzberg, pp. 112–113). In education, studies have confirmed that intrinsic rewards such as having exciting work, seeing students achieve, and fulfilling competently a task one views as important are consistently more powerful engines of performance than salary (Mitchell and Peters, 1988, p. 75). Acknowledging and thanking people for fulfilling intrinsic goals and ennobling purposes helps to reinforce the school's basic values and vision. It is here that real potential for improvement lies.

In schools, of course, neither extrinsic nor intrinsic rewards are adequate. Much thought has been given to correcting these through major structural improvements. Hygiene factors are so poor—so many dissatisfying conditions are so solidly entrenched—that there is a tremendous amount of catching up to do. There are those who continue to insist that the best way to motivate better performance and acceptance of change is through extrinsic incentives, such as merit pay, though the evidence is strongly against them.[1] Others have sought to improve intrinsic rewards, basing their proposals on corporate experiments with job enrichment. These call for, among other measures, offering workers greater autonomy over the design of their work (while still holding them accountable for results), maximizing the variety of skills a job entails, and assigning people whole tasks rather than robotic partial functions. The aim is to increase their sense of efficacy and hence their job satisfaction and motivation. In schools these proposals have generally focused on creating growth opportunities through participatory governance, collegial interaction, and differentiated staffing plans ("career ladders"). These offer teachers professional development without requiring them to become administrators. They can move to different ranks (Level I Teacher, Level II Teacher) by participating in special training and by assuming roles as mentor, team leader, trainer, study group facilitator, and the like. Though potentially more promising than merit pay plans, these, too, have had little impact.[2]

Structural changes like career ladders might conceivably play a role in an ultimate redesign of the entire teaching profession or a longer-term strategy for attracting to the field the most capable college graduates, but they would require shifts in national priorities and funding that seem most unlikely, and they offer little help for the present and the intermediate future. And they are beyond the reach of school leaders. Principals and superintendents need practical, economical ways to enhance recognition right now. From one perspective their task is easy. Though it is sad that teachers' work lives should leave them pathetically grateful for fragments of praise and validation, it creates an opportunity and points a very direct path for leaders: almost any kind of recognition will represent an improvement. Even small doses can go a long way toward raising teacher morale, performance, and investment in innovation.

Top-Down Recognition

A consistent leitmotiv in the leadership literature is the observation that leaders in all sorts of organizations know too little about recognition and minimize its importance. Many leaders find providing recognition soft and fuzzy rather than businesslike, more appropriate for children than adults. They act according to the old maxim that a job well done is its own reward. In schools, where management tends to be less hard-nosed, few administrators would profess such a belief. But there are still many whose use of positive feedback and acknowledgment is, at best, minimal and perfunctory. Authentic leaders, because they are such meritocrats, tend to avoid this failing. They maximize recognition, reinforcing effort and results wherever they can and reframing events to accentuate the positive. And they do so sincerely (or, where this is impossible, they acknowledge the reality of people's struggles and concerns).

The core principle of recognition is to apply it wherever possible. Authentic leaders tend to be natural (as opposed to calculated) reinforcers and validaters. They tend to be, as we have seen, enthusiastic, both about their goals and about the potential of people to fulfill them. Thus, though they are not always flamboyant, they do lots of modeling and encouraging, noticing and asking, approving and supporting. They are on the lookout for evidence of progress and improvement and are enthused when they see it—even in small increments. Far too much innovation is handled on an all-or-nothing basis, especially by administrators and school board members who favor what they see as a no-nonsense emphasis on accountability. These taskmasters want people to undertake the change and achieve it before they offer recognition. Especially with complex reforms, this is self-defeating. It misunderstands not only human nature but also the nature of new learning, which requires that people do *more* and *different* first and then start to do *better:*

> Responding to a rapid rise in the number of non-English-speaking students, principal Karl Mikkelson wanted to develop a special schoolwide emphasis on English literacy. Because the teachers' contract severely limited the number of meetings that could be held, he had to start by cajoling people to come to voluntary sessions. He sent personal notes to everyone who did. He stopped by their rooms later and asked them what they thought. If he overheard two people talking about a meeting or the literacy issue, he followed up with them. When he eventually got a pilot project going and needed volunteers from the faculty to try out new emphases on reading across the curriculum, he repeated the notes and follow-up. "I needed folks to give me some time and attention and then maybe take a stab at something new," he says. "This meant more work for them, and I acknowledged everybody who did *anything.*"

Change begins with getting people to try something new or to try the same thing harder. Smart leaders start by rewarding interest, curiosity, and exploration. They especially reward any kind of experimentation with new practices. Throughout the early stages of change, when uncertainty is highest, they provide steady confirmation of teachers' effort as well as their success, however modest.

Only thereafter do they move toward expecting real improvement in results (Mitchell and Peters, p. 75). Even then, it is often wise to employ "a strategy of small wins," in which the leader defines a major innovation in terms of a series of smaller stages and builds momentum "by encouraging participants to savor the joys of successive small accomplishments that signal milestones along the way toward achieving more ambitious goals" (Eden, pp. 186–187).

The key focus of this approach is to not penalize those who try but fail. The "excellence" literature is replete with examples of how America's top corporations reward their people for trying innovations and avoid punishing them if they come up short. In fact, they usually provide all sorts of inducements to encourage people to propose and try new initiatives, and they accept the inevitable error rate that comes with experimentation. If we truly want schools to become learning organizations, the immediate prerequisite is to achieve "an openness and reflectivity that accepts error and uncertainty as an inevitable feature of life in complex and changing environments." Leaders must see legitimate error as "a potential lesson rather than an occasion to allocate blame," part of the cost of research and development. Similarly, they must accept negative events and unexpected setbacks not just as inevitable but also as useful learning opportunities (Morgan, 1986, p. 91). Motorola sums up this orientation with a wonderful motto: "We celebrate noble failure" (Hammer and Champy, p. 106).

Identifying certain kinds of failure as noble is an example of an excellent recognition vehicle, reframing, which involves redefining a concept, behavior, event, or relationship by situating it in a different context, approaching it from a different angle (Watzlawick, Weakland, and Fisch, p. 98). A leader who regularly scolds her staff may do so because she dislikes or disapproves of them or because she loves them and wants desperately for them to do well. We often take literally so much of what other people say and do and become so locked into rigid frames of perceiving and understanding—remember the notion of culture as prison—that it is hard for us to see different dimensions, functions, and meanings in behavior. Reframing aims to help people break out of such a pattern, to give them a new perspective.[3] Here is a colorful instance:

During one of the many nineteenth-century riots in Paris, the commander of an army detachment received orders to clear a city square by firing at the *canaille* (rabble). He commanded his soldiers to take up firing positions, their rifles leveled at the crowd, and as a ghastly silence descended he drew his sword and shouted at the top of his lungs: "Mesdames, M'sieurs, I have orders to fire at the *canaille*. But I see a great number of honest respectable citizens before me. I request that they leave so that I can safely shoot the *canaille.*" The square was empty in a few minutes [p. 81].

Sometimes reframing is as simple as helping people see that a glass is half full rather than half empty. Sometimes it involves a more fundamental reappraisal of events. The point is not to insist that people stop seeing events in their old way but to offer a new way to make sense of events, broadening the context for understanding. This is especially important when setbacks occur during innovation. At these critical moments, when interim assessments of progress are made, leaders play a crucial role in shaping staff reactions (Eden, p. 186). Time and again I have seen groups benefit from being helped to see how a particular obstacle is inevitable or expectable in their situation rather than resulting from a failure of their judgment, skill, or will.

None of this implies that a leader's recognition should be false or forced. A strategic bias toward recognition means that positive feedback must be earned. That it can be earned by good effort, not just a good result, makes the task easier. But accentuating the positive, being on the lookout for small bits of progress, and reframing do not mean lying or laying on empty accolades. To do so simply saps a leader's credibility and weakens the impact of his genuine praise. Reframing can be a powerful way to support self-esteem, but only when it is truly meant and comes from an authentic leader. Within certain limits, a leader's saying something is so will make it so—provided that the leader has earned people's trust and confidence. But reframing has real limits. One cannot simply redefine any negative result, no matter how awful. Searching too hard for a thin silver lining in a thick dark cloud contradicts the core of authenticity: savvy and integrity. It makes one seem out of touch—or worse, insincere. And as we have seen, insincerity is hard to hide; a habit of it is fatal to trust.

One excellent way to ensure sincerity is specificity. Nothing is more genuine and meaningful than specific praise. Feelings are always attached to particular actions and words. Abstractions can be powerful, but they are always at their most intense when expressed in specific ways:

> Harvey Abel, one of the most effective superintendents I've met, is a slow, scholarly, somewhat shy man who is revered by his administrators and teachers because of his brilliance and his sincerity. He has what he calls a "weakness for the specific." He remembers small details about staff members' personal interests and recommends books he has encountered that they might like. He sends teachers notes praising the way they phrased particular questions in classes he observed. He sends memos to the administrative cabinet reflecting on a thoughtful question one of them raised at a meeting. As one of his principals says, "It's amazing how seriously he takes what you say and do. When Harvey thanks you, you always know why, and you know that he *knows* you."

In human interchange, God is definitely in the details.

Another way good leaders show sincerity is to align rewards with purposes. For example, authentic leaders tend to link advancement and special project roles to the pursuit and fulfillment of key school goals. Rather than awarding department chairmanships, team leader positions, mentor roles, and the like on arbitrary or "nonpurposeful" bases (seniority, politics), they are likely to offer promotions for demonstrated performance and commitment (Schlechty, 1989, p. 365). In a similar way, leaders who are committed to building participation and collegiality think not just about increasing recognition but about doing so in new configurations. One of the disjunctions in educational improvement is that we preach the importance of collegial and collaborative work, but we continue to recognize people (to the extent that we do so at all) the same way we evaluate them, as individuals (Mitchell and Peters, p. 77). A leader truly focused on enhancing morale, collaboration, and collegiality directs recognition and performance appraisal to collegial groups or work units, whether these be departments, teams, or a whole faculty.

If praise is not to be false, what does a leader do about disappointments in innovation, negative outcomes, or difficult impasses that do not lend themselves to reframing? This question brings us to the last aspect of leader recognition: it is not just praise that matters but acknowledgment, as Kathy Constanza's example above illustrates. A leader who schedules the periodic pulse-taking, how-are-we-doing meetings I recommended in the last chapter will surely hear complaints (provided that people trust her enough to speak candidly). If she can resist the urge to take each one of these complaints personally as either her fault or her responsibility to fix, she can help people feel better and cope better simply by acknowledging and validating the sincerity of their concerns. In her second year, Kathy began having such meetings and summarizes the experience this way:

> I heard all kinds of complaints, from sincere anguish to tedious whining. I would ask the person to give me an example, tell me what he found especially hard. I'd ask if others had the same concern. When I could modify my plan to suit them, I did. When I couldn't, I told them honestly. I restated what they wished, said I was sorry, repeated briefly why I couldn't agree, thanked them for doing their best, and hoped things would work out. A lot of what I said boiled down to, "Yes, I see that this is hard for you, but it's the reality and we have to face it." This felt inadequate to me at first, but it was in fact true. To my surprise, it made a difference. After each of these meetings, morale improved.

Just going through the motions of acknowledgment is condescending, but truly confirming that one has heard the extent and intensity of people's concerns and takes them seriously, even when little or nothing can be done, goes a remarkably long way toward improving effort and cooperation.

The Curious Case of Faculty Resistance

I can already anticipate principals and superintendents thinking to themselves, "This is fine in theory but hopeless with a real faculty." Many administrators have already tried to enhance recognition levels and ran into immediate trouble, stymied by the singular phenomenon of teacher opposition. Among all professional groups, in both the for-profit and non-profit spheres, teachers are, in my experience, exceptional in their resistance to recognition. Here is the typical scenario, versions of which have been enacted in schools throughout the country:

> Principal John Doe decides to improve recognition. At a faculty meeting he begins by saying that he appreciates how hard and effectively everyone has been working and that he wants to acknowledge several examples. He cites several teachers by name. ("Sally, I got a lovely note from Mrs. Cohen saying how much extra help you've been giving her son; Art, you helped me break up that fight in the cafeteria; Susan, you put so much extra work into directing the play. Thank you all very much.") After the meeting, each of these teachers finds John to tell him, in essence, "Don't single me out again!" Others find him to say, "What about me? I did just as much as they did, but you didn't mention me!" If John keeps it up, the complaints increase. If there is a powerful, assertive union, it may soon file a grievance against him. Eventually he stops, and everyone lapses back into the state of overworked, underthanked victimization.

Readers who are not educators might find this scenario eccentric, even preposterous. School administrators know better.

This curious behavior is, I believe, unique to teachers. I have encountered no corporations and no other human service agencies where this kind of resistance to public recognition for performance is so intense. It may be another instance of people who feel significantly deprived banding together in their deprivation rather than see a few of their number singled out for reward. It may reflect mistrust between labor and management. (A history of feeling manipulated or mistreated by administrators and school boards will make teachers doubt the good intentions of any leader who seems to want to give them something.) Another source could be teaching's history as a religious vocation marked by modesty and sacrifice. And through it all there is the we're-all-the-same norm of egalitarianism, which, though it seems absurd to many, does fit the independent artisan model of teaching (as we saw in Chapter Eleven). Whatever its roots, this resistance to recognition needs to be resolved if innovation is to have a chance.

The best approach is to go right at it, to address it directly— opening up the problem, insisting that it be corrected, and seeking the faculty's help in doing so. Authentic leaders, who have the courage of their convictions, are ideally suited for this task. Their message is:

> We have a serious problem. We're living by a ferocious double standard. We shower recognition on our students and we starve ourselves. We know that if we stopped acknowledging students for working hard and doing well, their performance and self-esteem would suffer. It wouldn't be fair or right. Yet I see many of you doing hard work and getting good results, but when I try to acknowledge you, you object. And I don't see much evidence of your recognizing one another. We need to talk about this. I need to understand your objections, and then we need to find ways to improve our collective recognition of one another—ways that will be meaningful to us all, not phony.

The typical first response is, "Write us notes," to which the answer is:

> Yes, I'm glad to do that, but it's not enough. You don't just write notes to your students. We need ways to honor ourselves openly. I am not interested in competition, in singling out one person at the expense of another. I am interested in celebrating examples of us at our best. If the outside world were lavishing recognition on us, I wouldn't be taking this up with you. But it's not. We need to take better care of ourselves if we're to keep taking good care of students. How can we do that in a way that will be meaningful to us?

If there is a history of distrust, even one that stems from a long-gone predecessor, it may be important for the leader to hear about this, to let veterans who remember the story retell it—and then for the leader to reiterate the need for teachers to do for one another what they do for students. Here are a set of questions that superintendents and principals can present to staff for reflection and discussion:

- As a teacher, what do you do best and enjoy most? Who else here knows these things about you?
- When was the last time you got specific recognition for your professional work?
- When was the last time you gave specific recognition to a colleague? What keeps you from doing so?

- What would make life more fun for us and help us to stop taking one another for granted?

Permitting people to talk about these questions in pairs and small groups and then as a whole faculty is an excellent way to stimulate ideas and suggestions and to start changing the group's dynamics. There is no set of ideal recognition techniques or procedures that should emerge from this discussion; all sorts of recognition are fine. The key is that they be meaningful to those involved.

Larger Goal: Meaningful, Lateral Recognition

What is also key is that they point toward lateral (not just vertical) recognition. An authentic leader's ultimate desire is not to be a magnificent, solitary fount of appreciation but to nurture maximal lateral recognition among her constituents. Her aim is to help faculty become adept at praising and acknowledging one another. Again, it matters little which method they favor, so long as it is significant to them. Here are four simple examples of recognition schemes that faculties have developed to acknowledge and encourage effort, excellence, and innovation:

- A small New England high school has a custom of awarding "parking days" in January in the deep of winter. They permit staff to park in the principal's parking place, right next to the front door (and he parks out in the snow bank, where the teachers usually leave their cars). Parking days are awarded by faculty vote to those who, in the judgment of their peers, have made an "above and beyond" contribution to the school. All fall, at staff meetings, they spend a few minutes considering nominations and voting before they turn to the serious business on their agenda. They have great fun with it, and they devote time at every meeting to considering who is contributing to the school.
- A growing number of elementary schools rotate faculty meetings among teachers' classrooms. Each meeting begins with the host teacher introducing the room and its layout and materials and offering a short summary of key emphases she is pursuing. Colleagues get a chance to see and hear, pick up an idea or two,

and offer feedback of their own. There is nothing formal or lengthy, but it offers a quick chance for people to learn about—and admire—one another's work.

• Many schools begin faculty meetings with a brief interval in which people can simply acknowledge or thank colleagues for something they have done. There is no obligation and no pressure, but there is an opportunity to share publicly the fruits of a colleague's labor.

• Teacher groups in a few school districts publish their own professional journals. Designed to celebrate teaching and teachers, these include reflections on the craft, profiles of individuals, and original fiction and poetry.

Whether the recognition vehicle is formal or informal, symbolic or substantive, serious or light, what is essential is that it pass the tests of meaningfulness (if not, it is just another gimmick or empty ritual) and laterality (if not, it leaves the whole task to the principal). The leader's role is first to mobilize it and then to foster its establishment among individuals and groups throughout the school community.

Caveats

Before leaving this topic, two points bear mention. First, though it is truly important that recognition be noncompetitive in intent, there is an inevitable risk of longer-term competitive effects. Recognition does not work if it is structured to inspire rivalry. Its focus must be overtly on "examples of us at our best," with repeated, explicit reminders that recognition is often directed at individuals who exemplify an aspiration, a belief, a strength, a skill, or a quality that is shared elsewhere in the school or is within the reach of others. However, as recognition becomes a more regular feature of school life, it is likely that over time some individuals will receive a great deal and others very little. Usually there are good reasons for the disparity, chief among them that those who are being "overlooked" are not earning any attention because they are actually marginally competent and minimally involved. They may make some periodic, lukewarm gestures toward participating in change and go through a few motions, but most likely they are treading water. Nonetheless, principals and superintendents who wish to improve recognition often hesitate to do so for fear of being accused of unfairness by these individuals. To such a challenge there are essentially three responses: one can lie by pretending not to have noticed the imbalance, one can apologize and promise correctives, or one can make use of it. For an authentic leader, the first two stick in the craw, and the third is a rare opportunity:

> When principal Jean O'Hara was challenged by a teacher who frostily complained that he never received any praise, she didn't miss a beat. "You know," she said, "I've noticed that. Why do you think that is?" (She asked this quite seriously, not sarcastically.) "Are we overlooking something? If so, you need to tell me, and I need to correct my mistake. I think we should sit down together and talk about all this." When they met, Jean elaborated: "What I *have* noticed is that you've skipped most of our faculty meetings where we discuss our school improvement plan, and you're one of the few who hasn't volunteered to try out any of our new curriculum units. I don't want to be unfair, but I don't think I or others can praise a contribution we don't see." The teacher admitted both a strong philosophical disagreement with Jean's change agenda and a strong personal dislike of two teachers she had promoted to project leader. He was convinced that his traditional practice had always been adequate and would be again if given "half a chance and better students." He was ultimately unwilling to seek common ground with Jean and decided to seek a transfer to another school.

Encounters like these are likely to be scarce and will not always have outcomes that aid school improvement, and they are certainly not the reason for raising recognition levels, but for leaders who are willing to capitalize on them, they can prove to be beneficial side effects.

The second caveat involves the injustice of asking school leaders to take the initiative in recognizing others when they themselves are generally the most recognition-deprived members of the institution. However harsh the teachers' level of deprivation, administrators' is almost invariably worse, largely because they are so isolated and cast in such parental roles as monitors, policymakers, bearers of bad news, and rule enforcers. Recognition is so relatively easy and cheap and its results so positive that it is unquestionably a sound bias for leaders, but it requires them to show even more care and consideration for others when they themselves receive next to none. Ideally, recognition would ultimately flow upward as well as downward and laterally. In my experience, this is rare. Too much of what a principal or superintendent does is unseen by teachers for them to genuinely appreciate it. Consequently, leaders need to arrange more occasions when they can gather as peers and share feedback, praise, and acknowledgment. Districts must acknowledge that the intensity and complexity of the burdens of school leadership necessitate higher levels of continuing support for administrators. It is increasingly important to provide opportunities for them to gather not in agenda-driven meetings or skill-training sessions but to share and reflect on their experience, to compare notes and troubleshoot common problems, to counter some of the isolation of their role, to regain some distance on their crowded work lives, and to renew their concentration on their own priorities.

This proposal, indeed this entire chapter, might be summarized as a call for a new reverse Golden Rule in schools: adults should do unto themselves as they do unto students. Amid all the obstacles they can't overcome, the double standard of recognition stands out as one they can. Even modest increases in genuine attention, praise, and validation enable authentic leaders to reinforce the meaningfulness of the educational endeavor, confirm the accuracy and adequacy of teachers' performance, and bolster teachers' self-esteem. Mobilizing broader lateral recognition has the potential to shift the tone and climate of a school, fostering a special kind of empowerment that can only improve the chances for change.

Notes

1. Though these schemes seem to exhibit a steady appeal for business executives, free-market theorists, and others, they have a persistently poor track record in schools (Yee, 1990, p. 3; Johnson, 1990, p. 320; Schlechty, 1989, p. 358). Still, because so many teachers are veterans and because extrinsic rewards become more important in midcareer, one might wonder if these proposals would appeal more now than in the past. Not so. They almost invariably provoke hostility. Most merit plans offer stipends that are too few and too small to stimulate real effort (Mitchell and Peters, p. 76). Moreover, so long as most educa-

tors' compensation lags well behind that of other college graduates and professionals, singling out a few teachers for minimal rewards is more likely to damage than raise morale (Schlechty, 1990, p. 109; 1989, pp. 352–353).

2. See Schlechty, 1989, p. 358 for a discussion of their faults.

3. For an example of reframing applied to school reform as a whole, see Deal, 1990.

Chapter Thirteen

Confrontation: Avoiding Avoidance

I've tried what you said, but there are still some people who refuse and some who still don't get it. What do I do after I've done everything right?
—PRINCIPAL

The strategic biases I have thus far recommended seek to reduce and resolve resistance, rather than to drive or drag people out of it, to foster followership, not to force obedience. But despite these constructive steps, some people continue to resist change. Even if leaders adopt every suggestion in this book, projecting clarity and focus with Lincolnesque skill, nurturing true participation with patience and persistence, and opening a river of recognition, they will still encounter those who, intentionally or unintentionally, overtly or covertly, fail to embrace or fulfill the new agenda. The question of how to respond to them—what to do after you've done everything right—faces any leader who undertakes major change.

The short answer is, It depends. It depends on the form of the resistance, whether it is indifference or incompetence or sabotage, and on the number, strength, and posture of the resisters, whether they are few or many, weak or strong, quiet or noisy. A few marginal teachers who just never get around to implementing a new priority pose a different problem than a larger, influential group who publicly challenge it. The answer depends on many other factors, too, such as the substance of the innovation itself and the strengths of the staff members who support change (and of the school itself as a setting), but most of all it depends on the leader's bias. All resisters test a leader's credibility and savvy. In myriad ways small and large they present a recurring choice: to avoid or to confront. The authentic bias is unambiguous: it is to confront significant resistance. Authentic leaders acknowledge and address opposition to their priorities, trying to surface the sources of conflict and foster an open, substantive debate on their merits (Badaracco and Ellsworth, pp. 170–171).[1] When these sincere efforts at resolution fail, they confront directly those who continue to resist, especially when this resistance becomes exceptional—that is, when it violates the school's essential purposes or basic norms.

"Exceptional resistance" does not refer to most of the phenomena I have thus far described in this book: the ambivalence, the initial preoccupation with loss, the need to find new meaning, the anxiety about competence, the expectable level of disagreement and confusion. These all lie within the normal range of resistance. And it does not refer to principled objection by people of good faith who candidly oppose a change because it clashes with their own philosophical commitments but are amenable to discussion, who have the greater good of the school at heart, and who generally respect institutional norms. (In times of radical change these individuals can experience—and cause—considerable anguish, and they can be a focus of much ferment, but in my experience most ultimately respond well, if slowly, to the authentic leadership reflected in the three biases I have already outlined.) Rather, exceptional resistance is opposition that is not based on principle or is marked by strong, boundary-breaking violation of school priorities or chronic misunderstanding and nonfulfillment of these priorities.

Figure 13.1 presents a way of schematizing exceptional resistance: it is my proprietary Innovation Responsiveness Kontinuum, or IRK Scale. It ranges from the hottest hot to the deepest freeze and measures two dimensions of responsiveness to innovation: commitment (whether people are invested in the change) and fulfillment (whether they are actually implementing it). At the top (left) side are the "red hots." They are cooking. They are the key members, the ideal performers, the individuals a leader wishes to clone. They are deeply committed to the innovation and are truly enacting it. It flourishes in their classrooms and in their

Figure 13.1. Innovation Responsiveness Kontinuum.

	Red Hot	Unfreezable	Cryogenic
Committed	yes	yes	no
Making it	yes	no	no

school behavior. In the middle are the "unfreezables," a group whose resistance is unintentional, sometimes even unconscious. They think they are implementing the change, but they are not. These are the practitioners of false clarity, of cooperative listening, those who actually believe they are innovators but don't really get it. I call them unfreezable because they are stuck but potentially responsive to unfreezing.

At the lower (right) side are the "cryogenics." Not only are they not accomplishing the change, they don't care. They are not even trying. Their resistance does not stem from a deep commitment (or indeed from commitment of any kind, except perhaps narrow self-interest). In some instances it seems to reflect a blanket negativity or contrariness; in others, selfish laziness; in still others, malice or vengefulness. Perfect examples are the Naysayers at Prospect High School (Chapter Seven), who represent all three. Resistance has other permutations, but the unfreezables and the cryogenics constitute the large majority of those who trouble leaders of school change.[2] We shall consider both, but first we must look briefly at the factors that dispose school leaders not to deal with them.

The Tradition of Avoidance

In school leadership the prevailing bias is toward avoiding any potentially serious conflict (and thus most forms of resistance to change). School leaders generally prefer to minimize friction and discord, overlooking them when they can, finessing and fudging them when they can't. Viewed from without, this tendency can seem unwise and cowardly—even shabby—but it has its own logic rooted in school structure and culture. We have seen that administrators are assigned exaggerated responsibility but given too little authority to accompany it. They cannot rely on, for example, most of the extrinsic motivators (salary incentives, promotion, demotion) prescribed in management theories and routinely employed in the corporate sector to motivate performance and reduce resistance. Most models of supervision and evaluation assume not only greater leverage than school leaders enjoy but also greater commitment and insight than entrenched resisters demonstrate. We have also seen that most administrators are trained to be maintainers rather than innovators; that, as a matter of pure practicality, they need to preserve positive relationships with staff rather than discomforting them; and that they are often forced to implement initiatives that they themselves dislike and that require them to change their own roles, causing them to be ambivalent and hesitant rather than confident and forceful.

Although these structural conditions alone exert a strong impetus toward avoidance, their impact is greatly magnified by school culture. Just as most schools are marked by a norm of egalitarianism that limits people's professional and collegial interaction, so too do they exhibit a strong norm of conflict avoidance that severely constricts people's direct criticism or overt disagreement with one another. In any organization, to challenge someone's resistance to a new program or practice is awkward and potentially messy and risks conflict, but in schools there is a powerful cultural prohibition against open friction. The frequency and candor with which disagreement and criticism are expressed, both colleague-to-colleague and leader-to-staff, is markedly lower than in most other workplaces. Though educators take this restraint for granted, it is, if not unique to schools, certainly far less common in other professional settings. In the business world, for example, the "friction baseline" is considerably higher, even in companies where conflict is generally discouraged. In the most sober and civil organizations where I have consulted—insurance companies, banks—the routine level of challenge and contention (not to mention belittling and threat making) far exceeds that found in most schools.

From a school perspective, the competitive corporate ethos can seem cruelly hard. From a business perspective, the school ethos seems childishly soft. I know well a number of teachers and administrators who came to education from careers in the private sector. All found themselves surprised by what one of them calls "the make-nice, don't-upset-anyone mentality." Years later, some of them still marvel at it. Says a high school science teacher, "If I take a colleague's opinion seriously but I differ on the merits, and I speak with half the frankness that was typical in the engineering company I used to work for, it's like I've committed assault and battery. Nobody here has any idea how people in the outside world disagree."

This norm of conflict avoidance has several sources. Education attracts the contemplative and the nurturing more than the competitive and the assertive, drawing people whose guiding occupational interests and values are more likely to emphasize service to others and job security for oneself than, say, entrepreneurial risk taking or the projection of personal power. More simply, people who work in schools tend to like people—and to want to be liked back. And many teachers, especially at the elementary school level, display a rosy, all-embracing optimism that can seem quite naive (Jackson, 1968, pp. 143–147). They are used to looking for the best in students because they look for the best in everyone. It is a trait most of us wish them to keep, but one that inclines them to fear and avoid negativity that in other settings would seem mild.

I do not mean to push these generalizations too far, or to suggest that schools are totally conflict-free or that educators have no competitive or aggressive strivings and never express differences. I do want to underscore that the avoidance of open disagreement or friction is thoroughly entrenched in the culture of schooling and that, coupled with the structural limits on leaders' leverage, it makes administrators' reluctance to address opposition understandable. Unfortunately, it also leaves them ill-prepared for one of the toughest truths of change in schools: failing to confront resistance cripples both their own credibility and their efforts to improve their school.

The Confrontation Imperative

Avoidance occurs in pure and mixed forms. The pure form is full denial (see-no-evil). Ignoring clear, repeated violations of a school's change agenda sends a powerful signal that a leader's own commitment is in doubt—she doesn't really mean what she says—or that she lacks the skill and courage to tackle tough issues. Imagine the impact when a principal disregards the disrespect and defeatism of the Naysayers or takes no action in situations like these:

> To pilot an extensive reform proposal, a large high school creates a small, self-contained "minischool" centered on new interdisciplinary courses and community service. After a very successful year, student interest grows. It appears that a second minischool may be needed, which means that more teachers will have to participate. A group of faculty whose practice is very traditional and who dread the spread of this innovation begin advising their students not to join the program and telephoning parents to warn them—falsely—that it lacks rigor and discipline and could damage students' chances for college admission.

> A middle school teacher who does not belong to the union and who six years ago crossed the picket line during a strike is appointed as leader of a new team charged with implementing a new interdisciplinary curriculum. Two staunch union members dry up and drop out. They sit mute in planning meetings, answering only direct questions and only as briefly as possible. They do the bare minimum required and collaborate only when pressed. As the year progresses, they increasingly avoid and snub colleagues who cooperate with the leader.

Ignoring such overt resistance can only cloud one's authenticity and undermine innovation. What may be less evident is that compromising with it is equally damaging.

The most common form of avoidance is not pure denial but compromise. Many school leaders rely on chronic compromise (resist-no-evil) as a basis for trying to manage change. Its risks are not always immediately obvious, because we associate it with both fairness and with political adroitness and because it can provide a kind of surface calm that passes for consensus. But all too frequently it means retreat and masks underlying discord. As a primary leadership practice, its consequences are quite damaging. It frequently fails at its aim, which is to enhance agreement and reduce friction, and ends up pleasing no one. It too often degenerates into a slippery slope, with one concession leading inexorably to another and, ultimately, to the betrayal of innovation. It encourages processitis by moving the focus away from a concentration on facts and toward a concern with the negotiation itself, such as whether a proposed decision balances everyone's position equally (Badaracco and Ellsworth, pp. 174–176). Consequently, a habit of compromise saps a leader's integrity just as surely as a habit of denial. It makes him seem at best wily rather than principled and at worst weak rather than authoritative. It is ultimately counterproductive, because it impairs true consensus and discourages followership.

The essential source of consensus in a school is not the finding of a middle ground on critical decisions but a shared commitment to core purposes and values (p. 168). This commitment does not develop through bargaining. It springs from the clarity and focus of a leader's vision and from people's discovering that their leader has the will and the power to make change work. "Leaders" who make compromise a persistent pattern, especially with respect to serious resistance, are not worthy of the title. They cannot truly claim to stand for anything and will not be taken seriously.[3]

The corollary to the danger of avoidance and compromise is the opportunity provided by confrontation. Few change agents welcome resistance, but it is not only inevitable and ultimately necessary to the embedding of innovation after it is implemented, it is also useful during the implementation process. Without it, designers have little chance to understand and correct flaws in an improvement plan. Resisters' complaints are often valid, and they deserve attention. And even when a complaint is technically wrong, its mere existence may signal a need for clarification and support. As I have argued at several points, surfacing and acknowledging the sources of normal resistance, such as the loss caused by change or the fear that one's competence will be invalidated, is the only way to overcome it and enhance the consensus for change. So long as resistance is within the normal range, it can be a useful guide and goad to the perspicacious leader. With exceptional resistance the picture is both similar and different: similar in that it involves many of the elements we have previously examined, notably the need for unfreezing and for leaders to apply pressure as well as support, and different in that it takes these to new levels of intensity, especially with hard-core resisters. Ironically, the value of such confrontation can be large even though the potential for changing the individuals involved is not.

The frank truth is that no model of change or leadership offers a way to convert cryogenics to the cause of innovation or transform unfreezables into red hots. Among those who are both uncommitted *and* protected, no input of any kind induces change; among those who are committed but not making it, skillful, hard, and lengthy input may induce modest, useful change. Though they are far fewer in number than the unfreezables, cryogenics exert a disproportionate negative influence against change. We will consider them first.

Confrontation Itself: Challenging Cryogenics

Unprincipled resistance is not amenable to rational explanation or equitable give-and-take. Nor is it responsive to technical assistance—teachers who don't particularly care about their work or their school and are not invested in a new priority have no motivation to make use of training. And it is immune, too, to performance appraisal, absent any clout on the part of the evaluator. In the face of teachers who don't care and who, thanks to tenure, needn't fear, a principal or superintendent cannot raise guilt at the failure to fulfill an institutional commitment or anxiety about continued employment. Nor is entrenched resistance amenable to the democratic, participatory approaches to conflict resolution enshrined in many school improvement plans. These, after all, depend on mutual goodwill and an enlightened, shared definition of self-interest; and, as we have seen, they are sharply limited in their ability to resolve the normal range of conflict surrounding school change, let alone hardened, unprincipled resistance. From virtually any perspective, cryogenics are beyond help.

(In corporate America leaders save themselves the trouble of even trying to help cryogenics; they fire them. This is precisely the leverage school leaders lack. In fact, because trying to remove tenured teachers, even for egregiously poor performance or gross insubordination, can take years and cost thousands, many districts shy away, even when an administrator is eager to take on the challenge of documenting the case.)

When termination is not an option, three choices remain, all of them poor. The most commonly used is forcible transfer. Its short-term local impact may be positive (at least for the school that "loses" such a teacher), but it inspires resentment in its targets rather than an appetite for change. It is seen, accurately, as a kind of avoidance and thus weakness on the part of the administration. And it rarely advances the overall prospect for innovation in a district. The second is seduction. Leaders with vast amounts of free time and a high tolerance for bad company can try to cultivate and convert their naysayers. Their return on this investment is likely to be slight. Cryogenics are not former superstars who have fallen on hard times; they are longtime deadwood performers who usually received tenure not out of merit but out of the earlier cowardice of conflict-avoiding administrators. The third is "voodoo death"— making people so miserable that they decide to leave. Theoretically, one might "stick pins" in resisters and drive them out by putting them in the most uncomfortable classrooms, assigning them the most difficult students and distasteful duties, and visiting informal humiliations upon them. In actuality, this is rarely possible or desirable—we don't want *any* students with such teachers, let alone at-risk students—although simply contemplating it can bring frustrated leaders a brief fantasy of strength and revenge.

There is, however, more than fantasy at their disposal. Though school leaders have far too little formal power vis-à-vis cryogenics, they are not impotent. Though cryogenics are beyond help, they are not beyond all reach. And though there is no perfect answer— no technique to metamorphose the truly negative into genuine contributors—there is an approach that offers some realistic promise and a genuine opportunity. Unprincipled resisters who actively oppose change can and must be vigorously challenged. They demand outrage. Authentic leaders are ideally suited to respond.

Authentic leaders care passionately about their purposes. They are committed to certain "nonnegotiables," common central values that compose the cultural core of the school, and they demand adherence to these. They may encourage broad freedom in the way these values are implemented, but they expect them to be actualized. When people ignore or violate these values, authentic leaders express their anger (Sergiovanni, 1991, p. 140). First privately and then, if need be, publicly, they convey their disappointment and disapproval and reiterate their commitment to the school's purposes and principles.

This outrage is not a ploy or a tactic but a heartfelt reaction. Its strength comes in part from the leader's positional power (even if a principal is not free to fire people, few like to be on the boss's bad side), but mainly it flows from its sincerity and its symbolism. It compels attention precisely because it is not a political maneuver but a true expression of strong feeling by the formal head of the institution. "Real toughness," as Sergiovanni says, "is always principle-value based." Leaders who have demonstrated their integrity speak with a moral force that their manipulative, style-based colleagues do not. This stature makes their confrontation "a symbolic act that communicates importance and meaning and that touches people" in powerful ways (1991, pp. 141–142). Here is an example:

> As the new principal at Carville High School, Ed Stone encountered a group of five negative veteran teachers. At an early faculty meeting he was soliciting ideas for school improvement. The group made a number of sarcastic remarks about both the suggestions that were offered and the teachers who offered them. The discussion dried up. The next day Ed found each of the five individually to ask about their comments and to say, in essence, "I was surprised that you were so critical and sarcastic. You have a right to your opinion, and I'd be interested to hear your views, even if you disagree with someone, but I don't think it's helpful or professional to treat colleagues disrespectfully."

> For two months the group was quiet. During this time Ed led the faculty in considering core values for Carville. One of the first they adopted was respect for others. Then, several teachers came to him individually to complain about new instances of the group's intimidating and ridiculing teachers at department meetings—adding, of course, "But don't use my name or tell anyone that I told you."

> Soon another episode occurred at a full faculty meeting, during a discussion about modifying the school's rigid tracking system. The next day Ed summoned the entire group of five to say, "I have already talked with each of you individually about my concern about the way you treat your colleagues. Yesterday was another example. Our discussion about tracking just shut down after you ridiculed the proposals that were made. I'm upset, and I need to understand why you did that." There was an uncomfortable silence, followed by a few halfhearted efforts to criticize the detracking proposals. Ed responded, "I'm not just talking about tracking but about respect. We made an agreement— you included—that respect for others would be one of our basic operating principles. I repeat: I'm eager for you to voice your own ideas or to take issue with others about this or any other issue. But I won't tolerate disrespect and public demeaning of others. I'm putting you on notice that if it happens again

I will have to start considering disciplinary options. I hope this won't be necessary, and I'm counting on you to be good contributors and colleagues."

For some time things were quiet again. Then Ed began to receive new complaints about the group members' comportment. This time he asked those who came to him why they were doing so and what they wanted him to do. None were quite sure, but they did want him to know. He asked how they had responded to the incidents. None had done or said anything, and again, none wanted to be named as an accuser.

Finally, in another faculty meeting the group made fun of a new teacher's naive but earnest proposal for improving discipline. Ed stopped the meeting and addressed the five. "I have spoken to each of you individually and then together," he said. "I'm repeating now what I said then, that you are free to voice your opinions about the substance of any issue but not to violate our norm of respect for one another, and that I will not tolerate this kind of unprofessional and demeaning behavior. I will meet with each of you tomorrow to discuss this."

Ed then turned to the teacher they had ridiculed. "On behalf of the faculty I want to apologize to you," he said. "I appreciate your proposal, I'm interested in it, and I want to make it the first item at our next meeting, but I am going to adjourn this one."

Ed met with each of the five teachers, placed a formal letter of reprimand in each one's personnel file, and threatened to seek dismissal if there were further episodes. In the following days, as the anonymous accusers came to thank him, Ed told them, "I'm doing my part. Now *you* need to do yours, to stop letting them get away with it. Don't come back to me with more complaints about these people if *you* haven't first spoken up."

By the end of the following year, the group was disempowered. None was transformed or happy, or a better teacher, and none liked Ed. Other faculty were now challenging not just their behavior in meetings but also other irresponsible actions, such as skipping assigned duties. Two of the five had taken early retirement, and the other three were mute and marginalized. "It's almost like we've left them behind us," said one teacher.

Ed Stone's example illustrates four essential aspects of confrontation. First, its aim is not to convert the truly negative but to limit their behavior and support the committed. Ed would have welcomed, but was not seeking, a radical change of heart among the five teachers. But for the reasons outlined above, this was most unlikely. The leader's immediate goal is to contain and reduce demoralizing sabotage and any other beyond-the-boundaries behavior. Too many principals and superintendents underestimate their ability to exert a small but significant restraint on a hostile minority and to simultaneously embolden a timid majority. Simply expressing outrage and going public, even when one cannot compel a behavior change, makes it harder for both sides to maintain their routine patterns of interaction.

The real target in a confrontation like Ed Stone's is not the recalcitrants themselves but everyone else, particularly those teachers who have committed themselves to innovation. To tolerate overtly negative sabotage makes a mockery of a leader's vision and demoralizes those who have responded to it. Ed Stone looks back on his confrontation as a combination of indignation and protection: "I don't seek fights unless I'm sure I can win. But I just couldn't stand to see a school dominated by people so unprofessional and so mean. Plus, there was a strong core at Carville with great potential. How could I urge those teachers to start on a new path and then not back them up? I wasn't sure I would win, but I knew I couldn't stand it if I didn't try."

Not all strong principals would react as Ed did, or as soon. Local political and situational factors may cause a leader to moderate or temporarily override a bias toward confrontation. But like Ed, most authentic leaders would prefer to lose honorably and, if necessary, move to another school than to tolerate the intolerable.

Second, Ed's confrontation was not an ad hominem attack but a defense of the school's core values. Ed stuck to issues of substance, not personalities. Though he surely caused the five embarrassment and distress, this was only because they refused to behave professionally. Even then, he treated them seriously and directly and not in the snide, derogatory way they treated their peers. He challenged them publicly only after he had tried to reach them privately, and he mounted his challenge in the name of a principle he viewed as central to the school's well-being, a principle that the faculty had also adopted.

Third, although Ed accepted the necessity of initiating the confrontation, he then moved to muster the majority of the faculty to act on their convictions, pressing them to stop their conflict avoid-ance. Just as recognition becomes vastly more effective when it spreads throughout a faculty, so too does the confrontation of saboteurs. It is in mobilizing such collective action that leaders help to truly change school culture. To build collective support over time for a norm of not tolerating unprofessional behavior creates a powerful shift in the daily climate and underlying values of a school.

Finally, Ed did not have to repeat his intervention over and over. Confrontation is a rare event, not a routine one. Leaders need not fear that asserting themselves will provoke the need for continuous challenging. A successful confrontation is such a dra-matic step that it usually needs little repetition. It often turns out to be a critical incident in a school's life and a defining moment in a leader's tenure. It becomes enshrined in the school's history, passed on to future teachers as part of the school's mythology, its impact magnified by its stark contrast to the usual pattern of avoid-ance. "My God, that room was quiet," one of Carville's teachers remembers. "*Intensely* quiet. Some of us were elated, some were not. But all of us were stunned, and none of us will ever forget it. It was a kind of turning point, and after that the positive forces in the school really began to emerge."

The Unfreezable: Successful Negative Feedback

If cryogenics are very few but very negative, unfreezables are more numerous and less individually problematic. They are never the first priority on a change agent's agenda. But though they present nothing like the corrosive threat that Ed Stone's opponents did, they can, over time, exert a strong drag on innovation. And though it is possible to move them in a positive direction, doing so is slow and sometimes painful work, and progress is likely to be modest at best, though beneficial nonetheless.

The unfreezable are exemplars of false clarity, individuals who believe that they are fulfilling a new priority or implementing a new practice but, like Shirley Wetherbee's social studies teachers (Chapter Ten), are not doing so, either because they misunder-stand the priority or practice or because they misapprehend their own behavior. To an informed observer they may seem to be in the earliest, rudimentary stages of transition toward new understanding and new performance, whereas they see themselves as having already mastered both. To change agents who have too much to do and to whom reform is so clear and logical, this apparent blindness is often maddening.

Unlike cryogenics, the unfreezables are not beyond help. They need unfreezing, which as we have seen requires the leader to disconfirm people's satisfaction with their own performance, to make them aware of the discrepancy between their apparent commitment and their actual practice, and to do so without humiliation, with caring and support. In this instance the unfreezing occurs at a less profound philosophical level than in our earlier consideration in Chapter Four. It is not usually a matter of challenging these teachers' beliefs about schooling, but rather their perception that they are fulfilling these beliefs.

This kind of unfreezing is essentially what most systems of performance appraisal call for. (In clinical supervision, for example, supervisory observations are targeted toward goals chosen by the teacher in conjunction with the supervisor, whose role is to provide specific feedback about the teacher's performance in the identified areas.) Unfortunately, there is an enormous gap between the textbook model and typical practice. Much research confirms that negative feedback is rarely handled well. It is one of the most common management problems in all kinds of organizations. A chief culprit, again, is avoidance. Many leaders typically sidestep a staff member's performance problems and delay negative feedback until they reach a point of frustration and anger. They then intervene in a hostile way, making broad generalizations that tend to blame the performance on personal failings (bad will, poor judgment, abrasive personality). This not only denies the individual timely, targeted information that could help him improve, it loads the encounter with tension that increases his defensiveness, damages his self-confidence, and encourages a negative self-fulfilling prophecy ("I'm no good; I can't do this job well") (Eden, p. 171).

If, by contrast, negative feedback is administered in a timely, thoughtful way, spells out the specifics of a problem, and offers concrete assistance, it can help people learn from their mistakes and can actually support their self-esteem and expectations, creating a positive self-fulfilling prophecy by conveying confidence that they will improve. Shirley Wetherbee's prompt, direct intervention with her teachers is an example. There is no shortage of methods and training available to the leader who seeks guidance in giving negative feedback. Some models advise elaborate improvement plans or intensive supervision; others advise less formal approaches. Many plans, like the one in this superintendent's district, are eclectic:

> Our supervisory message to people who aren't making it is, "Although I know you're committed to X, I don't see it in action in your teaching. I want to describe for you what I do see and then think together with you about how to achieve X." We offer concrete examples—"I counted eighteen students who raised their hands but never got called on at all" and so on. And then we move toward ways of helping, and here we are very flexible, whether this involves further direct supervision, pairing that teacher with a colleague, or sending him to a workshop. We want them to know we mean business but that we want to support them, not punish them.

Whatever their particular emphasis, virtually every model of supervision and evaluation teaches administrators to deliver specific, nonjudgmental summaries of their observations and, when performance is problematic, to offer recommendations, encouragement, and follow-up.

Because there is so much information available, I will not dwell on the theory and practice of this kind of confrontation. I do want to make three points that contradict the idealized case examples offered in textbooks and graduate courses on supervision and in formal plans for educational reform. The first is that though the effort does not involve the adversarial intensity of confronting cryogenics, it can be quite stressful. To disabuse people of the notion that they are fulfilling a commitment or that they are making a real contribution to innovation can cause them genuine distress and a serious loss of face. It is likely to make them sad or angry, and hence defensive, even when the negative feedback is delivered thoughtfully. Hurting people of apparent goodwill is an unwelcome prospect (another impetus for avoidance). And though the discourse with the unfreezable is less charged than it is with cryogenics, it is still charged—and it is often much more prolonged.

The supervisory input required to foster true change can involve repeated classroom visits and discussions. This may be manageable with one teacher, but as few as two or three constitute a daunting drain on a school leader's time.

This raises yet again the larger issues that plague all school improvement: time and money. Unfreezing is time-consuming, labor-intensive work. Unintentional resistance is so common—it occurs not just in schools, but wherever complex change is undertaken—that any innovation scheme must anticipate the need to address it. We cannot simply dismiss all those who unwittingly fail to fulfill the visions of change they appear to embrace. We must face the reality—and the price tag and the time implications—of having to help them truly approach the destination they think they have reached.

The third point is itself a contradiction: the potential reward for this investment of time and resources is often modest, but it is ultimately positive. Despite the optimistic models of performance appraisal and despite the fact that the unfreezable genuinely wish to participate in change, I have seen few cases of true transformation. Few such teachers are ever turned into red-hot masters of innovation. People who for several years can misunderstand the spirit and substance of a school improvement initiative or be unaware of a serious discrepancy between their beliefs and their actions may ultimately see the light when confronted in a direct, caring way. They may then modify their practice. But whatever clouded their comprehension or self-awareness is generally so pervasive—so "characterological," as psychologists say—as to limit their potential for growth. It is rarely a temporary blindness or a mere perceptual "glitch" that yields to a flash of insight, which then catapults them into the vanguard of innovation. They typically display either a cognitive concreteness or an emotional impulsivity that constrains their capacity for self-reflection and change.

This does not mean that addressing these teachers' unintentional resistance is futile. Instead, we must remember Senge's observations (Chapter Four) that people who merely—but genuinely—*comply* with an organization's goals behave much like those who truly *enact* the goals, and that an organization composed of genuinely compliant people would vastly outperform most of its competitors. Those who are beset by false clarity may never become outstanding, creative teachers, but helping them bring their classroom practice into genuine compliance with the essentials of a school improvement plan can produce a noticeable gain, year after year, in the learning of students.

Confrontation forms a matching bookend with clarity and focus. Each illustrates the value of authenticity and provides a powerful opportunity for a leader to demonstrate it. Each swims against the tide of school culture and demands the courage to fulfill one's convictions, to translate commitment into action. Each entails some risk, but with each the far greater risk lies in avoidance. Each involves triage, a choice of where to concentrate and which issues to pursue as a priority. (None of the successful school leaders I know ignore serious, active, cryogenic resistance, but many confront unfreezable resistance only as they can or when it embraces large numbers of teachers; none concentrate on resisters so much that they fail to emphasize the positive, foster recognition, and nurture a critical mass of support for change.) Finally, each reinforces the other. A bias toward clarity and focus permits a leader to confront resistance in the name of common purpose; a bias toward confrontation helps to clarify and confirm that purpose throughout the school community.

Notes

1. My framing of confrontation as a bias owes a great deal to Badaracco and Ellsworth.

2. There are some hard-core resisters who might be called "terrorists." Their opposition does appear to reflect a commitment to a philosophy of education, but to preserve this commitment and resist the change they seem prepared to break any rule; they are apparently willing to destroy the school to save it. They should be treated essentially as cryogenics.

3. Compromise has a place, to be sure—no leader can avoid it—but it is tactical, not strategic. It may play a role in deciding how core commitments should be carried out, and at what pace, but not in deciding which commitments should prevail.

Chapter Fourteen

Reach and Realism, Experience and Hope

What we need most is what good teachers give students:
real challenges—goals that stretch you, but that you can
reach; and real inspiration—encouragement to keep
trying no matter what.
—PRINCIPAL

In the face of serious problems that cry out for attention and in an era of fads and quick fixes, it is hard to stay true to human nature, to face the genuine complexity of real problems and the actual limits in our skills and resources. In trying to stay true to human nature, I may have seemed to some too sympathetic to resistance and too pessimistic about the potential for school improvement. I have, indeed, argued that resistance is a normal, necessary reaction to change, that it is embedded in individual psychology and organizational culture, and that it must be anticipated and respected. I have framed the tasks of implementation in this light, emphasizing that they are motivational before they are technical, that they require readiness before training, and that they depend crucially on the meaning of change to those who must implement it. I have asserted that school improvement schemes, including many of the reforms known as restructuring, tend to overlook these truths and to be overloaded and unrealistic, especially in light of factors that limit teachers' and schools' readiness for innovation. And I have highlighted ways in which traditional notions of leadership complicate rather than facilitate the implementation of change and the over-coming of resistance.

But I have also underscored that none of this denies the necessity of reform. On the contrary, all of it aims at making real change more possible. To me it is incontestable that many of our schools need broad, thorough renewal and that high standards are crucial to motivating performance for everyone involved in this enterprise. We cannot hope to transform schools without *reach*—a commitment to the highest levels of excellence and the most effective innovation.

At the same time, because the restructuring movement has generated such hope and such hype, we hugely overestimate how much change schools can accomplish, how fast they can accomplish it, and how much impact they can have on the young. And because leaders are known to be so vital to innovation, we hugely overestimate how readily they can make it all happen. Renewing schools could hardly be a more difficult undertaking; it demands perspective. If this book has any lesson to teach, it is that we must recast our expectations for leaders, for teachers, and for the larger task of improving schools. This does not mean lowering our standards or abandoning our goals; it means staying true to human nature, combining reach with *realism*—a frank acceptance of the baseline from which we depart and the complexity of the problems we must overcome. It means not expanding the horizon of goals faster than dedicated people can advance. And it means measuring gains up from our beginning position as well as up against our ideal outcome. Only in this way can we appreciate what constitutes true progress, strengthen the prospects for real change, and sustain hope.

Of all the factors vital to improving schools, none is more essential—or vulnerable—than hope. Each year I meet more and more educators at all levels who have never been working harder or doing more, but who go home at the end of the week feeling worse, not better, less adequate, not more. If deadwood and cryogenic teachers illustrate one kind of demoralization (a problem that needs to be fixed), the key members and red hots who have been pouring themselves into school reform pose another (a solution that is losing hope). Absolutely critical to the future of school improvement is to preserve and nurture genuine hope among them. Hence, my interest here is not on things to do but on things to think about, expectations for leaders of school change to carry in their heads, ways to balance reach and realism as they tackle the challenges of innovation.

Time and Pace

Perhaps the best way to achieve this balance is to ask, "How far, how fast?" To base plans and forecasts for change on need alone is futile. Few schools, no matter how desperate their shortcomings, are capable of rapid, radical transformation. The problems of loss, incompetence, confusion, and conflict, exacerbated by the problems of the veteran staff and of chronic institutional stress, virtually rule out such turnarounds. Whatever one might wish for our schools, especially for the most troubled, it is surely true that we must measure the magnitude of change in terms of the starting points of the individuals implementing it and that it is wise to do fewer innovations better rather than more innovations worse (Fullan, pp. 71–72, 104).

What precepts could be so sound and yet so widely ignored? The point here is not just that it is unrealistic to expect too much too soon but that it is counterproductive. Despite the rhetoric of instant excellence and world-class standards, and despite the fervent intensity of many committed practitioners, there are dangers to overreaching, to trying too much too fast: it literally overwhelms institutions and people, reinforcing resistance and burning out innovators. These dangers are recognized by most thoughtful organizational experts, including some who are widely praised as gurus of innovation. Senge, for example, observes that "virtually all natural systems, from ecosystems to animals to organizations, have intrinsically optimal rates of growth [which are] *far* less than the fastest possible growth." When pressured by excessive growth—he cites cancer—"the system itself will seek to compensate by slowing down; perhaps putting the organization's survival at risk in the process" (p. 62, emphasis added). Vaill frames this perspective graphically. He insists that we must cast our aspirations for excellence in relation to time. There is a balance between going too fast, guaranteeing resistance and disappointment, and going too slow, permitting stagnation. This balance is found in what he calls, felicitously, "the envelope of optimal realism" (1989, pp. 72–73).

The graph shown in Figure 14.1 implies roughly a five-year time frame for significant organizational change. Kaufman takes a more conservative view. At the end of a generation (twenty-five or thirty years), he says, any complex organization will be much the same as it was. "This stability is not a result of conscious choice or preference," he suggests, but "of the way the world is ordered. . . . The built-in tendencies of organizations not to change, and the dampers that come into play when change is nevertheless introduced, keep the number, magnitude, and importance of changes within rather narrow limits over [such a] comparatively short period" (p. 95). I don't believe I have met anyone engaged in school reform who thinks in terms of a decade—much less a generation—as a time frame for success. Two or three years seems to be the outer limit, especially in the case of many state reform plans.

Here is where the paradox of expectations, of reach and realism, begins to emerge. It is not just that inflating expectations is self-defeating (because it leads to demoralization, burnout, and the abandonment of innovation) but that limiting and focusing expectations leads to truly appreciating what is actually achieved and ultimately to accomplishing more. I have been careful to modify most of my earlier references to the chronic failure of school reform as "perceived" because in truth the picture is less grim than is commonly thought. Beneath the received wisdom that schools never change there is a different—but gradual, incremental—reality. Schools do change, but as Elmore and McLaughlin note, they change not through "highly visible, well-specified, sequential actions . . . but [through] subtle shifts over time" (p. 7). Because their account is so relevant and compelling, I cite it at length:

Take a given reform at a given point—say, the teaching of high school biology in 1962. What we typically find is a pattern something like the following: Leading experts and policymakers have observed the deplorable state of high school science instruction. A national initiative has resulted in earmarked funding, curriculum development, teacher workshops, and broad-scale dissemination of new ways of teaching biology. A substantial minority of biology teachers have enthusiastically adopted the current view of "best practice," but the majority of teachers are still doing it the "old

Figure 14.1. Vaill's Envelope of Optimal Realism.

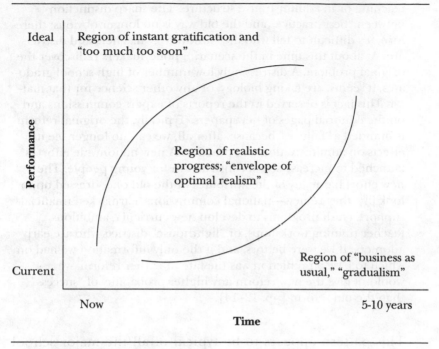

Ideal | Region of instant gratification and "too much too soon"

Region of realistic progress; "envelope of optimal realism"

Performance

Region of "business as usual," "gradualism"

Current

Now

5-10 years

Time

Adapted from Vaill, 1989, p. 73.

way." A considerable minority of school systems have successfully adapted to the principles of best practice by setting up district-wide programs, but the majority of school systems have not made a commitment to the change. Over time, some of these latter districts will make piecemeal adjustments to the new definition of best practice, some won't. At the state and federal level, advocates of reform alternately praise the fast adopters, chide the laggards, criticize state and local administrators for their unresponsiveness, and condemn the majority of high school biology teachers as poorly trained and hopelessly retrograde. At the same time opponents of reform express concern over the erosion of "local control" brought about by unwarranted intrusions of federal and state bureaucrats into the curriculum decisions of local administrators and teachers.

If we look at the same system twenty years later—say, 1982—we typically observe that the original reform has long since ceased to be an identifiable entity; some of its features have become part of the conventional wisdom of the field, others have not; but whatever separate identity it had as a "reform" is usually not discernible in teaching or in administrative structure. The sharp distinction between "best practice" and the old way is no longer obvious; therefore, it's difficult to tell who the "innovative" teachers and districts are. At about this time in the scenario, policymakers rediscover the original problem. A distressingly low number of high school graduates, it seems, are taking biology, or any other science for that matter. This fact is observed in the reports of expert commissions and on the editorial pages of newspapers. Typically, the original reform is branded a "failure," because, after all, we can no longer see its effects on administration and practice. A new nationwide effort is launched to increase science instruction for young people. The new effort has many of the attributes of the old one, dressed up to look like they're new—national commissions, earmarked financial support, crash programs to develop new curricula, ambitious teacher training workshops, or "lighthouse" districts who are early adopters. If we were bettors, and if the only information we had on which to base a prediction was the fate of earlier reform, we wouldn't give the new reform any higher probability of "success" than the old reform [pp. 12–14].

This pattern appears to be typical of all the major school reforms of the twentieth century. It does not necessarily reflect a failure of the individual change effort or of the educational system as a whole. Seeing it so represents a failure of perspective and expectation. For embedded in the ebb and flow of change and stasis, action and reaction, is "an enormously complex sifting and sorting process" (p. 12). Some of a reform's early goals and practices prove impractical or unwise and are discarded. Some are altered by external factors (political, demographic, economic) beyond the control of a given school or of the entire educational establishment. Others succeed and spread widely, becoming so standard as to be taken for granted. The notion of failure stems from seeing reforms as full packages, "discrete changes . . . that are either 'there' or 'not there'" (p. 13). But changing education, Elmore and McLaughlin suggest, is rather like changing a language: formal efforts to modify usage don't usually succeed at first and rarely turn out exactly as they were intended, but over time a language makes dramatic changes, incorporating a variety of new influences in diffuse and uneven ways.

I think it is likely that among the recent restructuring reforms there are similar instances under way, even though they may not yet be clear to us. One such may be the case of the Coalition of Essential Schools. What we might call the "full Coalition package"—its nine common principles, which call for a range of curricular, instructional, assessment, and governance changes—may not, over time, endure and spread *as a package*, that is, in the form of vast numbers of schools joining the Coalition and fully implementing the nine principles. But the Coalition has already sparked a variety of changes of the kind Elmore and McLaughlin describe. For example, one of its pioneering emphases has been on authentic assessment, the measuring of performance through a portfolio or other measure that demonstrates students' ability to use and apply their learning. In 1986 this was a relatively new concept—it was hard to find a school that was using portfolios. Ten years later, the concept is ubiquitous, and it is hard to find one that hasn't started doing so or isn't considering doing so. In addition to the eight hundred schools that have joined the Coalition, thousands have either embraced or are exploring one of its core concepts. Doubtless many of these schools are introducing portfolios only partially, and many may be doing so badly; the ultimate implementation may take a variety of forms, many of which fail to fulfill the Coalition's original intent. But the concept of authentic assessment appears likely to live on, embedded in educational philosophy and school practice. If so, it would be a classic example of how schools change.

Policy and Practice

Viewing school improvement as a gradual, incremental process has a vital implication for educational policy: the need for restraint, for respect for practice. As many observers have noted, there is in education a natural tension between policy and practice. Policymakers and experts, whose roles permit them an overview of the field, have a breadth of perspective that practitioners in individual school districts lack; they can see common needs and problematic trends, the forest instead of the trees. Hence, policy can serve as a helpful goad and stimulus to practice—pressure, as we have seen, is crucial to innovation. However, practitioners have hands-on experience, judgment, and craft knowledge. They know the trees. They know what works and what doesn't in the daily press of classroom life. When, as has happened in the 1990s, policy routinely ignores these realities and devalues this knowledge, it compounds the problems of schooling by intensifying the resistance of teachers and leaders.

In this regard there is a desperate need for clarity in educational policy. Without a basic "value consensus" about the purpose of education, substantial improvement in school performance is unlikely (Schlechty, 1990, p. 28). This is not a call for national curriculum standards but for better purposing at a fundamental level. As John D'Auria, one of the most thoughtful, dedicated principals I know, points out, such a consensus must emerge from a broad, deep understanding about goals for children. We need to bridge major fault lines in the foundation of American education between policymakers, who want educators to improve schooling rapidly across a broad range of areas, and educators, who want policymakers to stop multiplying requirements without providing supports. In the same way, we need to bridge the gap between parents, who also want educators to improve schooling, and educators, who want parents to improve their support for children's schoolwork. To reach mutually shared goals, D'Auria argues, we all need to be clear about what we want for our children, how we want them to grow up both as people and as learners. Only when we have clarified this will we know what we want from our schools (1995, p. 151).

This consensus, whatever it calls for, must not only be clear, it must focus the aims of schooling; it cannot consist of simultaneous multiple improvement. It is here that we see most clearly the need for policy to yield to practice. Policymakers and legislators must stop multiplying the tasks and mandating the methods of teaching and administering. The endless addition of new goals and the relentless prescription of the procedures by which these must be fulfilled are making classrooms unteachable and schools unleadable. The personal and institutional realities I have examined confirm a long-established organizational truth: the formula for success is to set mutually agreed standards and to hold people accountable for achieving them—but to free them to do so in their own way wherever possible. To do otherwise is to shackle schools and their leaders and to impede the very changes that are man-

dated. Thus, we need to ask of every proposed new policy and procedure questions like these: How will this change fit with those we
have previously imposed? Do wise practitioners find it necessary,
desirable, and feasible? How will it affect the school's "leadability"?
More generally, we need to ask, Are those of us outside schools
micromanaging them, even though we may not think so? And
above all, How will we empower leaders to fulfill the tasks we have
assigned them? ("Empower" does not mean "pack more techniques into"; it means "assign doable tasks and grant authority
commensurate with responsibility.")

A related policy implication is that we must improve the preparation of school leaders, but without going overboard and creating a new fad. The growing effort to standardize training and
certification requirements for principals and superintendents is
notable for its overreliance on rational-structural assumptions and
functional taxonomies. These need to be shifted toward an emphasis on strategic-systemic assumptions and the moral dimensions of
leadership. The lists of skills and styles need to be given a secondary role as tactical aides to effective leadership, not a primary
role as the core of the craft. That must be reserved for purposing
and for ways of building and sustaining consistency and credibility. This does not mean making a fetish out of authenticity. We
must resist the already evident urge to translate transformational
leadership into a quick fix, to imagine that a bit of "moral training" will enable school leaders to accomplish cultural turnarounds
in short order. Leadership that concentrates on meaning and motivation is by definition not amenable to such translation. It emerges
from within and is communicated over time in a steady stream of
actions—words and especially deeds—of the kind I have described.

The Triumph of Hope

There is, of course, little reason to assume that policymakers will
heed my advice any more than they have heeded similar recommendations made in the past by observers far more influential.
And even if policy were to begin showing a new respect for practice, those who have committed themselves to school reform may
find my notions of time and pace for change discouraging. Ebb
and flow, gradual accommodation, slow accretion—these can seem
tiny returns on a large and exhausting personal investment. And

if one accepts the idea of a generation as a time frame for significant impact, it is hard to be confident about one's own effectiveness as a contributor to that outcome. The serious pursuit of school change is chronically hard on one's sense of efficacy. Where does one turn for hope? The primary power of transformational leaders is moral. It derives from the power of the ideas, purposes, and values they stand for. But in the face of all the obstacles we have explored, uplift is hard to sustain. One of the largest problems I encounter among educators who are pressing for change is, as one teacher put it, that "it's just so hard to stay hopeful."

I began this book by suggesting that one might apply to school reform Samuel Johnson's sardonic jest about remarriage: the triumph of hope over experience. Even if reform's history is less futile than generally thought, it has often been a great frustration to its proponents. Today, when there seems such an urgent need for change and yet the prevailing conditions are so unfavorable, the potential for frustration is greater than ever. What we need is precisely a triumph of hope over experience. But we will not find it in false promises or forced confidence. Nor will we find it in naive optimism or pie-in-the-sky dreaming. Real hope doesn't ignore the dilemmas of real life; it is a commitment that bridges reach and realism. We can find it only in ourselves. The playwright and Czech president Vaclav Havel—a man who knows something about sustaining hope in the face of experience—defines it as "a state of mind, not a state of the world," an "orientation of the spirit," not a forecast:

> Hope in this deep and powerful sense is not the same as joy when things are going well, or willingness to invest in enterprises that are obviously headed for early success, but rather an ability to work for something to succeed. Hope is definitely not the same thing as optimism. It's not the conviction that something will turn out well, but the certainty that something makes sense, regardless of how it turns out. It is this hope, above all, that gives us strength to live and to continually try new things, even in conditions that seem . . . hopeless [1993, p. 68].

This is the kind of hope I would wish for all those who are working to improve and renew our schools. In a letter to H.G. Wells, Joseph Conrad made a related distinction: "You don't care for humanity," he wrote, "but think they are to be improved. I love humanity, but know they are not" (cited in Bennis, 1989, p. 46). School change requires a belief in the potential for improving people, but it also requires an acceptance—a love—of people as they are. To truly accomplish all that we can, we must hold fast to the core commitments that give life and education promise—but we must also appreciate what constitutes genuine progress toward our goals. Real change is always personal; organizational change is always incremental. In the best of schools, with the best resources and the most skillful leadership, the time frame for transforming culture, structure, belief, and practice is years. Success will require the highest strivings and the most down-to-earth expectations. Only if we maintain a healthy respect for the lessons of experience can real hope truly triumph.

References

Argyris, C. *Increasing Leadership Effectiveness*. New York: Wiley-Interscience, 1976.

Aronstein, L., and DeBenedictis, K. "Principal Power: Key to Site-Based Management." In A. Costa, J. Bellanca, and R. Fogarty (eds.), *If Minds Matter: A Forward to the Future*. Palantine, Ill.: Skylight Publishing, 1992.

Badaracco, J. L., and Ellsworth, R. *Leadership and the Quest for Integrity*. Boston: Harvard Business School Press, 1989.

Baker, P., Curtis, D., and Berenson, W. *Collaborative Opportunities to Build Better Schools*. Chicago: Illinois Association for Curriculum and Development, 1991.

Barth, R. S. "The Principal and the Profession of Teaching." In T. J. Sergiovanni and J. H. Moore (eds.), *Schooling for Tomorrow: Directing Reforms to Issues that Count*. Needham Heights, Mass.: Allyn & Bacon, 1989.

Barth, R. S. *Improving Schools from Within: Teachers, Parents, and Principals Can Make the Difference*. San Francisco: Jossey-Bass, 1990.

Basler, R. (ed.). *The Collected Works of Abraham Lincoln*. New Brunswick, N.J.: Rutgers University Press, 1953.

Beckhard, R., and Harris, R. T. *Organizational Transitions* (2nd ed.). Reading, Mass.: Addison-Wesley, 1987.

Bellah, R., and others. *Habits of the Heart*. New York: Harper & Row, 1985.

Bennis, W. "Transformative Power and Leadership." In T. J. Sergiovanni and J. E. Corbally (eds.), *Leadership and Organizational Culture*. Urbana: University of Illinois Press, 1984.

Bennis, W. *Why Leaders Can't Lead: The Unconscious Conspiracy Continues*. San Francisco: Jossey-Bass, 1989.

Bennis, W., and Nanus, B. *Leaders: The Strategies for Taking Charge*. New York: Harper & Row, 1985.

Bird, T. "Mutual Adaptation and Mutual Accomplishment: Images of Change in a Field Experiment." In Ann Lieberman (ed.), *Rethinking School Improvement*. New York: Teachers College Press, 1986.

Bissinger, H. G. "'We're All Racist Now.'" *New York Times Sunday Magazine,* May 29, 1994, pp. 26–56.

Blumberg, A. *School Administration as a Craft.* Boston: Allyn & Bacon, 1989.

Bolman, L. G., and Deal, T. E. *Reframing Organizations.* San Francisco: Jossey-Bass, 1991.

Bowman, T. G. "Last of the Suffering Heroes." *Phi Delta Kappan,* 1991, *73*(3), 251–252.

Brimelow, P., and Spencer, L. "How the National Education Association Corrupts Our Public Schools." *Forbes,* June 7, 1993, pp. 72–84.

Burns, J. M. *Leadership.* New York: Harper & Row, 1979.

Caplan, G. "Mastery of Stress: Psychosocial Aspects." *American Journal of Psychiatry,* 1981, *138,* 413–419.

Carnegie Corporation. *Starting Points: Meeting the Needs of Our Youngest Children.* New York: Carnegie Corporation, 1994.

Chira, S. "Survey: Teachers Want Parental Support." *New York Times,* June 22, 1993.

Cohen, D. K. "Revolution in One Classroom." *American Educator,* Fall 1991, pp. 17–48.

Coleman, J. "Families and Schools." *Educational Researcher,* August-September 1987, pp. 36–37.

Comer, J. *School Power.* New York: Free Press, 1980.

Conger, J. *The Charismatic Leader: Behind the Mystique of Exceptional Leadership.* San Francisco: Jossey-Bass, 1989.

Costa, P. T., Jr., and McCrae, R. R. "Personality Continuity and the Changes of Adult Life." In M. Storandt and G. R. Vandenbos (eds.), *The Adult Years: Continuity and Change.* Washington: American Psychological Association, 1989.

Cuban, L. *How Teachers Taught: Consistency and Change in American Classrooms 1890–1980.* New York: Longman, 1984.

Cytrynbaum, S., and Crites, J. O. "The Utility of Adult Development Theory in Understanding Career Adjustment Process." In M. B. Arthur, D. T. Hall, and B. S. Lawrence (eds.), *Handbook of Career Theory.* New York: Cambridge University Press, 1989.

D'Auria, J. "Tremors We Should Not Ignore." *Daedalus,* 1995, *124*(4), 149–152.

Deal, T. E. "Reframing Reform." *Educational Leadership,* 1990, *70*(5), 341–344.

Deal, T. E., and Peterson, K. *The Principal's Role in Shaping School Culture.* Washington: U.S. Department of Education, 1991.

Derr, C. B., and Laurent, A. "The Internal and External Career: A Theoretical and Cross-Cultural Perspective." In M. B. Arthur, D. T. Hall, and B. S. Lawrence (eds.), *Handbook of Career Theory.* New York: Cambridge University Press, 1989.

Diegmueller, K. "Nearly Half of Newly Hired Teachers Returned to Profession, Survey Finds." *Education Week,* September 5, 1990, p. 10.

Drucker, P. F. *The Effective Executive.* New York: Harper & Row, 1976.

Drucker, P. F. *The Practice of Management.* New York: Harper & Row, 1986.

Eden, D. *Pygmalion in Management.* Lexington, Mass.: D. C. Heath, 1990.

Elmore, R. F. "On Changing the Structure of Public Schools." In R. F. Elmore and Associates (eds.), *Restructuring Schools: The Next Generation of Education Reform.* San Francisco: Jossey-Bass, 1990.

Elmore, R. F., and McLaughlin, M. *Steady Work: Policy, Practice, and the Reform of American Education.* Santa Monica: RAND Corp, 1988.

Erikson, E. *Childhood and Society.* (2nd ed.) New York: Norton, 1963.

Evans, R. "The Faculty in Midcareer: Implications for School Improvement." *Educational Leadership,* 1989, *46*(8), 10–15.

Evans, R. "Making Mainstreaming Work Through Prereferral Consultation." *Educational Leadership,* 1990, *48*(1), 73–77.

Farber, B. A. *Crisis in Education: Stress and Burnout in the American Teacher.* San Francisco: Jossey-Bass, 1991.

Feistritzer, C. E. *Profile of Teachers in the U.S.* Washington: National Center for Education Information, 1986.

Feistritzer, C. E. *Profile of School Administrators in the U.S.* Washington: National Center for Education Information, 1988.

Feistritzer, C. E. *Profile of Teachers in the U.S.* Washington: National Center for Education Information, 1990.

Finn, C. E., Jr. "Education That Works: Make the Schools Compete." *Harvard Business Review,* Sept.-Oct. 1987, pp. 63–68.

Fisher, R., and Ury, W. *Getting to Yes.* Boston: Houghton Mifflin, 1981.

Frady, M. "Profiles (Jesse Jackson—Part I)." *The New Yorker,* February 3, 1991, pp. 36–69.

Fullan, M., with Stiegelbauer, S. *The New Meaning of Educational Change.* New York: Teachers College Press, 1991.

Gallagher, W. "Midlife Myths." *Atlantic Monthly,* 1993, *271*(5), 51–68.

Gibbons, T. "Revisiting the Question of Born vs. Made: Toward a Theory of Development of Transformational Leaders." Unpublished doctoral dissertation, The Fielding Institute, 1986.

Gilligan, C. *In a Different Voice.* Cambridge, Mass.: Harvard University Press, 1982.

Glass, I. "School Reform Proves to Be a Tough Sell to Faculty." *All Things Considered.* (Radio program.) National Public Radio, November 8 and 9, 1993.

Gleick, J. *Chaos: Making a New Science.* New York: Penguin, 1987.

Glickman, C. D. *Renewing America's Schools: A Guide for School-Based Action.* San Francisco: Jossey-Bass, 1993.

Goleman, D. "Major Personality Study Finds That Traits Are Mostly Inherited." *New York Times,* Dec. 2, 1986, pp. C1-C2.

Goodlad, J. *A Place Called School: Prospects for the Future.* New York: McGraw-Hill, 1984.

Gould, R. *Transformations: Growth and Development in Adult Life.* New York: Simon & Schuster, 1978.

Gould, S. J. *Bully for Brontosaurus.* New York: Norton, 1991.

Gray, F. P. "Chère Maître." *The New Yorker,* July 26, 1993, pp. 82–88.

Greenleaf, R. *Teacher as Servant.* New York: Paulist Press, 1977.

Greider, W. *Who Will Tell the People: The Betrayal of American Democracy.* New York: Simon & Schuster, 1992.

Hall, D. "Breaking Career Routines." In D. Hall and Associates (eds.), *Career Development in Organizations.* San Francisco: Jossey-Bass, 1986.

Hammer, M., and Champy, J. *Reengineering the Corporation.* New York: HarperBusiness, 1994.

Handy, C. *The Age of Unreason.* Boston: Harvard Business School Press, 1990.

Havel, V. "Never Hope Against Hope." *Esquire,* October 1993, p. 68.

Hemenway, C. "Meyers-Briggs Indicator Helps Us Know Ourselves and Each Other Better." *Resources.* Holyoke, Mass.: Human Resource Association of the Northeast, 1994.

Hersey, P., and Blanchard, K. H. *Management of Organizational Behavior.* Englewood Cliffs, N.J.: Prentice-Hall, 1988.

Herzberg, F. "One More Time: How Do You Motivate Employees?" *Harvard Business Review,* Sept.-Oct. 1987, pp. 109–120.

Hirsch, E. D. *Cultural Literacy.* Boston: Houghton Mifflin, 1987.

Hodgkinson, H. All *One System: Demographics of Education, Kindergarten Through Graduate School.* Washington: Institute for Educational Leadership, 1985.

Hoffer, E. *The Ordeal of Change.* New York: Harper & Row, 1967.

Houston, P. D. "School Reform Through a Wide-Angle Lens." *Daedalus,* 1995, *124*(4), 169–172.

Howe, H., II. "Families, Communities, and Children." *Harvard Graduate School of Education Alumni Bulletin,* 1994a, *38*(2), 10.

Howe, H., II. "The Systemic Epidemic." *Education Week,* July 13, 1994b, p. 40.

Huberman, M. "Recipes for Busy Kitchens." *Knowledge: Creation, Diffusion, Utilization,* 1983, *4,* 478–510.

Huberman, M. "The Professional Life Cycle of Teachers." *Teachers College Record,* 1989, *91*(1), 31–57.

Huberman, M. "The Model of the Independent Artisan in Teachers' Professional Relations." In J. W. Little and M. W. McLaughlin (eds.), *Teachers' Work: Individuals, Colleagues, Contexts.* New York: Teachers College Press, 1993.

Huebner, D. "The Vocation of Teaching." In F. Bolin and J. Falk (eds.), *Teacher Renewal.* New York: Teachers College Press, 1987.

Hughes, R. *The Culture of Complaint.* New York: Warner, 1993.

Jackson, P. *Life in Classrooms.* Austin, Tex.: Holt, Rinehart, & Winston, 1968.

Johnson, S. M. *Teachers at Work.* New York: Basic Books, 1990.

Jones, R. "The Loneliness of Leadership." *Executive Educator,* March 1994, pp. 26–30.

Kauffman, J. M., and Hallahan, D. P. (eds.). *The Illusion of Full Inclusion.* Austin, Tex.: Pro-Ed, Inc., 1995.

Kaufman, H. *The Limits of Organizational Change.* Tuscaloosa: University of Alabama Press, 1971.

Kelley, R. E. "In Praise of Followers." In *Managers as Leaders.* Cambridge: Harvard Business Review Press, 1988.

Kouzes, J. M., and Posner, B. Z. *The Leadership Challenge: How to Keep Getting Extraordinary Things Done in Organizations.* San Francisco: Jossey-Bass, 1987.

Kozol, J. *Savage Inequalities: Children in America's Schools.* New York: Crown, 1991.

Krupp, J. A. "Understanding and Motivating Personnel in the Second Half of Life." *Journal of Education,* 1987, *169*(1), 20–46.

Krupp, J. A. "Motivating Experienced Personnel, Adult Development and Learning." Presentation at ASCD convention, March 1988.

Lasch, C. *The Culture of Narcissism.* New York: Warner, 1979.

Lee, V. E., Smith, J., and Croninger, R. "Another Look at High School Restructuring." *Issues in Restructuring Schools,* no. 9. Madison, Wisc.: Center on Organization and Restructuring of Schools, 1995.

Levin, H. "Accelerating Elementary Education for Disadvantaged Students." In Chief State School Officers (eds.), *School Success for Students at Risk.* Orlando, Fla.: Harcourt, Brace, Jovanovich, 1988.

Levine, S. L. "Understanding Life Cycle Issues: A Resource for School Leaders." *Journal of Education,* 1987, *169*(1), 7–19.

Levinson, D., and others. *The Seasons of a Man's Life.* New York: Knopf, 1978.

Levinson, H. "Men at Work." Presentation at Cambridge Hospital, Harvard Medical School, Cambridge, Mass., January 23, 1991.

Lewin, K. "Group Decision and Social Change." In G. E. Swanson, T. N. Newcomb, and E. L. Hartley (eds.), *Readings in Social Psychology.* (Rev. ed.) Austin, Tex.: Holt, Rinehart, and Winston, 1952.

Lohr, S. "On the Road with Chairman Lou." *New York Times,* June 26, 1994, Sect. 3, pp. 1, 6.

Lortie, D. C. *Schoolteacher: A Sociological Study.* Chicago: University of Chicago Press, 1975.

Louis, K. S., and Miles, M. B. *Improving the Urban High School.* New York: Teachers College Press, 1990.

Maddi, S. R., and Kobasa, S. *The Hardy Executive.* Chicago: Dow Jones-Irwin, 1984.

Malkiel, B. G. *A Random Walk Down Wall Street.* New York: Norton, 1990.

March, J. G. "How We Talk and How We Act: Administrative Theory and Administrative Life." In T. J. Sergiovanni and J. E. Corbally (eds.), *Leadership and Organizational Culture.* Urbana: University of Illinois Press, 1984.

Marris, P. *Loss and Change.* London: Routledge & Kegan Paul, 1986.

Massachusetts Department of Education. *Principles of Effective Teaching and Effective Administrative Leadership: Special Draft of Proposed Revisions to Evaluation Regulations.* Boston: Massachusetts Department of Education, June 1, 1995.

Mathis, C. "Educational Reform, the Aging Society, and the Teaching Profession." *Journal of Education,* 1994, *169*(1), 84–97.

McAdams, D. *Stories We Live By.* New York: Morrow, 1993.

McClelland, D. *Power: The Inner Experience.* New York: Irvington, 1975.

McDonnell, L. M. *Restructuring American Schools: The Promise and the Pitfalls.* New York: National Center on Education and Employment, Teachers College, Columbia University, 1989.

McGregor, D. *The Human Side of Enterprise.* New York: McGraw-Hill, 1960.

Miles, M. B. "Forty Years of Change in Schools." Address to an American Educational Research Association meeting, San Francisco, April 23, 1992.

Miller, J. B. *Toward a New Psychology of Women.* Boston: Beacon Press, 1976.

Mintzberg, H. "Planning on the Left Side, Managing on the Right." In H. Mintzberg, *Mintzberg on Management.* New York: Free Press, 1989.

Mitchell, D. E., and Peters, M. J. "A Stronger Profession Through Appropriate Incentives." *Educational Leadership,* 1988, *46*(3), 74–78.

Mitchell, S. *Relational Concepts in Psychoanalysis: An Integration.* Cambridge, Mass.: Harvard University Press, 1988.

Mojkowski, C., and Bamberger, R. *Developing Leaders for Restructuring Schools: New Habits of Mind and Heart.* Washington: National LEADership Network, 1991.

Morgan, G. *Images of Organization.* Newbury Park, Calif.: Sage, 1986.

Moroney, T. "Harried School Nurses Offering Primary Care." *Boston Globe,* April 3, 1994, p. 28.

Mortimer, J. *Clinging to the Wreckage.* New York: Penguin, 1982.

National Commission on Excellence in Education. *A Nation at Risk: The Imperative for Educational Reform.* Washington, D.C.: U.S. Government Printing Office, 1983.

National Education Association National Center for Innovation. *It's About Time!!* Washington: National Education Association, 1993.

National Policy Board for Educational Administration. *Principals for Our Changing Schools: Knowledge and Skill Base.* Fairfax, Va.: National Policy Board for Educational Administration, 1993.

Neugarten, B. L. *Middle Age and Aging: A Reader in Social Psychology.* Chicago: University of Chicago Press, 1968.

Newmann, F. M., and Wehlage, G. G. *Successful School Restructuring.* Madison, Wisc.: Center on Organization and Restructuring of Schools, 1995.

Nicholson, C. "Henry Scattergood." *Germantown Friends School Alumni Bulletin,* 1995, *36*(2), 13.

Nisbet, R. *Social Change and History.* New York: Oxford University Press, 1969.

Nisbet, R. *The History of the Idea of Progress.* New York: Basic Books, 1980.

Ouchi, W. Z. *Theory Z.* Reading, Mass.: Addison-Wesley, 1981.

Peters, T. *Thriving on Chaos: Handbook for a Management Revolution.* New York: Knopf, 1987.

Rosenfeld, S. J. "Role of Schools for Handicapped Children at Issue." *Education Week,* February 8, 1989, p. 32.

Sacks, O. "To See and Not See." *The New Yorker,* May 10, 1993, pp. 59–73.

Saphier, J. and King, M. "Good Seeds Grow in Strong Cultures." *Educational Leadership,* 1985, *42,* 67–74.

Sarason, S. B. *The Culture of the School and the Problem of Change.* New York: Free Press, 1971.

Sarason, S. B. *The Creation of Settings and the Future Societies.* San Francisco: Jossey-Bass, 1972.

Sarason, S. B. *The Predictable Failure of Educational Reform: Can We Change Course Before It's Too Late?* San Francisco: Jossey-Bass, 1990.

Schein, E. *Career Dynamics.* Reading, Mass.: Addison-Wesley, 1978.

Schein, E. *Organizational Culture and Leadership.* (1st ed.) San Francisco: Jossey-Bass, 1985.

Schein, E. *Process Consultation* Vol. II. Reading, Mass.: Addison-Wesley, 1987.

Schein, E. *Organizational Culture and Leadership.* (2nd ed.) San Francisco: Jossey-Bass, 1992.

Schein, E. "How Can Organizations Learn Faster? The Challenge of the Green Room." *Sloan Management Revue,* Winter 1993, pp. 85–92.

Scherer, M. "On Our Changing Family Values: A Conversation with David Elkind." *Educational Leadership,* 1996, *63*(7), 4–9.

Schlechty, P. C. "Career Ladders: A Good Idea Going Awry." In T. J. Sergiovanni and J. H. Moore (eds.), *Schooling for Tomorrow: Directing Reforms to Issues That Count.* Boston: Allyn & Bacon, 1989.

Schlechty, P. C. *Schools for the 21st Century: Leadership Imperatives for Educational Reform.* San Francisco: Jossey-Bass, 1992.

Schön, D. A. "Leadership As Reflection-in-Action." In T. J. Sergiovanni and J. E. Corbally (eds.), *Leadership and Organizational Culture.* Urbana: University of Illinois Press, 1984.

Selye, H. *Stress Without Distress.* New York: New American Library, 1974.

Selznick, P. *Leadership in Administration: A Sociological Interpretation.* New York: Harper & Row, 1957.

Senge, P. *The Fifth Discipline.* New York: Doubleday, 1990.

Sergiovanni, T. J. *The Principalship: A Reflective Practice Perspective.* Boston: Allyn & Bacon, 1991.

Sergiovanni, T. J. *Moral Leadership: Getting to the Heart of School Reform.* San Francisco: Jossey-Bass, 1992.

Sergiovanni, T. J. *Building Community in Schools.* San Francisco: Jossey-Bass, 1993.

Shahan, K. E. *The Administrator's Role in Developing Innovations.* Unpublished doctoral dissertation, Harvard Graduate School of Education, 1976.

Sheehy, G. *Passages: Predictable Crises of Adult Life.* New York: Dutton, 1974.

Shils, E. A. "Charisma, Order, and Status." *American Sociological Review,* 1965, *30,* 199–213.

Sizer, T. R. *Horace's Compromise: The Dilemma of the American High School.* Boston: Houghton Mifflin, 1984.

Sizer, T. R. "Silences." *Daedalus,* 1995, *124*(4), 77–84.

Starratt, R. J. *The Drama of Leadership.* New York: Falmer Press, 1993.

Stewart, J. B. "Grand Illusion." *The New Yorker,* Oct. 31, 1994, pp. 64–81.

Tannenbaum, R. and Schmidt, W. H. "How to Choose a Leadership Pattern." In *Managers as Leaders.* Cambridge, Mass.: Harvard Business Review Press, 1991.

Taylor, F. W. *The Principles of Scientific Management.* New York: Harper and Brothers, 1911.

Taylor, D., and Teddlie, C. "Restructuring and the Classroom: A View from a Reform District." Paper presented at the Annual Meeting of the American Educational Research Association, San Francisco, 1992.

Thomson, S. D. "Leadership Revisited." *Education Week,* Oct. 16, 1991, p. 26.

Tyack, D. "'Restructuring' in Historical Perspective: Tinkering Toward Utopia." *Teachers College Record,* 1990, *92*(2), 170–189.

Usdansky, M. L. "Single Motherhood: Stereotypes vs. Statistics." *New York Times,* February 11, 1996, Sect. 4, p. 4.

Vaill, P. B. "The Purposing of High-Performing Systems." *Organizational Dynamics,* Autumn 1982, pp. 23–39.

Vaill, P. B. "The Purposing of High-performing Systems." In T. J. Sergiovanni and J. E. Corbally (eds.), *Leadership and Organizational Culture.* Urbana: University of Illinois Press, 1984.

Vaill, P. B. *Managing as a Performing Art: New Ideas for a World of Chaotic Change.* San Francisco: Jossey-Bass, 1989.

Vaillant, G. *Adaptation to Life.* Boston: Little, Brown, 1977.

Viadero, D. "Nation Is Still Falling Short in Meeting Education Goals, Progress Report Finds." *Education Week,* October 6, 1993, p. 5.

Watzlawick, P., Weakland, J., and Fisch, R. *Change: Principles of Problem Formulation and Problem Resolution.* New York: Norton, 1974.

Weick, K. E. "The Significance of Culture." In P. J. Frost and others (eds.), *Organizational Culture.* Newbury Park, Calif.: Sage, 1985.

Weick, K. E., and McDaniel, R. R., Jr. "How Professional Organizations Work: Implications for School Organization and Management." In T. J. Sergiovanni and J. H. Moore (eds.), *Schooling for Tomorrow: Directing Reforms to Issues That Count.* Needham Heights, Mass.: Allyn & Bacon, 1989.

Weiss, C. "Shared Decision Making About What?" Paper presented at the Annual Meeting of the American Educational Research Association, San Francisco, 1992.

West, C. "Market Culture Run Amok." *Newsweek,* January 3, 1994, 48–49.

Whitehead, B. D. "Dan Quayle Was Right." *Atlantic Monthly,* 1993, *271*(4), 47–84.

Yee, S. M. *Careers in the Classroom.* New York: Teachers College Press, 1990.

Zaleznik, A. *The Managerial Mystique: Restoring Leadership in Business.* New York: HarperCollins, 1989.

Index